C000065100

Nymph Fishing

A History of the Art and Practice

NYMPH FISHING

A HISTORY OF THE ART AND PRACTICE

Terry Lawton

SWAN·HILL
PRESS

Copyright © 2005 Terry Lawton

The right of Terry Lawton to be identified as the author of this work has been asserted in accordance with the Copyright, Design and Patent Act 1988

First published in the UK in 2005 by Swan Hill Press, an imprint of Quiller Publishing Ltd

British Library Cataloguing-in-Publication Data
A catalogue record for this book
is available from the British Library

ISBN 1 904057 65 9

The information in this book is true and complete to the best of our knowledge. All recommendations are made without any guarantee on the part of the Publisher, who also disclaims any liability incurred in connection with the use of these data or specific details.

All rights reserved. No part of this book may be reproduced or transmitted in any form or by any means, electronic or mechanical including photocopying, recording or by any information storage and retrieval system, without permission from the Publisher in writing.

Typeset by Phoenix Typesetting, Auldgirth, Dumfriesshire
Printed in China

Swan Hill Press
An imprint of Quiller Publishing Ltd.
Wykey House, Wykey, Shrewsbury, SY4 1JA
Tel: 01939 261616 Fax: 01939 261606
E-mail: info@quillerbooks.com
Website: www.swanhillbooks.com

Contents

Acknowledgements

I am surprised at just how many people have made a contribution to this book. I have been in contact with people all over the world and virtually everyone has been prepared to help in some way – some in a quite extraordinarily generous fashion. So in no particular order, I would like to acknowledge and thank the following for their help:

Robert Spaight for allowing me access to his very extensive and comprehensive library and much other help besides; and Richard Nelson for loan of books.

Sandy Leventon for allowing me unfettered access to the archives of *Trout and Salmon* magazine and Carmel Jorgensen and the Salmon and Trout Association for access to the archives of *The Salmon and Trout Magazine*.

Steve Cooper and Cookshill Fly Tying (www.cookshill-flytying.co.uk) for supplying many of the materials for tying the nymphs used for photography and also suggesting sources of supply of other materials and also Christina of Chevron Hackles for supplying some of the more unusual hackles used to tie Skues' flies (www.featherbenders.com). Together they made it possible to tie some of the historic patterns.

David Beazley, librarian, John Morgan, custodian and Cmdr Tim Boycott, secretary, of The Flyfishers' Club for such generous access to the Club's splendid library and museum. The librarians in my local library for dealing with equanimity with many requests for often seemingly weird and wonderful fishing books and Mary Carter-Hepworth, assistant archivist at Boise State University, for help with supplying information on and photographs of Ted Trueblood. Messrs A. & C. Black for permission to reproduce from the works of G. E. M. Skues.

Nick Sawyer and his father Tim Sawyer for permission to use photographs from Frank Sawyer's first book. Various Sawyer books are obtainable from Nick's website at www.sawyernymphs.com

Major Sidney Vines and friends for information on the pheasant tail red spinner and other information to do with Frank Sawyer. Theo Bakelaar for information on the recent history of goldhead nymphs and Dr Rob Sloane for putting me in contact with Mike Stevens who provided so much information about and all the photographs associated with and of R. H. Wigram.

Charles Jardine for allowing me to use some of his original illustrations. Kuba Chruszczewski for tying the Polish nymphs.

And last but very far from least, my good Swedish fishing and fly tying friend James Andersson for tying all the current and historic English flies.

Readers may be interested to know that there are two Oliver Kite videos still available: *Oliver Kite – Master Fly Fisherman*, and *A Tribute to Oliver Kite*. They are available from Edward J. Channell, 12 Newland's Avenue, Shirley, Southampton, Hants SO15 5ER. Telephone: Int +44 (0)23 8077-4837.

Every effort has been made by the author to contact owners of copyright material but in some instances this has not been possible; he will be happy to add any omissions to future editions.

PHOTOGRAPHIC CREDITS

Ulf Börjesson pages 44, 103, 141 and 144; Edward J. Channell page 86; Chris Hoelzer pages 33, 45, 56, 63, 70, 129, 163 and 164; Johan Klingberg page 90; Terry Lawton pages 4, 5, 52, 59, 71, 91, 92, 93, 94, 125, 127 and 167; Ron Lucas, Sr. pages 119 (bottom), 121 and 162; John Marchington pages 83, 85 and 88; Charles Ritz page 67 Jim Schollmeyer page 119 (top); Jan Siman pages 124, 126 and 128; Sidney Vines page 79; Boise State University Library pages 116 and 117; by kind permission of the estate of Frank Sawyer pages 67, 73, 74, 75, 76, 77, 78, 80, 81, 95, 153 and 161; by kind permission of the Fly Fishers' Classic Library page 40; by kind permission of The Flyfishers' Club pages 2, 53 and 111; by kind permission of Michael Stevens pages 134, 135, 136 and 138

Jacket

Front: Jan Siman   Inset: Chris Hoelzer

Back: Terry Lawton

Hook size conversion

PENNELL SCALE	REDDITCH SCALE
0000	18
000	(17)
00	16
0	(15)
1	14
2	(13)
3	12
4	(11)
5	10

NOTE: The odd numbered sizes, in brackets, are not normally available.

1 Prologue

In his short but delightful book about the Wiltshire Avon, *One River*, Brigadier General H. E. Carey summed up fly fishing very well: 'Fishing undoubtedly trains one's powers of observation, teaches the art of stalking, and demands the employment of tactics whereby the enemy may be outwitted.' Over the last hundred years or so, nymph fishing has changed from a 'minor tactic' – and one that was often considered little better than poaching – to being an accepted and increasingly popular tactic for out-witting fish.

What do we mean by nymph fishing? At one time a definition would have been limited to that of fishing, or casting, an artificial pattern to a fish seen to be feeding under water on nymphs. The artificial nymph would have been expected to represent the nymphs on which the trout was thought to be feeding. Today that definition can be widened to include fishing suitable imitations of most forms of underwater trout food including larvae, midge pupae and shrimps. This is not dissimilar to the changes and developments in dry fly fishing where the use of artificial terrestrial patterns, ants, beetles and even caterpillars is accepted practice. But 'nymphing' is now often used to describe a way or method of fishing flies sub-surface, regardless of whether or not fish are feeding on nymphs. It is used simply as an effective sub-surface technique and some might argue that this is a coarsening of a normally very delicate way of catching fish.

In *The Field* of 20 February 1909, when writing on 'The Antiquity of The Dry Fly', W. Fletcher declared: 'The wet fly is, in fact, a discovery, the dry fly an invention and in the case of the former we have not by any means fully realised as yet what we have actually discovered.'

Rules have evolved and developed as times have changed, and more people fish an ever-greater variety of waters. Brian Clarke wrote in an article in *Trout and Salmon* magazine in 1978, that those anglers who fished the gin-clear chalk streams of Hampshire in the early years of the twentieth century, outlawed fishing the water because it was usually possible to see feeding fish and then cast to individual fish, whereas fishing the water would frighten unseen fish. But when water clarity is less than perfect and fish cannot be seen so easily, then fishing the water must be an acceptable tactic. And two years later (1980) when his book, written with John Goddard, *The Trout and the Fly, A New Approach*, was published, he wrote: 'To impose constraints upon oneself that

Frank Sawyer with his wife Margaret and their dog

either prohibit fishing at all, or that are quite absurdly limiting, is not only ridiculous, but the cause of much bad fishing.'

A number of experts and well-known fishermen/authors have speculated that various early (fifteenth century) flies could have been representations of nymphs or were nymph-like artificial flies. But as no actual examples, paintings or drawings of these early patterns are available, such speculation must remain just that. Such speculations contribute little, if anything, to the more easily proven and documented history of nymph fishing.

For nearly fifty years – the first half of the twentieth century in fact – the history of nymph fishing was dominated by just two rivers: the Itchen in Hampshire and the Avon in Wiltshire. G. E. M. Skues developed and practised nymph fishing on the Itchen and Frank Sawyer took it to a new stage on the Wiltshire Avon. What would have happened if Sawyer had not been appointed to the river keeper's position on the Avon? Would he have achieved everything that he did on another river? Would Major Oliver Kite have also achieved his place in the history of nymph fishing?

Another dominating influence of the first thirty or so years of the same century was the disagreements about whether or not it was a sporting and fair way to catch fish and the arguments between Skues and F. M. Halford. While there was the occasional verbal confrontation between Skues and Halford, most of the disagreement was in Skues' writings often long after Halford's death. Moving forward to the 1960s there was a similar disagreement between Oliver Kite and Frank Sawyer who referred to Kite, in a letter to

Trout and Salmon magazine published after Kite's death, as 'one of my pupils'.

Major Sidney Vines who knew Frank Sawyer for the last twenty-one years of his life claims to know the definitive reason for what he described as the estrangement between the two one-time friends and collaborators. It was a woman and a car. The woman was Frank Sawyer's wife Margaret and the car was Kite's white Jaguar. In 1958 Oliver Kite had bought White Owl Cottage on the main street of Netheravon, directly opposite Court Farm House where the Sawyers lived. (Kite's cottage is still there while the farm house where the Sawyers lived was burnt down.) Kite joined the then Officers' Fishing Association which employed Frank Sawyer as river keeper. Sawyer introduced Kite to nymph fishing and in 1961 Kite spent nearly every evening over a six month period in Sawyer's house gleaning every bit of information that he could from Sawyer about nymphs and nymph fishing. Margaret Sawyer was left alone but neither she nor Frank ever seemed to have complained about it. The result of Kite picking Sawyer's brain was his book *Nymph Fishing in Practice*, published in 1963. In his appreciation of Oliver Kite in the new version of *Nymph Fishing in Practice*, Robert Spaight wrote that Kite's doctor recommend that he bought himself a comfortable car with an automatic gearbox and that was at a time when the choice for such a car was quite limited. Anyway the white Jaguar – bought, no doubt, with some of the proceeds from his new book – was obviously the pride and joy of its new owner. The fact that he had to park it on the road outside the front of his cottage, bang opposite the Sawyers' house, did not go down well with Mrs Sawyer. Mrs Sawyer never forgot what she considered was the way that Kite took advantage of her husband and profited in, to her, such an ostentatious way. Sidney Vines was told this story nearly twenty years later, in 1982, and Margaret Sawyer's eyes still burned with anger when she looked across the street.

In a *Trout and Salmon* series, Past Masters (number three, February 1986), Terry Thomas wrote about the 'enigmatic Oliver Kite' and how Kite had asked him to put on a casting demonstration at a field day for members of a local fishery. Thomas said that he would have been happy to do this but why didn't Kite do it himself? Kite explained that as he was already scheduled to give two talks, he did not want to hog the day for himself. When Thomas suggested that he ask Frank Sawyer, 'he made some sort of excuse. Perhaps it was then that the first signs of a rift between the two friends appeared.'

Wilson Stephens, who edited Frank Sawyer's book *Nymphs and The Trout, New applications of a technique for fly fishermen*, made some very interesting and informative comments on how fly fishing had developed, in his introduction to the first edition. As he wrote, a fishery owner has the right to impose his own rules whether they be for dry fly only, or to allow upstream nymphing. Crucially he noted 'that a "dry fly only" rule is most often encountered nowadays when the owner of the fishing either lives beside his water, or is in a position to spend extended periods there.' Halford was in that position and was able to decamp to Hampshire for two or three weeks at a time during the prime weeks and months of the season. For Halford and his peers if they spent a day on the water and no fish rose and they did not make a cast, no matter, there was always the next day and probably the day after too when the fish would rise with alacrity. But for the fisherman who was limited in his opportunities to fish, should conditions render dry fly fishing impossible or futile, Stephens was of the opinion that the fisherman 'should go down to the fish' and use a nymph and that 'nymph fishing is an acceptable, sporting method by which to achieve this'.

As nymph fishing knowledge and techniques developed, so the practical fishing season was extended and the number of months increased when it was reasonable to fish. In the latter years of the nineteenth century and early years of the twentieth century, certainly on the southern chalk streams, most anglers fished the Grannom hatches of April, the Mayfly in May and perhaps June and by the end of that month they were off the rivers, although Skues fished regularly in July, August and even September. Nymph fishing saw the season

White Owl Cottage in 2004. No doubt Oliver Kite parked his perhaps infamous white Jaguar where the Audi is parked. He had nowhere else to park a car. The Sawyers lived behind where I stood to take this photograph

The exceptional water clarity of an English chalk stream makes it very easy to spot fish

extended beyond June into July and August – the peak months for Frank Sawyer and Oliver Kite – and now all through September and on into October, where allowed. Stephens, too, noted that the use of the nymph extended the season after midsummer so giving fishermen more days of active sport. Even as recently as 1950, according to Gordon Mackie, members of the Wilton Club fished mostly in May and early June only. And there are still Hampshire chalk streams where the use of the nymph is not permitted before 1 July.

There are still anglers today who pretend to despise the use of Polarised glasses when fishing. They tend to suggest that the likes of Sawyer and Kite would 'turn in their graves' if they knew that today's anglers used such aids. In fact, they could not be more wrong as Oliver Kite recommended the use of such glasses although he did not need to use them himself, as like Sawyer and I am sure others who spend their days by water, he had a seemingly uncanny ability to see *through* water and into the river. In the first edition of his book *Nymphs and the Trout*, there are two photographs of Sawyer fishing in sun glasses.

There is also a continuing ignorance of and lack of understanding of how, when and why to fish nymphs, evident through the 1970s and right up to the present day. For example a book published in 2003, written by a well-respected angling writer, covered upstream nymphing in about two pages.

The author was quite dismissive of the intricacies and subtleties of the practice.

It is Sawyer's (and Kite's) method of nymph fishing that has stood the test of time and is used today, both in its original and purest form and much modified, rather than Skues' surface or slightly sub-surface approach. It is interesting that the Poles, followed by the Czechs, developed their own 'short nymph' technique, with no reference to the English style, and have succeeded in exporting it to many countries. This is in contrast to so many English-speaking countries which imported (or English anglers introduced) the English upstream method and then gradually adapted and modified it to suit local conditions better.

While researching this book it was very interesting and informative to keep coming across complaints of the increasing scarcity of fly life and hatching flies, the Mayfly (*E. Danica*) disappearing from stretches of the Itchen and other rivers, the reduction in numbers of rising fish and problems with low water flows. These complaints were being made in the latter years of the nineteenth century and for a number of decades into the twentieth century. For today's anglers with similar concerns, surely the response must be: don't worry over much, it has all happened before.

What is the future for nymph fishing? I am sure that the continuing developments of tackle will have as big an influence on the future as they have had on the past. Another important influence will be the increasing number of travelling anglers who will take their own countries' methods and techniques with them and also learn new ways in the countries that they visit and take home with them new patterns of artificial nymphs.

2 The Great Debate

'For years past now a controversy has raged over the subject, rising and waning, like a recurrent thunderstorm which keeps returning after one had supposed its declining mutterings meant it had left the neighbourhood for good.'

H. D. Turing, *Trout Problems*, 1948

The tenth of February, 1938 was the day that the great debate on nymph fishing took place at The Flyfishers' Club[1], then at No. 36 Piccadilly, known as Swallow Street, London. In 1914 G. E. M. Skues had written of opening the door on the left-hand side of Swallow Street and running joyously upstairs to meet the good fly fishers who usually congregated there. This event was unique in the annals of the small, enclosed world of fly fishing history. There had never been such a momentous event as this debate. And, perhaps more importantly, it is highly unlikely that such an event, such a debate, will ever take place again. The whole world, and the world of fly fishing, have both changed beyond imagination in the intervening years. Standards then were very different from today. We will all have seen photographs of G. E. M. Skues, F. M. Halford and their peers fishing in thick tweed three-piece suits and felt or even bowler hats. No shirt sleeves on a hot summer's day. And certainly no designer fishing shirts and baseball caps which are the accepted norm today. George Selwyn Marryat in his Tam O'Shanter must have cut quite an eccentric and even 'hippy' figure in his day. People's behaviour is different today and expectations have changed, mostly for the good, but not always. It is these changes to personal and sporting codes in particular that were the background to the debate and part of the reason for it.

In *G .E. M. Skues, The Way of a Man with a Trout*, which covers the debate very extensively, T. Donald Overfield wrote: 'The years immediately prior to the 1939–45 war gave rise to a rebirth of dry-fly purism and the rigid code of the Halfordian disciples was once more being pressed upon the southern chalk streams. Those who were advocates of the dry fly only school were almost unanimous in their condemnation of Skues and his nymphing techniques, being determined to see this practice removed from the chalk stream.'

The social and sporting attitudes that prevailed at the end of the Victorian era and early decades of the twentieth century were reflected in the purism and even ultra-purism of Halford and his fellow dry fly-only anglers. Charles Chenevix Trench in his book, *A History of Angling*, described Halford as '. . . the High Priest, the very *Ipsissimus* of the Dry Fly Cult'. G. A. B. Dewar, writing in 1897, did not consider that the rise of a trout bulging, or feeding on nymphs, was a fair rise. R. D. Baird in 1907, when at school at Winchester, would not have dared catch a fish on a sunk fly because he knew that a river keeper would consider such a fish to be little better than one that had been poached.

Before his death, Halford had managed to convince all his peers – with the notable exceptions of Skues, J. W. Hills, Dr J. C. Mottram (who did change sides as we will see shortly) and a few other enlightened anglers – that it was impossible to imitate the movement of a swimming nymph and, as a consequence, it was not worth even trying. It must be pointed out that Halford, whose dry fly only purism and condemnation of Skues' use of the nymph on chalk streams was one of the main causes of the debate, had died in 1914, some twenty-four years before it took place. His legacy is still with us today, to some extent, in the twenty-first century.

Skues was only too well aware of 'a recrudescence of dry fly purism' as he wrote in a letter of 28 December, 1936, to his friend Major J. D. D. Evans who lived in Wales. In this letter he recalled how one member of his Itchen syndicate had objected to his use of nymphs which he, the member, considered did not accord with their agreement with the landlord. As so many of the other members of the syndicate were against his use of the nymph, Skues had agreed not to fish them anymore that season (1936). Later in the letter he expressed his concern about how his nymph patterns had been bastardised by tackle dealers who did not tie them correctly, and dealers who sold other patterns that should not be called nymphs at all[2]. 'The fact is the genuine nymph fisher is up against an almost invincible flood of ignorance on the part of the fly fishing public, who accept these abortions and monstrosities in good faith and no doubt catch trout with them now and again.

'It seems to me that the best defence against this flood of abysmal ignorance and misconception is attack.'

As he felt that it was most unlikely that fishing magazines would publish articles attacking the professional fly tiers and the tackle shops that sold 'these abortions and monstrosities', he hoped that Major Evans would join him in writing a definitive book on nymph fishing, as now aged seventy-nine Skues knew that his energy was no longer inexhaustible. Evans declined the invitation and the idea for the book was put to one side.

Some six months later, on 24 June 1937, Skues wrote to C. A. N. Wauton, who also lived in Wales in Swansea, and raised the question of the possible demand for 'a small cheap volume devoted entirely to nymph dressing and nymph fishing' and whether or not it would help anglers to differentiate between the acceptable commercial nymphs and the unacceptable. This time there was an encouraging response and Skues started work on what was to be his last published work and, interestingly his first actual book (all his previous publications were collections of articles written for and published in various magazines). *Nymph Fishing for Chalk Stream Trout* was published in the spring of 1939.

During the run-up to the debate there had been considerable correspondence in the *Journal of The Flyfishers Club*, on the ethics of nymph fishing. It was this correspondence that led to the debate being held. The Club member who wrote to the *Journal* objecting to nymph fishing on the basis that he wanted to fish the dry fly only and catch rising trout feeding on duns on the surface was probably very typical. But his argument against nymph fishing ignored a key question. As stated, the writer was only interested in dry fly fishing and, if at the end of the day he had to admit defeat and give best to a fine trout, he wanted to be able to return another day to that fish, safe in the knowledge that some bounder had not been along before his return and caught 'his fish' on a nymph. But would he have felt better had that fish been seduced by a fellow dry fly purist?

If the debate was to be held today, no doubt one of television's grand inquisitors such as Jeremy Paxman – himself a (celebrity) fly fisherman – would have chaired it. It might even have been televised by one of the satellite TV channels.

The debate was notable for its vicious attack on an eighty-year old G. E. M. Skues by Sir Joseph Ball, and for former supporters of nymph fishing changing sides, perhaps most significantly Dr Mottram who maintained that nymph fishing led to the hooking of undersize trout.

In his 'cheerful and witty' opening address on the subject for debate, Nymph Fishing in Chalk Streams, Dr Walshe was reported in the Spring 1938 issue of the *Journal of The Flyfishers Club*, to have said: 'To begin with, it is clear that there can be no rational basis whatever for any such discussion. Beyond all cavil and by every standard of reason and sportsmanship the nymph has justified its use in chalk stream fishing' and then that 'Mr Skues has shown us in a series of lucid and delightful books and articles that nymph fishing fulfils all the canons of trout fishing' and 'Whoever is not convinced by his arguments and by his experience is not amenable to reason, and is the timid slave of outworn convention.' He ended his address, very favourable to nymph fishing, with a splendid repudiation of the dry fly purist: 'The fact is that the dry fly purist is a would-be dictator who presumes to decide how we shall all fish. We must whistle to his shrill and antiquated tune. He is an obstructionist who is trying to hold up the development of our art.'

Skues, in his address, based his argument on the fact that Halford 'had clearly never tried it (nymph fishing upstream) and was condemning a practice he had not tested on grounds which did not apply.' Did he muster the strongest arguments in his support that he could? Reading the report of the debate nearly seven decades later, it would seem that he did not defend himself as strongly as he might have done. But this opinion does, perhaps, not take into account fully the fact he was nearly eighty years old. In true, modern political spin doctor style, he had got his retaliation in first in an article, 'Halford and the Nymph', published in the *Journal of The Flyfishers Club*, Winter 1937/38 issue.

In that article, Skues set out a number of fundamental misconceptions of the late Halford about nymph fishing. They were stated clearly and dealt with succinctly. But in a lengthy address in response, Sir Joseph Ball, a barrister, revealed himself as a master of mis-interpretation, mis-understanding and the half truth. He could not conceive of Halford making a mistake, but mistaken he was and limited in his knowledge of nymphs. Because of a lack of understanding of the behaviour of the different types of nymph, because one particular nymph 'proceeds to the surface in alternate bursts of extreme energy and inertness', Ball assumed that all nymphs behave in such a way. As Skues wrote in another article, quoted against him by Ball, 'Halford was not

the man to go back and continually revise his opinions and to bring them up to date in the light of later experience. Once having established a proposition to his satisfaction it became fact.'

Ball stated that Halford had fished the nymph 'as long ago as 1884 – a quarter of a century before the appearance of *Minor Tactics*' and while this was true, Halford himself admitted that he was remarkably unsuccessful. Halford had, indeed dressed a nymph as a copy of a grannom larva taken from a trout's stomach in 1884 and which he gave to 'fellow anglers as the grannom-nymph'. R. B. Marston, in *The Fishing Gazette*, wrote: 'The Grannom is a fly which seems to kill almost any time except when the natural is on the water . . . Halford gives a pattern for the larva which he says the trout take ravenously, neglecting the fully developed fly.'

Ball maintained that Halford 'had considered, tried, and finally rejected the nymph long before the publication of the first edition of *Minor Tactics* in 1909'. How many anglers today, who have read Halford's books, would agree with this very biased interpretation of an author's words? Towards the end of his address he recounts a delightfully biased vision of how a dry fly man would fish a 'short stretch of first-class dry-fly water', casting only to rising fish, using a 'good imitation of the fly it is clearly taking', fishing only for part of the day, during a hatch presumably, and then leaving the stretch untouched for perhaps a week. He contrasted this with a nymph fisherman who cannot see what is happening, lines fish left, right and centre and because he cannot wait patiently for a rise, fishes all day and so covers much more water. He finished this part of his address: 'I know one magnificent dry-fly water that has been ruined by such methods.'

Why didn't Skues and Hills fight back and expose these half-truths, distortions and lies of Sir Joseph Ball?

Mottram maintained that as it was difficult to see when a trout took a nymph, unlike a fish rising to a dry fly, it was not possible to either drag the nymph away from a small fish or not strike, so many small fish would be hooked, fish that a dry fly man would have avoided. In his opinion a dry fly man left his fly on the water no longer than absolutely essential to cover a rising fish, whereas the nymph fisher would leave his fly and gut in the water as long as possible so that both would be wet, and so sink quickly, for the next cast. In this way more water than necessary would be fished and unseen fish disturbed, ruining the water for a dry fly angler following up behind a nympher.

The Rev. Percy Sheriffs stated that he had caught trout with the nymph 'we called them wet flies then' since 1868. His argument against nymph fishing, and even dry fly fishing in the 'many streams of the North and West, from May 15th till the end of June' was because too many fish were being caught and he was very worried that there would soon be no trout to be caught anywhere.

Where did Skues' support come from? J. W. Hills was convinced that 'the art of fishing the nymph' upstream only, 'was a far higher one than that of fishing the dry fly.' Major Phelps and a Mr Marling were said to be in agreement that nymph fishing was 'safe for experts only' which was somewhat back-handed support. And that seems to have been the extent of support for poor Skues in what appears to have been a very one-sided debate. So much of the argument against nymph fishing was based on ignorance, intolerance and prejudice. It was ever thus.

Perhaps the final word on this less than glorious debate should go to Skues himself near the end of his long life. In *Nymph Fishing for Chalk Stream Trout*, he wrote that 'the protagonist (Sir Joseph Ball) of the purists argued with a great show of authority that I was wrong and Halford right on every point on which I had challenged his dicta, in connection with nymph fishing – particularly on the question of the activity of the mature nymph on its way up to hatch – (I have already dealt with this aspect of the case). And then he went on to quote cases in which he claimed that first-rate Test fisheries had been ruined by the use of the nymph. It did not seem to strike him (or his hearers except me) that if Halford was right and the trout would not look at the artificial nymph, it would be curious that the fish should have been so affected by the use of the nymph that they (though of course not caught with the nymph) should have become un-amenable to the temptation of the dry fly. Had they been scared out of the lengths in question or had they become so nervous that they had been driven to bottom feeding? Information on these points was not afforded.

'Of course Halford was wrong in saying that the trout would not look at the artificial nymph. Not only I, but many others, have proved that over and over again. Therefore the grounds for objecting to the use of the nymph had to be shifted.'

Notes

1 The Flyfishers' Club was formed in 1884 as a result of a meeting held at the Caledonian Hotel, Adelphi, which had been called by Mr R. B. Marston. Prior to the meeting he had discussed the idea with some friends, W. Senior, H. Ffennell and Cholmondeley Pennell who were in favour of the idea.

   The first Hon. Secretary was J. Paul Taylor who had to retire through ill-health before the Club was really established. Marston was the first Hon. Treasurer and a busy recruiter of new members as were his fellow committee members including Messrs. Senior and Ffennell.

   The Club differed from most fishing in clubs in that it was started for purely social reasons. It had 'nothing to do with competitions of any sort, and does not endeavour to provide its members with a fishery.' The Club met on Thursdays and Saturdays. From the start it seems to have had a very well-stocked library: 'very valuable books, both ancient and modern, besides some hundreds of ordinary angling works', initially under the care of a Mr Norris. Members could use the Club 'to conduct their correspondence or to meet their friends.' J. P. Taylor described the Club room, with its stuffed fish, pictures of fish and tackle cases as 'an enlarged "Angler's Den".' The annual dinner was attended by 'hundreds of members and guests'.

Members covered all levels of experience and competence and included 'Every sort of fly-ishing has its representative advocate, from the head centre of the inner brethren, who thinks it is almost profane to speak disrespectfully of the dry fly, to the reckless advocate of crude whipping with three formless insects on the tumbling waters of a Devon stream.' One idea that still has validity today was the provision of a query and suggestion book 'in which the more experienced or more travelled angler can answer questions placed therein by neophytes.'

2 Robert Bragg had the pleasure of serving Skues in September 1937, when working for Ogden Smiths Ltd. He wrote: '[Skues] was not enamoured with the tying of our nymphs'.

3 Why did nymph fishing take so long to develop? 1600 to *c*1900

'No mode of angling can be more fascinating, more exacting or more rewarding in intellectual satisfaction.'
Eric Taverner, *An Introduction To Angling*, Beaufort Library, 1953

Fly fishing has been an accepted way of catching trout for some thousands of years – no-one is sure for just how long – and equally, no-one is sure where fly fishing started. The earliest fly fishermen fished flies that would have floated when they were first cast upon the water, because they were dry, but would have started to sink as soon as they absorbed water. They did not seem to have worried whether they were fishing wet flies or dry flies for many hundreds of years. Quite simply, they were happy to be fishing whether it was for sport or for the pot.

Nymph fishing started as a very English way – but a hesitant and fumbling way – to catch trout when they could not be caught in what was then deemed to be the proper, or correct way on English chalk streams, on or with dry flies. But within a few decades of these first early fumblings between about 1890 and 1910, nymph fishing was established as a legitimate – if not still universally acceptable – way of catching trout and had started to spread around the world. Within forty years it was a method of catching trout (and other fish) feeding below the surface on nymphs, larvae, pupae and other sub-surface food forms that had gained international acceptance and no longer just a 'minor tactic' as described by G. E. M. Skues.

Like so many aspects of fly fishing for trout, nymph fishing has its origins in days much earlier than one might imagine. As long ago as 1600, John Taverner, a surveyor of woodlands for King James I, published his observations on the hatching of nymphs in a book called *Certaine Experiments Concerning Fish and Fruite* which was reproduced in two issues of the *Salmon and Trout Magazine* in 1928. This seems to be one of the earliest known references to actual nymphs. In this book Taverner described how he had observed what he called a young fly swimming backwards and forwards in the water, trying to break through the water surface and then take to the wing. 'I have scene a young flie swimme in the water to and fro, and in the end come to the upper

An emerging nymph

crust of the water and assay to flie up: howbeit not being perfectly ripe or fledge, have twice or thrice fallen downe againe into the water; howbeit in the end receiving perfection by the heate of the sunne, and the fat water, hath in the ende within some halfe houre after taken her flight, and flied quite awaie, into the ayre. And of such young flies before they are able to flie awaie, do fish feede exceedingly.' Crucially he was very well aware of the fact that fish fed heavily on these 'young flies' or nymphs. This seems to be one of the earliest descriptions of the underwater activity and hatching of nymphs but Taverner's vital observations appeared to have gone unnoticed for more than two centuries.

Another notable seventeenth century angler and sportsman, Colonel Robert Venables, who wrote *The Experienced Angler: or Angling Improved*, which was published in 1662, knew that a range of fish, including trout and grayling, would 'sometimes take the fly much better at the top of the water, and at another time much better a little under the superficies of the water; and in this your own observation must be your constant and daily instructor'. Here we have an example of an obviously observant angler passing on his knowledge and some sound advice too. Being observant all the time was not the only sound advice he had for his readers. In the final chapter of this short book (it runs, in facsimile to only sixty-one pages), general observations number twelve reads: 'The first fish you take, cut up his belly, and you may then see his stomach . . . and with a sharp knife cut it open without bruising, and then you may find his food in it, and thereby discover what bait the fish at that instant takes best, either flies or ground-baits, and so suit them accordingly.' In his next general observation on the fact that 'Fish are frightened with any the least sight or motion', he discusses the problems and merits of fishing upstream compared to downstream. Although he says that you can 'angle upwards' in small brooks, in big rivers you would have to wade – because of the length of line used – with the attendant risk of getting sciatica (a result, presumably,

15

of wading without waders or waterproof footwear of any sort), his considered opinion was that it was better to fish downstream. John Waller Hills, in *A History of Fly Fishing For Trout*, credited Venables with being the first writer to mention fishing upstream.

Venables' final piece of advice that is relevant to the history of nymph fishing was also far in advance of its day. This was on how to choose the correct colour of materials used for tying flies. 'When you try how to fit your colour to the fly, wet your fur, hair, wool, or moccado, otherwise you will fail in your work; for though when they are dry, they exactly suit the colour of the fly, yet the water will alter most colours, and make them lighter or darker.' Such considerations seem to have been ignored for the next two hundred and fifty years or so until anglers such as Dr J. C. Mottram stressed the importance of the appearance and colour of the *wet* artificial nymph.

Charles Cotton, in 1676, wrote about fly fishing with either live flies or artificial flies in the second part of *The Complete Angler*. This he described as fishing at the top. For fishing with artificial flies, Cotton recommended using a line up to two yards longer than the rod, which might have been anything up to sixteen or eighteen feet (4.8 to 5.5m) long, depending on the width of the river to be fished. His 'first and principal rule for trout-angling' was 'to fish fine and far off'. The fly would have been cast both up and downstream, depending on the direction and strength of the wind. If there was not too much wind, then Cotton said to keep as much line as possible clear of the water. But on windy days 'you will then of necessity be compelled to drown a good part of your line to keep your fly in the water'. Note that he used the word 'in' rather than 'on' the water. His flies seemed to have had bodies dubbed with fur, and wings but neither hackle nor tails. As no potions were available for keeping flies dry nor had, as far as we know, false casting been invented for both extending your casting line as well as drying wet flies, these basic hackle-less flies would have floated very low in the water, when dry, and then slowly deeper as they absorbed more water.

Moving forward just over one hundred and fifty years, John Younger in his book *River Angling for Salmon and Trout*, published in 1840, described 'the trout when feeding on flies swims about in middle-water, or rather nearer to the surface, picking and choosing the fly most agreeable to his taste.' That is, most definitely, a trout feeding on nymphs or nymphs about to hatch into duns. Three years earlier he had extracted three hundred caddis nymphs from the stomach of a trout. He also told his readers how to convert a wet fly into what he described as 'the maggot released from its case on the bottom stone and on its ascent to the surface.' He recommended mutilating the wings of a wet fly by pinching off about half the length, or by tying the wing down near the tail of the fly, so that it looked like the ascending nymph and then letting the fly sink as deep as possible in the water. This method was 'most likely to succeed in getting a few trouts'. One can imagine that some of his modified wet flies must have looked very similar to some of today's bubble wing and similar emerger patterns. Well chewed flies continue to seduce fish. Of equal import was his concern that the materials used to tie flies had to have the right look when wet. This point will be repeated many times during the story of the development of nymph fishing. One fly he tied with a blend of watermouse fur mixed with an equal amount of fine yellow wool or mohair, a blend which resulted in a killing colour when wet.

But in 1829, Richard Penn, writing his *Maxims and Hints on Angling, Chess, Shooting and Other Matters* (which was not published until 1855), advised on the pros and cons of fishing upstream and downstream and determined that the angler had a better chance of setting the hook when fishing upstream and there was a further advantage that a fish, when hooked successfully, could be played and brought downstream away from other feeding fish. He also gave advice on the benefits of whether to fish with only one fly on the cast or two. One very pertinent piece of advice, or indeed maxim, was that if fellow anglers claimed not to have seen a rise all day, do not rush to the conclusion that the fish had not been feeding on the fly. These maxims and hints were written before 31 May 1829 at Rod Cottage, River Side, the date and place recorded at the end of the introduction to his book.

H. D. Turing, then editor of the *Salmon and Trout Magazine*, wrote an interesting book called *Trout Problems* which was first published in 1948. In the chapter titled 'The Problem Of The Dry Fly', he quoted from a book, *North Country Angler*, written by an unknown author in 1786, a section on fishing with two flies, one a dry fly on a dropper and a sinking fly on the point. The author was obviously observant and a good fisherman. Turing quoted him as writing 'But the end fly I let sink two or three inches sometimes, having observed that it is often taken rather a little under water, than on the surface, the reason of which, I suppose, is that these flies are bred in the water under stones and among gravel; and as soon as their wings are grown they come to the top of the water, before they can fly, and are an easy prey to the lazy trouts who feed on them under the surface.'

Now Turing quoted from that passage as a very early example of the use of a dry fly. But surely it is of even more importance as an example of an early and basic form of catching fish feeding on nymphs, even if only 'a primitive form of nymph fishing'? Here we have an eighteenth century angler aware of nymphs and that trout feed on them yet Skues, the acknowledged founder of nymph fishing, was seemingly unaware of nymphs and their significance until the 1890s. Did he not read old fishing books – Turing's unknown author was not the first to observe nymphs underwater as we know – and benefit from them? In his later years Skues seems to have gained a reputation for producing very well researched articles and correspondence yet it took him so long to discover the nymph and its importance. Dr Tony Hayter, in *F.M. Halford And The Dry-Fly Revolution*, wrote of Skues' 'encyclopaedic articles on the history of fly patterns and other aspects of tackle and practice began in 1910 and were to continue to the end of his life. He spent long hours in the Reading Room of the British Museum burrowing back into the old-time authors to establish profitable lines of thought'. Writing in *The Way Of A Trout With A Fly* (first published in 1921) about when the use of a wet fly on a chalk stream was considered to be wicked, Skues referred to searching 'a number of more recent writers for light and leading on the subject', admittedly in vain. The way that the North Country Angler fished with a dry fly and a wet is not so different from some current practices where a dry fly on a dropper is used as both an indicator and a fly in its own right, or a nymph is tied to the bend of the hook of a *dry* fly, a technique much practised in New Zealand and now in other countries.

Comments here questioning assertions made by Skues' contemporaries and many other later and notable fly fishermen and writers as to his remarkable powers of observation leading to making the right deduction are not made with any intention of sullying or besmirching the old master's long-established and justified reputation as one of England's finest anglers, but simply that there are too many occasions – certainly prior to the early 1920s – where the evidence simply does not support these assertions.

Later in the same chapter, Turing wrote 'that flies like the G.R.H.E. and tup are fished *in* the surface film and are probably taken for nymphs hatching out.' Again we read of an angler appreciating the importance of hatching flies, or emergers as they are termed today. But not the full import, hence the use of the word 'probably'.

H. C. Cutcliffe wrote about fishing upstream in *Trout Fishing on Rapid Streams* in 1863. If he did not fish directly upstream he advocated fishing up and across and recommended using two flies and I suggest that very often he used the top, or bob fly, as an indicator if he was not always able to see a fish turn as it took a fly. 'From your fishing up-stream, your fly will most often be a little underwater, and there the fish takes it'. For him the point – or stretcher – fly was the critical one as it was the one most often a 'little underwater' but 'The bob is a useful appendage to take stragglers'.

In 1867, when Francis Francis's 'treatise on the art of angling in every branch,' *A Book on Angling*, was first published, there were two ways of fly fishing for trout: with a dry fly or with a wet fly. The dry fly was preferred on the chalk streams of southern England and the wet fly more popular in the north. But the wet fly was often recommended on chalk streams in rough, windy weather. In his instructions to the novice angler, Francis has him cast upstream 'parallel and as close as he conveniently can to the bank on his own side of the stream' and then he states that the novice must keep raising his rod tip steadily, as his fly floats back to him, 'so as to keep the fly near the top of the water'. 'Some people work their flies; but unless the fly be sunk rather deeply in the water (when it is mistaken rather for some quick darting water larva than a fly), this is bad, and often destructive of sport.'

He then wrote: 'When fish are only on larva don't worry them with fly or you spoil them. When the fly is well up [i.e. hatching] they will change from larva to fly; then you will find your account in your abstinence . . . It is not at all an uncommon thing to catch a fish on fly, when you open him to find the contents of his stomach a mass of larvae with about half a dozen flies, which he has only just got on to. You cannot mistake when a fish is only larva hunting. He never breaks the water.'

Here we have an early example of not only the impossibility of catching fish feeding on nymphs, or bulging fish as they were to be described for the next forty to fifty years, but also the fact that it was thought to be harmful to the sport to try to catch fish feeding below the surface. This was at a time when it was announced by *The Field* that its angling matters were to be dealt with by 'a fisherman who had "whipped half the streams of the United Kingdom" '. This is believed to have referred to Francis Francis who seems to have started work for the magazine in either 1856 or 1857. In his piece in *The Field* 'Gossip About The Hampshire Streams' (12 December, 1857), Francis wrote about the benefits of fishing with a dry fly and how it was impossible 'to imitate the motions of a live fly, that skips, hops, and whirls along the top of the water, as most flies do' but, by comparison the dun is immobile and there was, therefore, no motion to imitate. He continued: 'Anything more utterly unnatural than the jerks, wallops, and wabbles that the ordinary fly-fisherman gives to his wet fly an inch or more underwater (where any natural fly would be as-quiet as death could make it), under the supposition that he is making it appear alive – cannot be.' Later in the same article he writes of a small stream that enters the Solent opposite Osborne, where there were 'deep reaches and angles' and it was difficult to get the fish 'up to the top' so he resorted to 'biting a shot on at the head of the fly, and letting it sink to the bottom, and then working it up by short jerks'.

Francis maintained that 'The judicious and perfect application of dry, wet, and mid-water, fly-fishing stamps the finished fly-fisher with the hall-mark of efficiency'. Although his description of how to fish a wet fly upstream is very similar to fishing a nymph (apart from the actual design of the artificial fly that he would have used) and he knew that fish fed underwater on larva or what we know today are nymphs, why he feels that trying to catch fish feeding subsurface will spoil them is difficult to understand. (To read a little further in this section of his book offers an explanation when he advocates fishing large wet flies in a manner similar to how one would fish a streamer today and no doubt, small fish were caught on outsize hooks and may have been damaged when they were unhooked.) It was this belief that fishing a wet fly would spoil fish – and that it was not an effective way of fishing – that led to Halford and his peers decreeing that only the dry fly should ever be used on chalk streams. Yet Francis Francis was only too aware of the fact that trout fed on nymphs. It is also surprising that other anglers, including, once again Skues, were, seemingly, so ignorant of this fact.

In Scotland, David Webster *(The Angler and The Loop Rod*, 1885) liked to fish the loop line as it was less dependent on the wind direction. He was another very firm advocate of the necessity to fish upstream, particularly in clear water. In fact, he went so far as to describe fishing downstream as an 'antiquated method' although English fishing books of the period still promoted fishing downstream. Webster was promoting fishing upstream at least fifteen years before W. C. Stewart's book *The Practical Angler* was first published, but it was the latter's work that had the greater impact south of the border. It is interesting to read David Webster's claim that John Younger was also fully aware of the principles underlying the practice of fishing upstream, as was Richard Penn in his *Maxims and Hints*.

In his book *Ogden on Fly Tying*, published in 1879, the author James Ogden wrote about how he had caught mayfly nymphs, kept them in boxes underwater and then found drowned, hatched mayfly duns.

Red Spinner, in *The Field* of 3 October 1891, wrote at length on 'A Wet Fly Chalk Stream'. He had had a fortnight's angling ramble north of the Trent where he had fished a chalk stream 'in which the trout habitually take the wet fly, and upon which rainy and windy days are hailed with welcome instead of execration.' And that the favourite pattern was 'the well-known hackle made of partridge feather, with an orange body'. This fly he described as a killing fly in all parts of the UK and 'never out of the book of nine anglers out of ten in northern England and Scotland'. This lead him to write that successful wet fly fishing in the Hampshire chalk streams would be dependent on the choice of the correct pattern. Apart from a couple of days on the Test in wet and blustery weather, he admitted that he 'never gave the wet fly a fair trial'. He knew a brother angler who had tried the Test, Itchen and Kennet and that if these rivers were 'treated to the proper flies, the sunken method would be as successful as it was in the old days'. Some years later, in *The Field* of 30 December 1899, Skues wrote: 'In years gone by anglers used to get good baskets on Itchen and Test with the wet-fly. They will have to come back to it again. Some day they will learn to combine a judicious admixture of wet-fly science and dry-fly art, and then –

'There will be the time for some new development. In the meanwhile, why not?'

Later in his wet fly article, Red Spinner described a day on the Test at

Kimbridge with 'Mr Halford' when the fish were 'rising recklessly and madly in all directions, but will take no sort of fly that you may give them . . . nor was it possible to observe what the fish were rising at' and neither caught a fish. He had observed a similar 'hullabaloo' on the northern chalk stream mentioned at the start of the article. There he had the advantage of a high bank to stand on to observe the fish and he saw 'that the commotion made on the top of the water was made not by their noses, but by the dorsal fin or the extreme tip of the tail, as they ploughed about just under the surface of the water' of every shallow for about half an hour. Other anglers had seen similar activity and not one had caught a fish although there had been a few duns and midges which all the fish ignored.

George A. B. Dewar's book *The Book of the Dry Fly* was published in 1897 and contains some remarkable information. Writing in a chapter entitled 'Gross and Aggravating Feeders' about the 'three well-known and distinct habits of feeding trout', bulging, tailing and smutting (or cursing), he stated: 'The "bulging" trout appears to the casual or unsophisticated observer an earnest, straight-forward fish, taking winged flies of some kind or other.' And then he continued: 'A trout is described as "bulging" when he is taking the *nymphae* of the Duns or May-flies just beneath the surface, and consequently just before they hatch out into the *sub-imago* state. To catch the tasty morsel before it reaches the surface, and bursts through its husk, evidently requires activity on the part of the fish. He cannot stay in the same place and lazily draw in his food as when he is taking Duns in a slow-flowing backwater, but must needs rush hither and thither, a foot or more each time perhaps, and seize his victims in the nick of time. These quick movements close to the surface make a commotion in the water, and very often indeed this commotion is quite similar to that caused by a fairly rising trout. I have frequently seen a trout "bulging" in exactly the same place time after time, over no doubt a particularly good find of *nymphae*, and it is a fish like this which may now and then deceive even an old hand.' Note the use of the phrase 'fairly rising trout' which suggests that a nymphing fish is not playing the game according to the rules.

Dewar then posed the question 'what is the best thing to do with "bulging" trout?' 'Some recommend a remedy for the evil in a bright-coloured or fancy fly' and then in a footnote, 'Mr Halford recommends a gold-ribbed Hare's Ear as about the best fly, owing to its possibly being mistaken by the fish for a *nympha.*' Now we know that nymphing fish were considered evil, unsporting creatures that would, at best, take a fly fished dry but only in mistake for a nymph. Dewar's remedy, short of blasting the thing out of the water with a shot gun, was to move on and find another fish. He then admitted that some anglers have success with a wet, or sunk, fly with the wings cut off as such an artificial has a resemblance to a nymph. But he was not convinced as, like

According to Dewar tailing fish should be fished for with a long line down-stream and the fly worked with a series of little jerks, somewhat as in salmon fishing

Halford, he could not conceive how you impart 'the necessary movement in the water'. This, of course, was Halford's conviction too. But Skues knew that when fish were bulging – 'the vicious and reprehensible practice of bulging, or feeding on the nymphae about to hatch' – that the angler who wished for success must 'give it to them wet'. But the wet fly must be delivered with the same precision as a dry fly – not raking the water across and down.

But what of tailing trout? Surely another example of a fish behaving unfairly and in an unsporting fashion. You could not be more wrong! In Dewar's experience, tailing fish were, as a rule, easier to entice than bulging brutes. 'He must be fished for with a long line *down-stream* [my emphasis], and the fly worked with a series of little jerks, somewhat as in salmon fishing.' He is writing about fishing the hallowed chalk streams of Hampshire and Hertfordshire, would you believe. He maintained 'To kill "tailers" in broad daylight and in low water is quite an art in itself'. But he rather contradicts himself when he states that for the true dry fly fisherman it is not 'the real thing' and if a fish starts to rise to duns, then the tailer should be abandoned immediately.

So, here we had a knowledgeable angler who was only too aware that trout feed on nymphs, feeding on them particularly at the start of a hatch, that they can be difficult to catch but caught they can be, and the beginnings of a method of catching them using wet flies with the wings amputated. Why did neither he nor his peers set about developing better ways and means of catching bulging fish? There were, seemingly, two reasons. Firstly anglers in the late 1890s had convinced themselves of the impossibility of imitating the movement of nymphs in the water and secondly, that wonderful concept of the unsporting fish, that a fish bulging was not rising, or feeding, fairly and that they were an evil. Dewar was happy to sanction fishing across and down to tailing fish on dry fly waters but not upstream to nymphing fish. What a wonderfully muddled and confused sporting doctrine.

Harry Plunkett-Greene, the opera singer who wrote so lyrically about the little river Bourne – a tributary of the Test – in his book *Where the Bright Waters Meet*, was an out-and-out dry fly man by his own admission but by 1907 he had modified his opinions. He knew that he was 'a fool to stick to the winged fly' when his own experience and of others had proved 'that the hackle fly is the more deadly killer' and that his 'prowess with the nymph is still negligible, but my prejudices have suffered a sea-change'. He also felt that 'the true prophet of the nymph has the right to be proud of his creed'.

The attitudes of dry fly purists such as Halford, his peers and successors played a major part in the strangulation of the development of nymph fishing, as did a lack of understanding of the life cycle of up-wing flies and the importance of nymphs as food for trout although there was sound, documented evidence going back many years on both aspects, as we have discovered. For a long time leading anglers were profoundly ignorant and thought that flies fell onto the water: they did not know that most flies lay their eggs in the water, the eggs hatch into nymphs which then make their way to the surface of the river where they hatch into duns. This extraordinary misconception was still rife in the middle of the nineteenth century.

The growing understanding of nymphs and emergers in the life cycle of emphemeroptera and their importance to a trout's diet, played a significant role in the development of 'wet' flies. This is perhaps a pertinent place to state that upwing, or mayflies, progress from the egg, to nymph and then to winged insect without going through a pupal stage. This is known as an incomplete metamorphosis as they are considered to be of a primitive order. Sedges, or caddis, are a more advanced order and go through a complete metamorphosis from egg, to larva, to pupa and winged adult. These differences affect the way nymphs and caddis pupae look and behave underwater, which, in turn, dictate how the angler represents and fishes them. Towards the end of the nineteenth century, traditional wet flies were starting to be dressed without wings and many of these would, eventually, evolve into nymphs. That said, North Country spiders and similar traditional wet flies were and still are very good imitations of hatching sedges, in particular, and are fished as such. In his history of fly fishing, *The Fly*, Andrew Herd wrote about one T. E. Pritt and said: 'According to Pritt, a man who clearly understood the value of the nymph at a time when many fishermen were ignorant of its value, north country fishermen had abandoned the winged wet fly completely by 1860'. While that is probably a somewhat strong statement on the death of the winged wet fly, it does show the way the design and tying of wet flies was thought to be going.

Around the turn of the nineteenth century there were expert anglers who considered wet fly fishing to be an art form. Edmonds and Lee, in *Brook and River Trouting* (1916), maintained that an angler who had only mastered fishing downstream or even the dry fly, had an incomplete education. Such an angler would not be able to fish the rapid broken waters of the north country streams but the angler who had 'thoroughly mastered the art of fishing the wet fly *upstream* would be able to quickly adapt himself to the conditions and surroundings of the home of the dry fly.' Although wet fly fishing was often derided as 'chuck and chance', the skilful upstream angler cast 'to a definite point, not necessarily to a rising fish, as in dry-fly fishing, but successively to each of the many little runs, eddies, channels and slack water behind boulders, which his experience teaches are likely to hold feeding fish'. Flies were often fished *slightly* submerged.

(Today's anglers who scorn the use of take or bite indicators when nymph fishing may be interested to know that they have a long history. Edmonds and Lee advocated the use of a pinch of sheep's wool gathered from a fence or bush, fastened between the end of the fly line and cast, or leader, and used as an indicator when fishing the upstream worm. The wool was used as an indicator and not a float which is the case with some of the very large, buoyant indicators used by so-called nymph fishermen currently.)

Skues wrote about wet flies being taken 'perhaps as flies in the act of hatching' in *The Way Of A Trout With A Fly*, and 'The hackled North-Country pattern does not necessarily represent a submerged fly, but one in process of hatching or hatched out, and caught by the current and tumbled'. Skues had felt for quite some time that wet flies were taken for nymphs 'in the very act of hatching', or when fish were taking larvae, but when he discovered, in trouts' mouths, nymphs with 'no show of wing', he started to dress flies with very short hackles to represent nymphs specifically. He was only too aware of the ignorance of even highly-skilled and proficient fishermen 'of the very existence of the nymph, its form and character'. Dry fly anglers persisted at casting at rising fish seemingly breaking the water but these were often fish feeding on nymphs and not interested in the hatched, floating fly. Even though it took him a long time to realise that many of the fish he caught on wet flies fished upstream were nymphing, he later modified earlier pronouncements that such fish mistook his wet flies for hatching nymphs to suggest that they *might* take them for nymphs just about to hatch. But when he found nymphs in fish with no sign of wings, or hatching, he started to experiment with short hackled patterns.

On a blazing hot day, when the river was covered with smuts and small pale wateries, he caught four and a half brace of fish between one o'clock and three o'clock although the rise had, to all intents and purposes, finished. He had caught his fish on a half-sunk big dark olive. When he opened the stomachs of some of these fish, there were masses of smuts and not a trace of an olive of any sort. He had published his finding in a letter to *The Field* which was published on 10 Octobers 1891.

J. W. Hills was of the opinion that anglers had, thanks to the publications of Skues' book *Minor Tactics of The Chalk Stream*, a much better understanding of underwater fly life and that various nymphs had been identified including the olive dun, blue winged olive, iron blue and pale watery dun, and that copies were 'being built on new lines, copying more closely the original' without the wing and hackle of the traditional wet fly and that these new artificial nymphs were being used 'with success in the shyest chalk streams.' Although Skues used the same quote in *Nymph Fishing For Chalk Stream Trout*, he did not include Hills' comment that Skues thought that they would not be successful!

In his series of articles in *The Field*, 'Hints to Young Anglers', in June 1907, H. T. Sheringham wrote on smutting and bulging trout and told his readers to fish a fly wet and to press water into it with the fingers so that it would fish just under the surface and then to watch the reaction of the fish cast to. He wrote that it was not dry fly fishing but 'a perfectly legitimate way of catching trout on dry fly streams when they are obviously not taking surface food'; he added that it was very fascinating and not an easy way to catch fish. He also advised oiling the cast, bar the last foot (30cm), so that it would indicate a take if the fish could not be seen.

The second fundamental reason for the lack of development in nymph fishing was the tackle available through the nineteenth century in particular. At this time fly fishermen used very long rods and short lines and suffered from the very limited casting ability that they provided. Lines were made of horse hair which limited the practical length of line that could be made. A long rod meant that the fly could be placed closer to a fish in the middle of a river or well away from the bank. These rods and lines would not cast a fly into the wind and so, on everything but windless days, fishing was across and downstream, taking advantage of any favourable wind, and upstream only when the wind blew upstream. Even mixed horse hair and silk lines did not aid casting to any great degree as the rods were still not designed for casting. But Alexander Mackintosh did encourage readers of his self-published book of 1806, *The Driffield Angler*, to fish up and across. He wrote that by casting into the wind to

25

the opposite bank the angler would be able to kill more trout than any other angler. 'The wind and stream will bring the flies more naturally down and cross-ways on the stream than throwing downwards.' Casting somewhat upstream would also result in the fish being hooked more firmly and thus more likely to be landed.

One benefit of the long rod was that it could be used to hold a reasonable length of line clear of the water. This was important because methods of water-proofing fly lines had not yet been developed, nor was it possible to water-proof flies to prevent them from sinking. A waterlogged line soon pulled a fly underwater. Most anglers started a cast with a dry fly and as it absorbed water, they ended up fishing a wet fly. For many decades, and probably even centuries, they were not too fussed.

But Skues had witnessed the efficiency of fishing with a short fixed line in Bosnia in September 1897 and wrote about 'Bosnia – The Turco as a Fly-Fisher' in *The Field* of January 1898. Skues and a companion saw their first Turk fishing 'the dazzling blue waters of Bosnian Pliva' with 'a wand of some eight or nine feet, and casting among the cascades a short but accurate line'. Other 'Turkish sportsmen of the peasant class' were seen casting 'pre-Waltonian flies towards the river's edge', some of whom fished with a cast of four flies. The casts, or leaders, were made of horse hair which was very fine and strong and came from the local pony stallions. The local flies had wings 'of soft wild goose' or feathers from under the wings of geese, owls or eagles, no legs and bodies made of raw silk.

Skues was in the country for sixteen days and he found all 'the natives', even on different rivers, were using the same tackle. Rods were one piece and made from 'a singularly hard type of wood', no reel or winder or running line, the aforementioned horse hair casts and a team of flies. 'With these flies fished down stream I have seen the natives yank a three-quarter pound grayling from the water and catch it in the left hand.' Skues speculated on the possibility of the Yorkshire and North Country use of soft hackles coming from 'some marauding Norseman who brought his plunder from the Balkans.' An interesting thought. Towards the end of his life he mentioned his visit to Bosnia in *Nymph Fishing for Chalk Stream Trout* but that it had no affect on his 'progress towards nymph fishing in chalk streams'.

When long, tapered silk lines started to come into regular use, it was soon found that the then standard procedure of whipping a fixed line back and forth was not able to extend the new lines fully. Fly fishermen had to develop new techniques and new casts. Many of today's casts are based on these developments. One of the keys to successful nymph fishing is accurate casting, being able to place a nymph in a fish's feeding lane and far enough upstream to allow the artificial to obtain the required depth. Such accuracy was difficult to achieve with nineteenth century trout rods which were often twelve (3.6m), fourteen (4.2m) and sometimes more feet long and double handed. As well as being very long, and heavy, the action was usually very soft and pliable. Even single hand rods were still twelve feet long and cripplingly heavy to fish with all day. I used the word cripplingly quite intentionally as Halford wrote that dry-fly fishermen might have to make up to thirty false casts to dry their flies satisfactorily and they were often unable to fish all day without taking long periods of rest. In *F. M. Halford and the Dry-Fly Revolution,* Tony Hayter wrote: 'Marston once recorded that his wrist had become so numb on a chalk-stream expedition that he did not have the strength to strike at a rise . . . Halford came upon his guest Thomas Andrews sitting on a stile nursing his right hand and complaining that he could no longer hold the rod.' These must be the first recorded examples of that modern curse RSI or repetitive strain injury. Skues referred to one of his rods as a 'wrist-breaker' at the time that he acquired his first lightweight Leonard rod, and other contemporary rods as 'those terrible wrist-breakers, hand-paralysing, blister-producing flails of the [eighteen] eighties and nineties.' A graphic description of what must have been very unpleasant items of fishing tackle.

Rods were made from a variety of different woods and in many different combinations of wood, often with a whale-bone tip. It was the discovery that a new material – bamboo – could be split with a knife and the resultant strips shaped and glued together that led to the production of the first split- or built-cane rods. Early split-cane rods were not without their faults such as being very heavy and over stiff. They were also made from only three or sometimes four sections of cane. In America Samuel Phillippe, of Easton, Pennsylvania, built what is said to be the first six-strip cane rod in 1848 or 1849. It soon became evident that rods made from less than six strips were very difficult to cast at all, let alone with any real accuracy. Incidentally, H. D. Turing suggests that 'North Country Angler' may have invented built-cane rods – or at least established the method – nearly one hundred years earlier. His rod was made from split elder which had the advantage that the knots in it come on alternate sides of the branch so that long strips could be obtained by cutting sections from alternate lengths. 'North Country Angler' may not have used, or even known about cane, but he may have been the first to use this method of construction.

Hexagonal split-cane rods did not achieve any real popular success until Hiram L. Leonard made a rod, in 1869, of ash and lancewood, in Bangor, Maine. One of his friends suggested that he send it to a Boston sporting goods shop. The owners of the shop, Bradford and Anthony, were impressed with the rod and its workmanship and commissioned Leonard to build four-strip cane rods for them. Leonard then adapted the six-strip principle to his cane rods and these rods were to be the very first commercially-manufactured built-cane rods as we still know them today.

One key factor that contributed to the success of Leonard's rods was a machine that he designed to cut the sections of each rod with a precision and accuracy that had never been achieved before. His rods also used compound tapers which he calculated mathematically and he also discovered that of all the many varieties of bamboo available, Tonkin cane was far better than any other. Tonkin cane was much lighter than the Calcutta cane that he started with. Leonard moved his factory from Maine to Central Valley, New York, in 1881 and it was here that many other famous rod makers were to learn their trade. After Leonard's death in 1907, Thomas Bates Mills bought the remaining interests in the H. L. Leonard Rod Company and the factory was run by Arthur C. Mills III, his great-grandson.

Hexagonal cane rods were available on both sides of the Atlantic by the end of the 1870s. As always seems to be the case with most new developments, the high cost of these new rods, compared to a top-quality greenheart rod, slowed acceptance of them.

Skues fished with Leonard rods but even so there were times when he felt that the wind 'was too much for my little nine-footer'. On one such occasion he was fishing the Itchen with T. J. Lamorna Birch, an artist and first-rate fly fisherman, who used a ten foot (3m) Leonard. Skues was 'immensely impressed by the straightness of the line he drove into it [a stiff downstream wind] and by the accuracy of his casting'. The rod that Skues was using was probably his Leonard rod, built in 1905, that his fishing friend C.L.C. 'styled WBR, which, being interpreted, means World's Best Rod'. It was nine feet long (2.75m) and weighed five ounces (142 grams). Skues had acquired his first Leonard rod, a ten footer weighing six ounces (170 grams), in 1903. He continued to use the WBR right up until 1945, when he passed the rod to his brother Charles who was to present it to the Flyfishers' Club where it is still on display in a glass case.

In the *Journal of The Flyfishers Club* of 1917, Winter issue, Skues wrote an interesting article on fly rods. 'I think the chief part of the ecstasy of fishing with the fly is to be found in the qualities of the fly rod, and if I am right in this, the more exquisite the rod the keener and more perfect the pleasure to be derived from the sport, a strong argument in favour of perfection in one's weapon for the particular game in hand. It may be, indeed it is, better to fish with any old rod than not to fish. But to fish with the most perfect of gear raises the satisfaction to the sublime. . .' Skues knew that, in his day, there was no such thing as the perfect fly rod for all purposes and that 'perfection must be sought in relation to the purpose for which the rod is used'. He played a leading role in the introduction of lightweight American rods in the UK. He admits to having tried a number of 'the cheaper American split cane rods which come into the English market' and was 'struck by the scientific character of their taper'. He found many of these rods a delight to handle and although he did have his doubts about their durability, he felt that all English rod makers 'might with advantage take their cue from the States'. These scientific tapers produced rods which were much smaller in diameter than comparable English rods, without any loss of power or performance and there were no 'Such abominations as the lock-fast joint'; these factors resulted in the American rods being so much lighter than their English counterparts.

Fortunately for fly fishermen as quality horsehair lines were becoming more difficult to find, silk came along as a replacement. At this time fly lines were similar to modern shooting heads in that they consisted of a heavy, plaited 'casting line' with a thinner, long back or running line. But the advent of machine-made plaited silk lines gave fly fishermen longer one-piece lines. These lines were soon superseded by oiled silk lines which lasted well into the middle decades of the twentieth century. Tapered silk lines could be cast well, and farther, and controlled properly both on and off the water so that an angler could cast his fly where he wanted and manipulate, or mend, his line to keep the fly floating in the required direction.[1] One problem with some of the early silk lines was that they were too heavy for many rods, some of which broke under the strain of trying to cast these lines.

The tackle and flies available also had an influence on the way rivers were described – as either dry fly rivers or wet fly rivers – and how rivers and streams were fished. Fast, turbulent rivers were very difficult, if not impossible, to fish with dry flies because it was very difficult to tie flies that floated well on fast water. Suitable materials were not available and the best ways to use what materials were available were still in their early stages of development.

Dewar, in 1897, was well aware of the availability of treatments to make lines and leaders float better. 'But paraffin has a rival now in vaseline, which some use in preference for anointing line and gut.' But he and some of his peers frowned on the use of paraffin as they felt that it made angling too easy and luxurious. Believe it or not, some anglers even objected to fishing the evening rise, I imagine because of the difficulty of seeing your fly and the size of fish in failing light.

The history of nymph fishing is one of a continuing failure to connect observation with practice. Observers included Ronalds, Skues and Halford. It was Skues who, eventually, made the necessary leap of imagination. As long ago as the start of the second decade of the nineteenth century in his *Fishing Diary, 1809–1819*, the Rev. Richard Durnford of Chilbolton, Hants, was fishing with a point fly and sometimes a bob fly as well, depending on the wind, in particular, as well as the water. Skues had a copy of the *Diary*, which was not published until 1911, and wrote about it in the *Fishing Gazette* on 8 April 1916. Skues' most significant comment on *The Fishing Diary* was 'I have little doubt that the (point) fly was generally taken either for a nymph about to hatch or in the act of hatching. The diarist was not one of those anglers who imagined that the fly descended on the water from the air. He was acutely conscious of the nymph.' Durnford fished with his point fly just under the surface and he recorded taking trout that were 'absolutely gorged with nymphae of the gnats taken as they were descending through the water, their wings being imperfect' (8 May 1911) and then in June he caught trout with nymphs in their throats. When one considers how anglers like to meet and fish and talk together, to discuss tackle, flies and fishing methods and so on, why had no one else appreciated Durnford's observations in the near one hundred years that passed before publication and Skues getting his hands on a copy? Did the Rev. Richard Durnford have no fishing contemporaries who took account of his what we now know to have been very profound observations? It is not easy to discern from his diary exactly how Durnford fished and whether or not he attempted to imitate the nymphs that he had seen. On 17 April 1817, he wrote that 'A Bob (sic) fly should never be used so long as the wind will allow the end fly to be distinctly seen' and he also used a Bob fly when fishing in a strong wind.

Then in 1836, when Alfred Ronalds' book *The Flyfisher's Entomology* was published, he too knew about the life-cycle of emphemeroptera and mentioned nymphs by name. 'For all Ronalds' careful observation, hung in his tiny observatory, he missed a golden opportunity and unintentionally led fly fishermen into a dead end; because if his down-wing wet patterns weren't intended to represent nymphs, they didn't imitate duns very well either . . . Yet despite all his laborious observations, this great man missed his chance. Ronalds had seen enough to be able to make an inspired leap and discover nymph fishing, but he did not.'[2] In a similar vein, H. T. Sheringham, who edited and wrote an extended introduction to the 1921 printing of his book commented: 'He observed so closely, and knew the ways of flies and trout so thoroughly, that he must have been ever on the verge of enlightenment.' Although Sheringham's comment was written in connection with the development of dry fly fishing, it is, none the less, just as applicable to nymph fishing, as the quote from Andrew Herd's book *The Fly* demonstrates. Ronalds had designed and built an observation chamber that he suspended from a bridge over the river Blythe in Staffordshire. 'Its form was octagonal, and it had three windows, which being situated only four feet and a half above the surface of the water, allowed a very close view of it. The middle one commanded a *Scour*, each of the two others a small Whirlpool or Eddy. The curtains of the windows were provided with peepholes, so that the fish could not see his observer, and a bank was thrown up, in order to prevent a person approaching the entrance of the hut from alarming the fish.' His observations, although they helped him to design flies that were much more modern in concept than contemporary nineteenth century patterns, did nothing to advance the methods of fly fishing, whether dry fly fishing or nymph fishing.

Through the early years of nymph fishing, there was a common complaint that it was very difficult to buy properly-designed and made artificial nymphs. Even though the creative anglers such as Skues and Mottram produced good designs and flies themselves, many of the commercial tyings of these patterns were awful and did not find favour with their inventors. Even today some commercially-tied flies are unrecognisable when compared to the original tied by its inventor, such as Frank Sawyer and others.

Notes

1 In the USA Ted Trueblood, for many years angling editor for *Field & Stream*, who helped develop fly lines for Scientific Anglers, maintained that the introduction of the AFTMA system for calibrating and designating fly lines by weight – replacing the old system based on diameter – was the 'one thing [that] did more to take the mystique [out] of fly fishing than any other in the preceeding 100 years'. This introduction was followed by rod makers marking their rods with the correct line weight. In a letter of 29 January 1973, Trueblood wrote to Leon L. Martuch of Scientific Anglers about an old line 'my first good fly line' which was 'an oil-finished, double-tapered, Halford HCH, for $8.00 in 1931 and fished with it *only* until after World War II'. He emphasised that he used no other line during those years. Unfortunately his wife used both ends of the line to truss a Thanksgiving turkey!

2. *The Fly* by Andrew Herd.

4 The beginnings of nymph fishing 1880 to *c*1935

'. . . nymph fishing, new certainly in its modern dress, but in essence as old as fly-fishing itself. . . . . But nymph fishing is being practised more, and understood better, each year.'

J.W. Hills, *River Keeper*, 1934

'Fashions in fishing change every bit as much as they do in anything. Methods which were looked on with horror a few years ago are today accepted without question. While nowadays we are apt to be startled and surprised at some of the rigid, orthodox views expressed by our fathers, and while there are many instances in dry-fly-fishing, one which is of considerable interest is underwater fishing in a dry-fly stream' wrote R. D. Baird in *A Trout Rose*, which was published in 1946. The use of the phrase 'underwater fishing in a dry-fly stream' is interesting and the word underwater is used by other angling writers.

As we know now, in the early days of nymph fishing in the latter years of the nineteenth century and the beginning of the twentieth, one of the main reasons for the dry fly purists objecting to nymph fishermen was the latter were thought to, or accused of, flogging the water with a wet fly and not casting to an individual, rising – and thus feeding – fish. Because they were thought to be fishing at random, the purists were certain that any hungry fish which were not caught by these floggers, would be put-down and so would not rise to a dry fly. The descriptions of what was then still known as wet fly fishing as described and practised by Skues (who did, in fact fish with wet flies and spiders before and as he developed his range of artificial nymphs) and Mottram was the complete antithesis of the old-fashioned notion of wet fly fishing, casting and fishing across and down with a team of flies. It was the start of upstream nymph fishing as is practised today around the world.

Many nymph fishermen today may be very surprised to know that F. M. Halford did experiment with nymphs. He met George Selwyn Marryat on 28 April 1879, and together they experimented with nymphs, using a mayfly pattern of Marryat's – Marryat was not as dogmatic as Halford – and another of Mosely's[1]. Marryat was born in 1840 and after leaving Winchester he joined the Army and served with the 6th Dragoon Guards. He returned to

A modern interpretation of Marryat's Mayfly
nymph. Colonel Harding fished nymphs, including
Mayfly nymphs, tied by Marryat but never had a
touch with them

Hampshire when he was thirty years old. Marryat collaborated with Henry
Hall, of Winchester, on the development of eyed hooks and then with Halford,
particularly on fly tying. According to Skues, Marryat was dressing nymphs
before 1883. Halford often sought advice on fly tying matters from Marryat
who had learnt much of his fly tying knowledge and practice from Mrs Cox,
a professional fly tier. Without Marryat's help and encouragement it is likely
that Halford might not have written his first book, although Marryat had no
wish to have his name attached to that book. Marryat died at the early age of
fifty-six, during a major flu epidemic on 14 February 1896 and was buried in
Winchester Cathedral.

Halford was very aware of bulging trout, particularly on the Itchen, in the
late 1880s, and he was also only too well aware that trout took most of their
food underwater but was soon to convince himself that this food could not be
imitated successfully. Also he could not understand why artificial wet flies
should have wings because he had never seen any flies that had been drowned
by the flow of a river or stream. In his book *Dry-Fly Fishing*, published in 1889,
Halford wrote about 'Some authorities' who recommended fishing a large
sunk fly to bulging, or nymphing, fish. He admitted that he had never had any
success doing this, quite understandably because he had no confidence in
fishing a large artificial to fish feeding on small naturals. 'I have tried it in a
half-hearted way, and without any faith in the experiment.' He does admit to
having heard and 'once or twice I have positively seen such things occur'
which was a 'comparative novice' catching bulging trout, and grayling, 'with
wet-fly dragging, or even fished downstream'. His admission of having
witnessed such methods is interesting when compared with his later, rather
petulant remark in *The Dry-Fly Man's Handbook*, 'I am told, however, that there

is a school of fly fishermen who only fish the sunk fly over feeding fish or one in position if it will not take a floating fly. This, they urge, is a third method of wet-fly fishing, the other two being the more ordinary of *fishing the water* with sunk fly either upstream or downstream. Candidly I have never seen this method in practice, and I have grave doubts as to its efficacy.' *The Dry-Fly Man's Handbook* was published in 1913, after Skues' *Minor Tactics* and some thirty years after his own failed attempts at fishing an upstream sunk fly to nymphing trout. Halford's biographer, Dr Hayter, stated that the idea of a somewhat vague rumour having reached Halford's ear was nonsense and that he 'had read *Minor Tactics* and indeed everything else on the subject in his own journal *The Field* and elsewhere'. Proof of that can be had in Halford's own words on the sunk fly fisherman catching a fish on a chalk stream: 'He might go away and talk of having wiped the eye of the dry-fly man, or even fly into print and proclaim *orbi et urbi* that he had made the astounding discovery that the dry-fly men are all fools, and that the sunk fly will at all times kill on these south-country chalk-streams.' But he felt that this would be mere delusion and although many years ago odd fish had been killed with wet flies fished across or even downstream, it was only on what he described as 'happening days'. This is, or course, complete nonsense as dry fly fishing was a relatively new practice whereas fishing with wet or sunk flies has been prac- tised since time immemorial.

Who ever wrote the review of *The Dry-Fly Man's Handbook* for the *Salmon and Trout Magazine* of July 1913, did not mince his words in condemnation of some of Halford's more intolerant outbursts. 'The strange and even embittered intolerance shown in several passages towards critics and opponents of the purist and most rigid cult of the dry-fly, is certainly a blot upon the book.' The reviewer then suggested that a friend should have advised Halford to exorcise those comments, or failing that to at least temper them. The reviewer described Halford's comments as being a 'contemptuous dismissal' of those who disagreed with him. In Halford's obituary, published in April 1914, we read that Halford and his fellow dry fly purists would often consider the fishing of an artificial of the wrong sex of the fly that was 'up' was certainly a blunder and verging on a crime.

He wrote that a bulging fish was a feeding fish and as such he felt that 'a slightly showy pattern, such as an *orange bumble*, floated occasionally over the feeding fish, may be successful'. But for Halford the very best fly to use for bulging fish was a Gold-Ribbed Hare's Ear which he felt that even a novice could see, when nymph and artificial were compared side-by-side, was a very good representation of the nymph. G. E. M. Skues wrote of Halford being of the opinion that the Gold-Ribbed Hare's Ear was taken by a trout as 'a hatching nymph standing on its partially discarded shuck'.

A little further on in the same chapter, 'Studies of Fish Feeding', we get to the very heart of the concern that nymph fishermen prick and scare fish. There are two sentences that must be quoted in full. 'It has been darkly rumoured that some anglers are invariably able to get sport among bulging fish, and that the plan adopted is to cast up-stream with a good-sized sunk fly put directly above. The slightest movement of the trout is answered by a quick and some-what violent strike, the effect of this action being to drive the hook into some part of the moving fish, but certainly not into his mouth.' What he described was nothing other than attempting to snag fish. This was poaching, not fishing. For Halford, 'there is no word in the English language strong enough to express the utter contempt which a true sportsman should feel for the pot-hunter who would descend to such a strategy.' Obviously if such a practice was to have been allowed on any water, it is not surprising that fish would be pricked – or worse – and so put off feeding, but only for a short while because, as Halford admitted, trout do not have any long-term memory. But Halford would seem to have been unable to distinguish between snagging fish and fishing for them legitimately (although in a way that he did not approve of and was unable to practice successfully) and because his pronouncements were taken as law by his disciples and admirers, it is little wonder that nymph fisher-men were to be accused of and condemned for supposedly pricking and harming fish for so many years.

In *The Dry-Fly Man's Handbook* he wrote that 'Years and years ago' he and Marryat had dressed 'most effective patterns to represent the nymphs of duns and mayflies' and that they killed some fish with them. On 5 May 1908, on the Test at Mottisfont, Halford actually caught a trout on one of Martin Mosely's nymph patterns. He experimented further with nymphs that year and the following year (which was to be the end of these experiments) and although he knew that fish fed profusely underwater, he was of the opinion that such food – nymphs – could not be imitated successfully. He knew of the importance of nymphs, larvae and shrimps to the trout's diet through the many autopsies that he had carried out, yet he chose to ignore this evidence. In the chapter 'Autopsy', Halford wrote: 'It has been already shown that by far the larger proportion of the contents of the stomach of a trout or grayling consists of larvae[2], nymphae, caddis, shrimps &c., which are invariably in the middle and lower depths of the water, from which fact inferences must be drawn that the major part of their food is taken below the surface. At first glance, a natural deduction from this would be, that the sunk fly would be more likely to tempt than the floating one . . . Unfortunately very few of the disciples of the dry fly practise, even if they understand, *the art* [my emphasis] of fishing with sunk fly, which may account for the fact that as a general rule when tried in the Hampshire streams it has not proved successful.' Later in the same chapter he wrote about 'how small a proportion of the fish's insect food is taken when floating, and how large a proportion belongs to the middle and lower depth of the stream.' And then: 'A natural [conclusion?]from this would be, that the sunk fly would be more likely to tempt than the floating one.' And elsewhere 'It may also parenthetically serve to teach him why our wet-fly fishing brother can at times get such good sport, and it might possibly convey hints to the fly-dresser for new and perhaps killing wet-fly patterns.' In the same book in 'Studies of Fish Feeding', he described a fish ' . . . when feeding on larvae or nymphae it is described as *bulging* from its motion through the water.'

So why was he so against trying to catch nymphing trout? 'The difficulty does not lie in dressing an artificial grub fairly resembling the dun nymph, but in imparting to that imitation the motion and direction taken by the natural insect at that stage of its existence.' As we know, he had tried large sunk flies with no confidence or conviction and thus no success. In spite of this, he wrote in the chapter 'Selection of Fly', of 'a most efficacious [pattern]' evolved by Mr Marryat to be used for fish feeding on Mayfly nymphs. 'The fly should not be too dry, although, at the same time, it should not actually sink below the surface', yet another example of what, today, would be known as an emerger pattern fished in the surface film. It is interesting that Halford and Marryat were happy to attempt to catch trout with mayfly nymphs when one considers Major Oliver Kite's condemnation of the practice in *Elements of Nymph Fishing, Theory and Practice*: 'The use of a large artificial Mayfly nymph . . . is undoubt-edly an effective method of butchering fish but whether it can be considered sport is another matter which the individual fly-fisher should decide for himself.'

Halford seemed happy to write or say one thing and then do another. He tried to be very understanding of and not wishing to condemn the wet fly man's skills – he even referred to it as an art no less – yet this understanding and seeming generosity of spirit was not always borne out by his actions. And he was quite prepared to ignore the evidence of his own eyes and experience and the experiences of his fellow anglers too. He and Marryat stopped fishing with nymphs for two reasons. The first was that they considered them to be essentially wet flies and using them on a water reserved for dry fly fishing only was, therefore, a breach of the ethics of the dry fly. His second reason, which he thought that more anglers would understand, was that where and when-ever they fished nymphs, they hooked and lost an inordinate number of fish which resulted in these fish becoming so shy as to be unapproachable. Whatever his stated reasons were for stopping fishing with artificial nymphs, I believe that a very convincing case can be made for Halford's hatred of nymph fishing based on his admitted inability to catch fish on wet or damp flies fished upstream and his conviction that nymph fishermen set about catching fish by snagging them and not aiming to catch them in what we now know is both a fair and an artistic way. These facts must have gnawed and eaten away at his pysche like a cancer. If he could not stop all upstream fishing with a nymph or wet fly, then he was going to do nothing to help those who insisted on fishing this way either.

Fortunately not all his peers felt quite the same way. Baird was a pupil at Winchester in 1907 when day tickets for the Itchen could be bought for a small sum from 'what is now Mr Chalkley's shop'. Winchester scholars were allowed to fish at any time as long as it did not interfere with games or study. He claimed that in those days the fishing was 'exceedingly poor and very difficult, for it was not preserved, and, in consequence, was heavily poached'. Also the water meadows so close to the town were the playground for the good citizens of Winchester, their children and dogs. Two years later, Dr Burge, then head-master, and 'that most wonderful of all Wykehamist fishermen, Sir Edward Grey – somehow one can't call him Lord Grey when talking of him as a fisher-man', a fishing club was formed 'and the college took over all the water downstream to St Cross'.

Baird was on the committee of the club when its rules were drawn up. One rule was that dry-fly fishing only was allowed and anyone caught fishing a wet fly would be expelled from the club. In the early years of the twentieth century such a rule was all but universal on the chalk streams 'though here and there people with more advanced views were beginning to make themselves heard and put their audacious theories into practice, maintaining that Itchen trout fed underwater in addition to rising to surface fly, and that when feeding in this way should be fished for in a like manner.' As Baird said in a few sentences further on, he would not have dared to even think of using anything but a dry fly because he knew that such behaviour would have been considered beyond the pale. The old river keepers considered fish caught on wet flies or under-water to be little better than fish that had been poached – a true Halfordian view.

Baird knew that it was often a waste of time to try to catch nymphing fish on a dry fly. Anglers, in his opinion, had to make up their minds to fish under water or sit and read a book, or benefit from any other distraction, while waiting for the trout to start feeding on the surface on the floating fly. 'Fishing with an artificial nymph is certainly very good fun. It is also exceedingly diffi-cult – probably more so than with dry fly – and this is particularly so in striking correctly when the fish takes the nymph.' Another problem that he identified was that it could be difficult to get the artificial nymph to sink. Remember that this was in the days before weighted nymphs had been developed in England and 'the half-dozen or so preliminary casts through the air, to get out enough line before the cast proper is made' were often enough to dry the fly so that it would then float. Baird's remedy was to apply a little glycerine to the nymph, in much 'the same way that a little oil is used to make a dry fly float'.

In his chapter on 'Flies and Nymphs', R. D. Baird ended by discussing why, if nymph fishing 'is such good fun and such good value, should it be frowned upon, if not actively opposed?' He wondered if the reason might be that it was a 'relatively modern' method but, as he said, fishing underwater with a wet fly was actually much, much older than dry fly fishing. Another reason might be that it was deemed to be unsporting and a fish was not given a fair chance. He countered the unsporting argument by his prognosis that nymph fishing is more challenging than dry fly fishing. In his view one needed to look for a completely different answer. And he felt that reason to be 'tolerably easy to find'. It is based on the individual angler's approach to fly fishing: is fishing simply a means of catching fish, or is fishing 'an art, to be enjoyed and appreciated according to certain rules?' If the object of fly fishing was only to catch fish, then there would be no restrictions on methods used. Such an angler – and sadly there are still many of them – is often known as a fishmonger, or on occasion, an otter. But Baird was of the opinion that because chalk streams were relatively few and far between, that 'no other streams offer such wonderful opportunities to put into practice the art of dry-fly-fish *in all its purity* [my italics], and because a man who fishes a chalk stream is not solely a man who wants to catch fish, but rather an artist indulging his craft'. Although he felt that it might be argued that fishing with a nymph debases the purity of fishing and catching chalk stream trout with dry flies only – in his opinion a unique experience – he did believe that it was, ultimately, down to the individual angler to fish to his own personal rules and values. He maintained that the nymph should be fished to trout feeding on nymphs, and only then, because 'a chalk stream is essentially a dry-fly river'. Although his book is undated, he stated in the preface that he wrote the book immediately after the end of the Second World War, in about 1946 or possibly 1947. I mention this because he must have been only too well aware of the great debate on nymph fishing and its outcome when writing his book.

Even in the 1920s there were enlightened trout fisherman who were prepared to encourage fellow-anglers to fish the nymph particularly when the 'use of the correct nymph' was the only solution to a problem. B. W. Powlett (see chapter six and footnote) wrote a short but interesting contribution on nymph fishing for a book called *Fisherman's Pie, An Angling Symposium*. His opening sentence was prophetic: 'The nymph is destined to play a most important part in both dry and wet fly fishing.' He then offered his thanks to Dr Mottram and Mr G. E. M. Skues for making the use of the nymph so well known but felt that it was not being used as often as it should be. Powlett felt that the dry fly man was more likely to use the nymph more often than the wet fly angler but it was the latter who would gain the most benefit and pleasure from fishing with nymphs. For Powlett, and the wet fly man fishing rapid rivers, 'The charm of the nymph . . . is that it enables him to fish the rise in rough or smooth water, even in heavy waters where the wet fly down-stream has so far reigned supreme.' He had also noted that, throughout the season, 'when the fly is up and the rise is in full swing' that trout were often to be caught when they were feeding just below the surface and that they fed on emergers just as much as hatched duns on the surface. For him 'Such conditions are suitable for the employment of nymphs'. He advocated using very small patterns and, unless visibility and water clarity were both very good, he oiled his cast to within nine inches (23cm) of his fly. Oiling the cast, or leader, to make it float helped suspend the fly at the required depth as well as making it easier to see when a fish had taken the nymph. Finally 'no fly fisherman should be without these tiny imitations of the favourite and most general food of the trout'.

The first contributor to the same book, J. W. Dunne, ended his article, written for tyro fly fishermen, with a nice piece about how to deal with the curse of the tailing trout. Such a fish will pay no attention to any flies passing over head on the surface of the river. Dunne felt that the 'proper angling implement for such a fish is a harpoon' although he knew one would not be permitted on 'really good dry fly water'. He advocated three possible courses of action, namely to 'Leave the brute to his evil enjoyment', 'Call up another beginner and indicate to him the priceless opportunity' and finally to read Skues' 'delightful description of the one and only way of tackling successfully a tailing fish'.

In 1932 Dr E. A. Barton published *Chalk Streams And Water Meadows*, a collection of his articles, poems and twelve photographs selected specially by the author from his collection. In the penultimate chapter, 'The Loaded Nymph', Dr Barton wrote of his experiments with weighted nymphs. He first used fine copper wire which he rejected as too springy and rigid and, after 'much trial I find that the best wire is fine lead-compo wire such as is used for very light fusing of electric globes. It is soft, ductile, has no spring, cuts easily, and is altogether most satisfactory.' He had been tying nymphs with a few turns of wire round the hook shank for a number of years. That he found copper wire to be too springy, with a tendency to unroll when he cut it, seems to suggest that he was not tying it in and covering it with turns of tying thread as is common practice today. He also wrote of the care needed to cast a loaded nymph so that it did not make an excessive splash as it hit the water, compared with an unweighted fly. He finished by writing that he had introduced loaded, weighted nymphs to many of his friends and that, although they were then widely available in fishing tackle shops, he maintained that it was better to tie one's own artificials.

Another early exponent of the art of 'modern wet-fly fishing' was Dr J. C. Mottram (1879–1945), who although much younger, was fishing at the same time as Skues. And he had another similarity with Skues in that his early writings were published in magazines such as *The Field* (his first article on 'Dry Flies and White Hackle' on the purpose of the hackle, its colour and the colour of wings, was published on 17 July, 1909) under the pseudonym of Jim Jam, the *Journal of The Flyfishers Club* and *Salmon and Trout Magazine* before he wrote a book. Mottram's first book was his most important and contained much that was to be crucial to the history and development of nymph fishing. It was first published when he was thirty-six in 1915, after Skues' first book, *Minor Tactics of the Chalk Stream*. He was ahead of his time and, to some extent, ahead of Skues too when it came to assessing and understanding the importance of the nymph to both trout and trout fisherman. Although he realised the importance of the nymph and upstream nymph fishing, as we know he turned against Skues and the nymph fisherman in the last years of his life. He had had his disagreements with Skues in about 1912, when he wrote in one of his early contributions to *The Field* that he did not agree with an article Skues had written on tying nymphs because he, Mottram, was of the opinion that

J. C. Mottram –
'Jim Jam'

swimming nymphs kept their legs tucked close to their bodies. He then wrote that further observations had convinced him that nymphs could float motionless with legs and gills spread so he had started to tie his flies with legs emerging from the thorax and not in front as was the case with Skues' hackles. But two years later Skues did think that nymphs might be better tied without hackles if the hackles were not needed to break the fly's fall (*The Field*, 14 February 1914). Mottram mentioned in his article that he had read Skues' piece when fishing in New Zealand. In a follow-up letter in response to Mottram's piece, published on 19 October 1912, Skues wrote that Mottram's contribution was another 'nail in the coffin of the theory that the nymph cannot be effectively imitated because it is too lively'. In view of what was to happen in 1938, it was perhaps unwise of Skues to describe Mottram's swimming nymph as looking 'deader than mutton'!

The Field's angling number for 1911 contained a full-page on 'The Wet Fly on Chalk Streams', by Seaforth and Soforth (one of Skues' many pen names) and T. E. P., in 'Some Wet Fly' notes, referred to nymphs: nymphs with hare's ear bodies ribbed with gold oval tinsel and the Blue Upright which represented a whole series of dun nymphs. In his article, Seaforth and Soforth advocated changing back and forth from dry fly to wet to get the best of a day on the river, particularly for those anglers who were not always able to choose when they fished. Seaforth and Soforth wrote that 'The fly must be specially constructed to sink.' And should be tied sparsely with a 'soppy dubbing'.

Dr Mottram was a scientist and radiologist and was involved in developing treatments for cancer in the early years of the twentieth century; he was director of the research laboratory at Mount Vernon Hospital, Northwood, Middlesex. He died a very unpleasant death from cancer of the kidneys in Northwood on 4 October 1945. Thus he approached his fly fishing and writing with a scientist's mind. He was possibly one of the first, if not the first, scientists to write at length about fly fishing. In the introduction to his first book *Fly-Fishing, Some New Arts and Mysteries*, he wrote: 'It is useless to argue the question as to whether or no, fly-fishing is worthy of serious thought. A definite conclusion can never be arrived at because so much can be said for and against.' For him, as a scientific angler, '. . . fishing is a series of experiments: facts are noted, conclusions drawn, laws made . . .'

How much – indeed if at all – was Mottram influenced by Skues' writing? Those who espouse Skues' profound powers of observation and deduction (I can accept that he was a good observer but he did not seem to me to always make the right deductions, or, as he himself admitted in his later years, it had often taken him a very long time to arrive at the correct deduction), may suggest that Mottram was influenced by Skues, but as we will see, he was very quick to act on his own observations and developed two nymphs that were far in advance of most of Skues' representations. In his book *The Way of a Trout*

41

with a Fly, Skues wrote that Jim Jam had published in *The Field* and his book, 'a description of a method of imitating nymphs which he found successful'. Skues felt that his method did not present the right line of approach because he was of the opinion that these 'patterns were intended to be fished down stream and dragging'. Sadly Skues must have failed to read Mottram's book properly in which he described how the flies should be cast upstream. But Skues' comments would suggest that he did not feel that Mottram had copied his ideas.[3] We know that each read the other's published articles and often disagreed, and Skues quoted Mottram at quite some length in his book *Nymph Fishing For Chalk Stream Trout*, even though by that time Mottram had reverted to strict dry fly purism.

Mottram stated that the Resting nymph should be cast 'upstream to dimpling fish precisely like a dry fly, except that the last link or few inches of gut should, if possible, be made to sink.' A dimpling fish was one that was feeding on floating nymphs just under the surface. For bulging fish which he attacked with his Swimming nymph, a different approach was required. For such fish, he did feel that it was best to cast across and above a fish at an angle of forty-five degrees. He discussed the problems of fishing or casting directly upstream but he dismissed this approach as the leader would be seen too easily by the fish, fishing upstream at an angle of forty-five degrees was likely to result in the fly coming 'down in an inert, dead manner'. Fishing straight down was only too likely to end with the fly being pulled out of the fish's mouth. Casting from directly opposite was a possibility but he felt that fishing at forty-five degrees and placing the fly 'two or three yards above the fish and beyond it, so that as it swings down and round with the current it will cross in front of the fish' was the best choice. Is this method 'dragging' as Skues maintained? Mottram does, in the next sentence, refer to drag but my interpretation of his use of the word is the problem is likely to be caused by casting across water flows of differing speeds.

Mottram knew of the importance of presentation and also developed his own form of what is, today, known as the induced take. In *The Journal of The Flyfishers Club* in 1935 he wrote about fishing an artificial leaded nymph: 'As it passes the fish, gently draw on the line, causing the nymph to ascend through the water in imitation of a natural, and if all goes well the trout will follow it up and take it.'

Compared to Skues, Mottram seems to have been much readier to put his observations into practice. For example, fishing in New Zealand on the South Island in 1911, he saw a trout, in Diamond lake, 'pick something off the bottom so I waded out over the sand to investigate; there I found on the bottom a small green beetle which probably had settled on the water during the night, been drowned, and sunk to the bottom. I had soon tied a green-bodied beetle, this I cast out into a sandy bay where two or three large fish were cruising, and let it sink; then I sat and waited. At last a fish saw my fly, upped tail and downed head; a puff of sand and, pandemonium.'

Fishing the Clinton river, also on the South Island, he saw a fish bulging which would not take a dry fly. 'Instead of troubling to tie a nymph, I cut down a small March Brown I had in my fly box; quite a good nymph can be made in this way . . .' What an example of seeing the problem and coming up with an answer to it. And the right answer too as he caught the fish on the third or fourth cast. This is in such contrast to Skues' hesitancy in similar circumstances on the Highland Burn of the river Itchen.

Then fishing the Waikato river below Lake Taupo one evening, he returned from the river quite nonplussed by the fact that he had not caught a fish although the river was covered with duns and was boiling with fish. On his way home in the dark he realised that he had never seen a dun taken: the fish were all bulgers. 'The next evening I went fully armed with ephemera nymphs and slew many fish.'

Current opinion seems to be that Mottram was most likely to have been one of the first, if not the first, angler to have fished a nymph in New Zealand although there is no evidence that his visit had any lasting effect on the way New Zealanders fished for trout.

Mottram also fished nymphs on the Usk, certainly in 1929, and probably other years too, when he found that different patterns and sizes of nymph were required compared to the flies that he fished regularly on the Test.

Now to get to the meat of Mottram's book we need to turn to chapter twenty-two, 'Nymphs and Bulgers'. 'I believe the day is not far distant when the dry-fly fisherman may have to give up or share his throne with another; and to acknowledge that it is difficult to deceive a trout in its own element as in air, if not more. I have yet to find a water where the wet fly will kill but not the dry, but there are many of which it is said, "The dry will kill but not the wet" – in my opinion, an acknowledgement that it is easier to kill with the dry fly. The antipathy between wet and dry fly fishermen does not lie here. The dry-fly purist objects because he believes that his fish are made shy and bad risers by slogging of his water with a wet fly; and undoubtedly he is right, but only as regards the old school of wet-fly fisherman. Against the modern school, this objection cannot be raised. The modern wet-fly fisherman does not slog the water; he casts to a single feeding fish just as the dry-fly fisherman does, and he uses a single fly or lure which is an imitation of the insect on which the fish is feeding under water. This method, I maintain, does not render fish either particularly shy or bad risers: in fact, if a portion of a stream were set apart for modern wet-fly fishing only, I should expect the fish to become particularly free risers.'

It is worth noting the phrases 'easier to kill with the dry fly' and 'the old school of wet-fly fisherman. Against the modern school, this objection cannot

'The next evening I went fully armed with ephemera nymphs and slew many fish.'

be raised.' There are still many anglers who either do not, or are reluctant to fish with nymphs, because they believe that it is too difficult for them. Mottram says in a paragraph or two after the extended quote above: 'There is one other fact in favour of wet-lure fishing: it is, in my opinion, more difficult than the dry-fly fishing.' Nymph fishing can be extremely challenging and on other

Mottram was one of the first, if not the first, anglers to fish nymphs in New Zealand

days very easy. We will look at modern methods for fishing nymphs later in the book.

By the time that he wrote this chapter, Mottram claimed that every fisherman knew that nymphs rose from the weeds and river bed to the surface where they would shed their skin to become sub-imagoes or duns. He urged all anglers to spend time observing nymphs in rivers, particularly as it was said that most nymphs moved rapidly through the water. His observation, particularly of light-coloured (and thus easily seen) pale watery nymphs: 'The nymph will be seen coming down with the stream, but often diverging to one side or the other, at the same time, rising slowly to the surface; the motion is quite slow and even, not in the least fast or jerky.' This gives the lie to Halford's assertion that the action of a swimming nymph could not be imitated successfully. In *Dry-Fly Fishing*, Halford had written: 'the difficulty does not lie in dressing an artificial grub fairly resembling the dun nymph, but in

Top left: Resting nymph *Top right:* Swimming nymph
Bottom left: Caddis nymph, *Bottom right:* Diptera nymph

imparting to that imitation the motion and direction taken by the natural insect at that stage of its existence.'

Observation of what we call nymphing fish – or bulging as was the word of the day – by Mottram showed him that fish moved from side to side to intercept nymphs coming down stream, rather than chasing them. He also knew that fish bulged *before* a hatch began. They would feed on the nymphs as they made their way to the river surface to hatch. He also observed fish feeding on nymphs in or just under the surface film, on the point of eclosion. Fish taking nymphs below the surface, swimming nymphs, he described as true bulgers and those taking what we would call today hatching nymphs and emergers, as dimpling fish It is sometimes difficult to remember that this was written in the second decade of the twentieth century.

Mottram developed what he called a Resting nymph to imitate the nymphs that dimpling fish fed on. His imitation had legs – four rather than the requisite six but he and we know trout cannot count – and tails extended in the resting position. Different nymphs could be imitated by tying this basic pattern with different colours of floss silk for the body and in a range of sizes. His two patterns of nymph were much more advanced than any of Skues' nymphs and very much closer to the nymphs used today.

In his tying instructions, Mottram stressed the importance of using floss silk 'of the correct shade when wet' to match the colour of the natural nymph. In 1971 in their important work *Selective Trout*, Doug Swisher and Carl Richards too stressed that it is 'the colour and appearance of the artificial when it's *wet* that is important'. This serves to confirm how perceptive Mottram was and how far ahead of his time in much of his thinking and writing.

Bulging fish required, he knew, a different pattern. One that represented swimming nymphs, with no legs 'because nymphs, when swimming, keep their legs pressed close against their body; motion is obtained by rapid vibrations of the tail'. His nymph would still be effective today, particularly the neat touch of 'on the top of the thorax tie on the tips of two dark grey cock hackles pointing backwards – these are to represent the wing cases . . .' He also ran experiments with soft feather to replicate the undulations of the abdomen of swimming nymphs. He knew that the fly had to be cast upstream from the target fish, how far depending on the strength of the current. Accuracy was crucial as he wrote that the first cast was often the last, and more so than with an artificial dry fly. He knew, too, of the difficulty of knowing when to strike as 'usually no rise is seen'. As he wrote, when you can see the fish and your fly, life is easier. At the end of the chapter he wrote that 'The dry-fly fisherman who takes to this form of fishing will at first be very surprised at seeing a fish come a yard, or it may be two or even more yards, after his nymph, at seeing the fish fearlessly gulp it down, and then return to its station behind the weed-bed. . .'

Mottram's second article published by *The Field* (18 September 1909) was a very thorough illustrated guide to carrying out autopsies on trout. 'The staple food may be said to consist of snails, shrimps, small fish, caddis, duns and nymphs.' He also kept nymphs in jam jars – as did Halford – but he arrived at the right conclusions which, we know, Halford so singly failed to do. Through keen observation in rivers, Mottram discovered that nymphs do not all move rapidly through the water. Some move only slowly and evenly as they rise to the surface to hatch. Mottram also observed bulging fish 'not chasing nymphs, but moving quickly now to this side, now to that, in order to meet the nymphs coming down.'

Mottram described the modern wet-fly fisherman as someone who 'casts to a single feeding fish just as the dry-fly fisherman does, and he uses a single fly or lure which is an imitation of the insect on which the fish is feeding under-water'. He recommended that when fishing for rising fish 'taking floating duns', use a dry fly. For fish taking nymphs just below the surface, use his Resting nymph and for bulging fish taking nymphs swimming to the surface, his Swimming nymph.

One wonders how a man who had learnt so much and perhaps more signif-icantly, was prepared to act on his observations, was, twenty-three years after the publication of his very important and still very readable book, prepared to deny everything that he knew, had learnt and practised. Mottram finally 'put the boot in' in his last book, *Thoughts on Angling*, which was published just before his death. In 1937 he wrote on 'The Ethics of Nymph Fishing' and maintained that catching trout on nymphs would mean that there would be fewer fish to catch by 'other methods of fishing' and that 'a trout killed on a nymph in a chalk stream is one lost to the dry fly'. Did he and his peers not want to catch fish and even catch and kill fish on the dry fly too? By the end of his life he had also decided that nymph fishing was 'a less delicate art' and an easier art – even a too easy way to catch chalk stream trout – as drag was less of a problem to be overcome when fishing underwater and so gave less sport. He was also of the opinion that the improper use of artificial nymphs would be harmful to the sport of fly fishing. He now felt that there was very little difference between wet fly fishing and nymph fishing and that nymph fishing was only wet fly fishing but under a cloak. At this time there were the ultra-purists who would cast *only* to rising fish positively identified as feeding on duns. So if there were no fish rising, the ultra-purist could spend a whole day on the river and never make a single cast. He also had another wonderful idea that a fish pricked by a dry fly might be put-off feeding on duns but could revert to feeding on nymphs, and thus stay alive, but the fish pricked by a nymph would be put–off feeding on nymphs and, one assumes, end up on a starvation diet. This is wonderfully warped reasoning: if fish pricked by dry flies were going to be put-off rising to and feeding on floating flies, what was the point of keeping them alive (by feeding on nymphs) when he and his chums would not fish for them with a nymph? We know this is quite wrong because fish, particularly on catch and release waters today, are often caught many times in a season and do not die from starvation. Admittedly some do die from other causes but I doubt any die because they stop feeding *per se*. Skues did reply with a detailed and thorough demolition of his arguments and he was also supported in a letter from the American angler Eugene V. Connett.

If he had kept the faith and lived longer, what fun he would have had with the vast range of modern fly tying materials and also techniques such as wiggle nymphs with two-piece articulated bodies as he had given thought to tying artificials which would have movement. During his life Mottram demonstrated the talent, knowledge and aptitude to have made a much greater and more enduring impact than he did on the development of nymph fishing and possibly more significant than Skues. But he failed to ensure his place in the history of nymph fishing and is today, a largely forgotten and unsung hero of fly fishing.

G. W. Borlase, whose writings were subject to valuable criticism by 'the late Mr G. E. M. Skues', was another angler of the post-Halford period when the dry-fly purists and ultra-purists still ruled the world but he felt that 'The purist who condemns the use of the Nymph is not always quite consistent. Since it is the very foundation of his creed only to present to the fish a pattern representing the fly on which it is feeding, he should surely offer a Nymph below the surface to a nymphing fish rather than bombard him with floating flies.' One of the interesting things in this quotation is the reference to bombarding fish with floating flies, for this *was* allowed and surely if anything is going to spoil a fish, it is hammering one with an entirely unsuitable artificial? He was also unable to see how fishing a nymph upstream or across to an individual fish could do more harm than fishing with a floating fly.

Borlase found that the most difficult aspect of nymph fishing was knowing when to fish a nymph, that is identifying trout feeding on nymphs. He knew that when you saw a fish moving gently from side to side, over a weed bed, and just under water but not breaking the surface but bulging, that it was taking nymphs. He also knew that carrying out an autopsy on a fish would show that a trout's stomach usually contained more nymphs than other food forms, and there must be other occasions when they feed on nymphs. We are then introduced to the study of the 'rise form', to use Eric Taverner's term for the ways in which trout take insect food under varying conditions.

A tip that he passed on to his readers was to moisten your artificial nymph and 'the last foot or two of the cast so that it will sink quickly'. Further, he advocated that the nymph and gut leader should be allowed to land in the water at the end of each forward false cast, to keep the fly and leader wet. This was a technique favoured by Skues and Borlase probably copied him. Fortunately we have no need for such a guaranteed fish-frightening technique today. He also advised casting straight upstream either to the left or right of your quarry but not directly over him, as he felt that such a cast was less likely to drag compared to an up-and-across cast. He felt that surface drag was almost, if not quite, as detrimental as in dry fly fishing. Very perceptive.

Borlase knew, too, the difficulty of detecting takes. His preferred method was to watch his cast (leader) where it entered the water and keep his 'eye skinned for any sudden acceleration of the pace at which the fine end of the cast sinks. This indicates that a fish is at your fly, and you must strike at once or he will be away.' This is the Oliver Kite doctrine of watching what he called the dipping point.

'Certain of the feeding trout, sometimes nearly all of them, are not taking floating food, but something below the surface, probably "nymph", an earlier stage of development of the winged insect.' So wrote Sir George Aston in *Letters to Young Fly-Fishers*. He encouraged all young fly fishers to carry some imitations of these nymphs but he did wonder if using them was dry fly fishing. 'To be quite candid, it is not; but it is an art now practised by most dry-fly anglers under such conditions.' He advised that the best way to get a 'counterfeit of a nymph' to sink quickly was to anoint it and the end of the leader with glycerine. He also advised that if you were casting to a visible fish it was possible to tell when he had taken the artificial and you could tighten accordingly. But if you could not see the fish, but knew where he was, 'the best that you can do is to watch the floating part of the cast of gut on the water (if your eyesight is good enough to see it), and to tighten up when you see it go under'.

Sir George Aston felt that anglers would 'do better if they tried to copy the movement of real nymphs, which lie on the bottom until ready to turn into winged flies and then move *upwards* towards the surface. A little touch of some chemical which would make a bubble of gas when wet might cause an artificial nymph to do this.' He did not know of anyone who had tried this idea and he admitted that he did not know enough chemistry to try it himself. As he felt that it was not possible to imitate movement, he advised his young readers to try 'imitating exactly the colour, form, and size of the real water-insects.'.

H. D. Turing in his book *Trout Problems* (1948) advanced an interesting idea that imitations of spent flies should be fished wet so that they lie waterlogged 'on or near the surface, which effectively disposes of the contention that the dryness of an artificial is an essential quality in dry-fly fishing.' and in a previous chapter, ' . . . outspread wings lying in the surface film with the body below.' This is very close to Halford's description of how Marryatt's Mayfly nymph should be fished. Robert Hartman (author of *About Fishing* published in 1935) took what must have been a pretty radical approach to his choice of artificial nymphs. Whereas Skues designed and developed a wide range of patterns, Hartman recommended the use of but three. These were a Mayfly and a brown nymph and a green one. The Mayfly nymph was dressed on a mayfly hook with green-yellow wool, with a hump behind the head. The fibres from any soft, dark feather were passed over the hump to represent the wing cases and then 'spread out at the head to represent the legs'. The brown nymph was tied with a mixture of yellow and brown wool and the green nymph with a mix of green-yellow wool, these two patterns 'give us a light and a dark pattern with which to ring the changes'. This minimalist approach was very similar to that to be adopted and developed by Oliver Kite nearly thirty years later.

By 1924 J. W. Hills was able to write in *A Summer on The Test*, 'More and more each year does nymph fishing become a part of the modern angler's equipment, and he who does not possess the art is gravely handicapped. And at the same time has come the realisation that this art is both difficult and delightful.' Hills appreciated that nymph fishing required different skills and qualities in the fisherman and that it was a very exacting practice as he found that trout were harder to catch underwater than on top. Hills felt that he had an advantage over other would-be nymph fishermen in that he had grown up fishing 'a not too easy north country river where the practice was to fish up-stream' and where 'you had to strike your trout before you felt him and often without seeing him rise or take. Therein lies the art.' A keen eye was important for seeing fish in the waters of a chalk stream and for seeing when a fish took.

Although Hills claimed that he was still experimenting and was yet to be convinced that the 'modern nymph type beats the old-fashioned copy', ('Nymphs are modern young ladies, whose fashions are not yet fixed.'), he had first tried a nymph in 1914 at Ramsbury, on the Test, and had caught his first fish on this river in 1890. His time spent fishing the waters of the Houghton Club under the tutelage of the head keeper, William Lunn, were to prove invaluable to him. He knew that a day spent with Lunn when fish were nymphing would be a real education. 'Even to-day the importance of the nymph is not realised: if you examine the stomach of a trout clearly taking duns, you find more nymph in it than fly. Just as the river life of a nymph is the real life of the ephemerid, so nymphs, not duns or spinners, are the real food of trout. Hence nymph fishing, new certainly in its modern dress, but in essence as old as fly-fishing itself.' Lunn, like so many other famous river keepers was blessed with exemplary vision, although he wore glasses, an ability to know how deep a fish was feeding and due to his knowledge of the river and its insect life he had a pretty good idea what it would be feeding on if it was not obvious, and above all, 'Lunn seems to know when a fish takes, by instinct rather than visible manifestation.' These remarks would suggest that nymph fishing had become fairly well established and acceptable on this part of the Test, if not on the whole of the river, in the mid-1920s to early 1930s.

It is now time to explore the actions and writings of the man who, for many, is the accepted father of nymph fishing, George Edward Mackenzie Skues. Skues was born in St Johns, Newfoundland, on 13 August 1858 and was the eldest son of his father who was surgeon of the Newfoundland Companies. Skues, who had seven siblings, was about five foot seven inches (1.70m) tall, well built but with sloping shoulders, and a slow walk. Throughout his life he demonstrated great persistence and stamina, often walking great distances up and down the river bank. He arrived in England when he was three after his first and what was to be only crossing of the Atlantic. He won a scholarship to Winchester College in 1872 and it was while at school there that he had his first experience of fly fishing for trout on the river Itchen in 1875. He saw the Itchen for the first time – and fell in love with it immediately – from the train to Winchester when aged six. It was in July that year that he caught his first trout, a trout 'with manners of exceptional violence when hooked'. During his years at Winchester Skues did all he could to retain his individuality and to resist the pressure to mould him 'to a pattern'. This early rebellious streak was to serve him well in his life-long battle with the dry fly purists and ultra-purists. And it may even have been the very reason that he set off down that road.

After Winchester he started as an articled clerk in the firm of his family's solicitor, Mr James Powell, in 1878. In 1894 he and his sisters went to live in South Croydon, which would have been quite rural then, and the next year he was made a partner in his law firm. During his long working life, he would take the train to Winchester to fish his beloved Itchen until his last season in 1938. The Itchen at Abbots Barton was leased by Irwin Cox, one of the proprietors of *The Field*, from 1883 until 1917 and he invited Skues to fish regularly as a guest. After 1917, Skues joined H. T. Sheringham in forming a syndicate[4] that was to lease the fishing right up to 1953. In 1940 he retired and moved from Croydon to the Nadder Vale Hotel – having given up his Rod on the Itchen – where he stayed until the hotel closed in 1948. He then stayed in Wilton for a short time before moving to 23 Kilsy Park Road, Beckenham, Kent, to be nearer his youngest brother. He died suddenly in August, 1949, within a week of his ninety-first birthday after an internal haemorrhage. At Skues' request, his ashes were scattered on the banks of his beloved Itchen at Abbots Barton by William Mullins, his old friend and river keeper for his former syndicate.

In the *Journal of The Flyfishers Club* for the winter of 1935, Skues wrote: 'For many years it never occurred to me that F. M. Halford and his distinguished associates could be wrong, and it was not until after that volume (*Minor Tactics of the Chalk Stream*) was published that I began to realise, increasingly as the years went on, what an immense proportion of the food taken *at the surface* was nymphal, and that much of the trout's subaqueous food was taken there and not at the bottom or bulging in the weeds as Halford clearly believed.

'In view of my own slowness to deduce the true facts it would ill become me to cast a stone at any brother angler. But I cannot help thinking what a difference it would have made to the last half century of fly fishing for chalk stream trout if Halford and his friends had realised the truth as it has latterly appeared.' His slowness in developing 'his keen power of observation that made him such a master' was confirmed by his brother C. A. M. Skues in 1950.

In *Itchen Memories* he wrote of his first encounter with 'the great man' on the Itchen in September 1891 and how Halford tried to tell him what patterns of fly to use. Skues persisted in using what he thought were the correct patterns and out-fished Halford pretty comprehensively. This experience 'encouraged me to rely most on my own observations and not attach undue importance to authority'. Admittedly he was writing with the benefit of hindsight although he felt that Halford's recommendation was wrong and he also commented on the coarseness of the gut to which his fly was attached. (Halford had cast his fly across the river so that Skues could see what he was using.)

Going back to his slowness in deducing 'the true facts', perhaps part of his

G. E. M. Skues' famous marrow scoop. Once he had discovered the marrow scoop, he was able to tie his artificial nymphs 'with due attention alike to shape, colour and dimensions, and the blue macaws and other experiments went into discard'. The cork was to stop it sinking if he dropped it in the water

G. E. M. Skues in
old age. Colonel
Harding credited
him with restoring
tolerance and
sanity to the sport
of fly fishing

problem was the fact that Skues does not seem – at least in his early fishing days – to have been a great entomologist and he did not have his first encounter with a trout and nymphs until the spring of 1888 when he was fishing an Itchen carrier known as the Highland Burn. On the Saturday he rose a trout to a Pink Wickham, struck too hard and broke his cast, leaving the fly and a length of gut in the fish. He returned to the river on the following Monday when he hooked and landed a trout from which he recovered his fly and gut. But of more interest and significance was the fact that 'the mouth of the fish was dotted with a number of tiny pea-green creatures, which I later learnt were nymphs'. Although it was to be quite some years before he realised fully the significance and profound importance of this discovery, in September that year he fished the Coquet and caught a trout on a nymph with a body 'of dyed flat tawsy gut wound over the bare hook shank'. This fish and his earlier experience on the Itchen suggested that nymphs could be tied with similar gut bodies and he discussed his ideas with George Holland. In a number of old letters to the editor of the *Journal of The Flyfishers Club* that were published many years after they were written, Skues confessed to have been thinking of dressing nymphs in the 1880s. George Holland, in a letter of October 1888, had referred to tying larvae with Marryat but these flies never caught any fish.

His observation was to take on an even greater importance when he discovered the marrow scoop that allowed him to sample the contents of the stomachs of trout that he caught, without having to cut them open. In *Itchen Memories* he wrote a piece entitled 'On The Way to the Nymph', where he recounted how he acquired some 'eyed hooks with sharp points, and a variety of quills, blue and red macaw and others'. He used these to tie a number of fancy flies. At weed cutting time, rafts of weed floated downstream and anchored themselves against the bank on his side of the river. He was to observe trout patrolling the edges of the rafts, picking off nymphs which were escaping from the floating mass. Skues wrote that the trout were not learned enough to realise 'that these blue macaw bodied things were not real nymphs, with the result that, fishing close to the margin of these rafts, one collected quite a few unsuspecting trout which took these fancy nymphs. But in those days I had not discovered the marrow scoop. When I did – oh, when I did – the edge of the weed raft grew even more profitable.' In 'An Early Phase in the Evolution of the Artificial Nymph' he wrote of his observation of fish that 'were obviously feeding on something below the surface' and were cruising up and down, as they did not rise in the same place twice. Once he had discovered the marrow spoon, he was able to tie his artificial nymphs 'with due attention alike to shape, colour and dimensions, and the blue macaws and other experiments went into discard'.

He did not discover the 'real' use of the marrow scoop, or spoon, until June 1921. At his breakfast table one morning were some huge marrow bones and a long, narrow spoon with two ends, 'one containing a bowl of about five eighths of an inch the other an equally long bowl of about three eighths of an inch in width.' Such an instrument was used to remove the marrow from inside the bones. This, he decided, was the ideal means of extracting the contents of a trout's stomach, without having to cut it open. The marrow spoon was to accompany him to the river side where it was put to good use.

Earlier, in 1899, he had written in *The Field* that he felt that anglers should fish a wet fly upstream when there were no fish to be seen feeding on the surface and so could reasonably be expected to take a dry artificial: 'when your fish are bulging, give it to them wet.'[5] His prophesy at the end of the article that there would have to be 'a judicious admixture of wet-fly science and dry-fly art' took a very long time to be fulfilled. In *Minor Tactics of the Chalk Stream* he wrote that in 1892 one day in September he fished all day without success, despite using gossamer gut and all the generally accepted dry flies. He then changed to a shop-tied Dark Olive Quill, tied with a dyed hen hackle which increased its ability to soak-up water and sink. With this fly he proceeded to catch four and a half brace in the next hour or so. The stomach of the first fish that he caught contained 'a solid ball of black gnats, and not a dun of any sort'. This was similar to the other fish caught. He then wrote 'It was a lesson which ought to have set me thinking and experimenting, but it didn't. I put by the experience for use on the next September smutting day, and I have never had quite such another.' He had other similar experiences around this time but it would be another ten or more years before he combined his experiences and came up with the right answer.

Minor Tactics was, in essence, all about re-introducing in a new, modern form the ancient practice of wet fly fishing on chalk streams – 'a wet-fly modification of the dry-fly method of upstream casting to individual fish.' Skues could not believe that the feeding habits of trout had changed so much as to make fishing a wet fly upstream a waste of time. For his early nymphal fly patterns – and how to tie them – he sought and found help and inspiration in local patterns for the Clyde and Tweed and the soft-hackle patterns of Yorkshire.

Much of Skues' early experience of nymph fishing was using wet flies, but fished upstream rather than in the traditional manner of across and down and definitely not as understood by Halford. This was, of course, at a time when wet fly fishing on chalk streams was deemed by most anglers to be beyond the pale although it was the original method of fly fishing before the development of the dry fly. Again to quote from *Minor Tactics* 'What is left to the wet fly angler? I venture to say a mighty pretty, delicate and delightful art which resembles dry-fly fishing in that the fly is cast upstream or across, to individual fish, or to places where it is reasonable to expect that a fish of suitable proportions may be found, and differs from dry-fly fishing only in the amount of material used in dressing the fly, in the force with which the fly is cast, and in the extreme subtlety of the indications frequently attending the taking of the fly by the fish, compared to which there is a painful obviousness in the taking of the dry fly.' What better description could there be of upstream nymph fishing as we know it today? For Skues nymph fishing was not ' a sport by itself. It is auxiliary to the floating fly.'

The Itchen was not the only river that helped his early, tentative steps towards the development of nymph fishing. Unlike Halford, Skues fished many different rivers during his lifetime, both at home and abroad. A river in Germany, in 1905, played a role: 'It was in Bavaria on a stream know to readers of the *Field* as "The Erlaubnitz" because of the ease with which permission was obtained, that I first began to have some glimmerings of the idea of working-up a wet-fly theory for chalk streams on dry fly lines'. Although

Skues ended up with an extensive range of patterns of artificial nymphs. This is a selection of modern tyings of his patterns for which the right materials are still available.

1st row from left: Large dark olive of spring, May and throughout the season when the small darkish watery dun is on, July and August, Iron Blue Dun

2nd row: Medium Olive, Medium Olive Dun 4, Medium Olive Dun 5, Medium Olive Dun 2

3rd row: Pale Watery Dun 3, Pale Watery Dun 4, May to August 2, May to August 3, Blue Winged Olive 2

there are references to wet fly fishing and catching fourteen good trout on a wet version of a little Pale Blue Dun and in a subsequent article about a later visit to the river, in 1909, there seems to be no real indication of what these glimmerings might have been. He fished this limestone stream quite regularly between 1905 and 1909 and in his last book, he recorded that to his surprise 'that a large sunk Alder was very successful and that small wet flies often did better than small floaters.' But in his original article although he referred to the alder being very successful at the end of May – but just before the Mayfly were hatching – he did not mention whether it was fished wet or dry but in *Nymph Fishing For Chalk Stream Trout*, he wrote that his large Alders were fished sunk. The Alder produced both quantity – eight and a half brace (seventeen fish) to one friend – and quality, 'a trout of twenty inches (51cm) in peerless condition and over four pounds (1.8kg)'. More is revealed in *Minor Tactics* when he tied an imitation of a live alder larva that he had borrowed, in a tube, from Martin Mosely who assured him that they were of no interest to trout as they lived in the mud. He was rather pleased with his imitation and he fished it successfully although he did not know whether or not German, or indeed any, trout would be familiar with the larva of the alder. He wore out his three artificials very quickly and that was the end of that particular experiment as he did not feel that it was quite right to fish such an imitation, probably because it was too close to a maggot. He refused to publish his dressing for this reason. He also tied a caddis imitation which he tried but once, with great success for a few minutes, but gave up 'conscience-stricken' that it was too close to a maggot. He also tied some freshwater shrimp patterns which he never used.

Skues was only too well aware of the ignorance of even highly-skilled and proficient fishermen 'of the very existence of the nymph, its form and character'. Dry fly anglers persisted in casting at rising fish and seemingly breaking the surface of the water, but these fish were often nymphing and not interested in the dry fly. It was little wonder that they did not catch many of them. We know that Skues took a long time to realise that when he caught trout on sub-surface flies, fished upstream, these fish were feeding on nymphs and not duns. He also thought that his winged wet flies were taken as hatching nymphs (he later modified this to 'might' be taken rather than were taken), but when he found nymphs in fish and no sign of any hatched flies, he started experimenting with short hackle nymphs. For Skues 'An artificial nymph is a pattern dressed on a hook to attract trout and grayling, and representing in size, colour and appearance one or other of the types of natural nymphs.'

In *Nymph Fishing for Chalk Stream Trout*, Skues quoted a section from Capt. Robert Hartman's book *About Fishing*, in part as follows: 'Considered ethically there can be no difference between fishing with an artificial ephemera designed to represent the insect the minute before it becomes a dun and fishing with one which represents the same insect a minute after it has ceased to be a nymph.'

Although much of the time Skues fished his fly in or just under the surface film, he also used flies tied on double hooks. These double hooks, which were a single eyed hook with a second hook, without an eye, tied to the first, sank quicker and deeper than a standard single hook. This suggests that he was likely to have fished deeper than in or just under the surface film. 'When immediate sinking in rather fast water is required, additional weight can be got by tying on a second hook.' One of his first experiments with a true artificial nymph in July 1908, was with a Tup's Indispensable tied on a double hook. (He was only too well aware of the danger of double hooks being used for snatching or snagging fish but he claimed that he did not have a problem with fish being foul hooked.) On another day that month, on the Itchen, he caught a trout one afternoon which had a dark olive nymph in its mouth. He had his fly tying kit with him and set to work to tie an imitation using seal's fur an 'admixture of bear's hair, dark brown and woolly, from close to the skin'. In his eye, the result was an exact reproduction of the colours of the natural insect. The fly was completed with soft, short dark blue whisks, or tails, the body dubbed with the seal's fur/bear mixture, 'bunched at the shoulder to suggest wing cases', part-ribbed with fine gold wire and two turns of a very short, dark rusty dun hen hackle to complete the fly. He tied it with well-waxed bright yellow silk. Strangely he did not use the new pattern until the next morning when he caught five of six fish rising in a shallow in a few minutes, between ten and eleven o'clock, and packed-up with three brace in his bag when driven from the river by heavy rain.

By 1921 when he published *The Way Of A Trout With A Fly*, Skues had been fishing imitation nymphs on chalk streams for some fifteen years. He had decided that a nymph without a hackle was not as effective as patterns with a short, light hackle which he maintained were taken for natural nymphs in the act of hatching. Although at the end of the previous century Dewar had advocated applying paraffin or the then-new rival vaseline to line and leader to help them to float better, Skues was introduced to this idea – known as the wet-fly oil tip – by his younger brother, Charles, when fishing in Germany. He knew that treating his cast, barring the last foot or two, so that it would float would make detecting takes much easier, particularly in difficult light conditions. He wrote about the take of a trout 'often the indications which bid you pull home the hook are so subtle and inconspicuous for the miracle which is evidenced by the hooped rod and protesting reel.'

Contrary to the accusations of those who condemned him for nymph fishing and that the practice resulted in catching only small fish, Skues recorded that he caught fish of two pounds (1 kg) more frequently on nymphs than on dry flies and even the odd three pounder (1.4 kg). In *Nymph Fishing for Chalk Stream*

Trout, in the chapter 'Pros and Cons', Skues discussed whether or not nymph fishing was, indeed, fly fishing. He had a friend who claimed that it was not although the old practice of wet fly fishing on chalk streams had always been known as fly fishing. The old wet fly anglers must have caught, on a wet fly, many a trout that thought it was about to sup on a tasty nymph, although these anglers did not realise it. One of Halford's arguments against nymph fishing was that it 'was a breach of the ethics of the dry fly'. As a lawyer Skues was able to demolish this argument pretty convincingly: if the rules of the water stated that the dry fly only be used, then Halford's statement was irrelevant as

Nadder Vale. [illegible] Wilton

Salisbury. 21. VIII 43.

Dear Mr Eastham,

Thank you for your letter of the 19th returning me Knight's letter & the prescription for a floating dun. I hope both may be of use to you. I tied yesterday a fly by this method winging it from hen blackbird secondaries. It took up amazingly smartly. One of these same fast patterns was tied as follows.

Hook B7364? (see Side Lines for No)

Tying silk Yellow

Hackle Pale ginger cock

Whisks 3 strands of same

Body Yellow floss going greenish when oiled or wet

Wings Hen blackbird.

The first time I used it on the [illegible] I got before 12 my limit of 3 brace weighing 12lb 6oz.

You both the angling [illegible] having here and got a No 2 kingfisher from the stores. I amused myself by whipping a loop at each end.

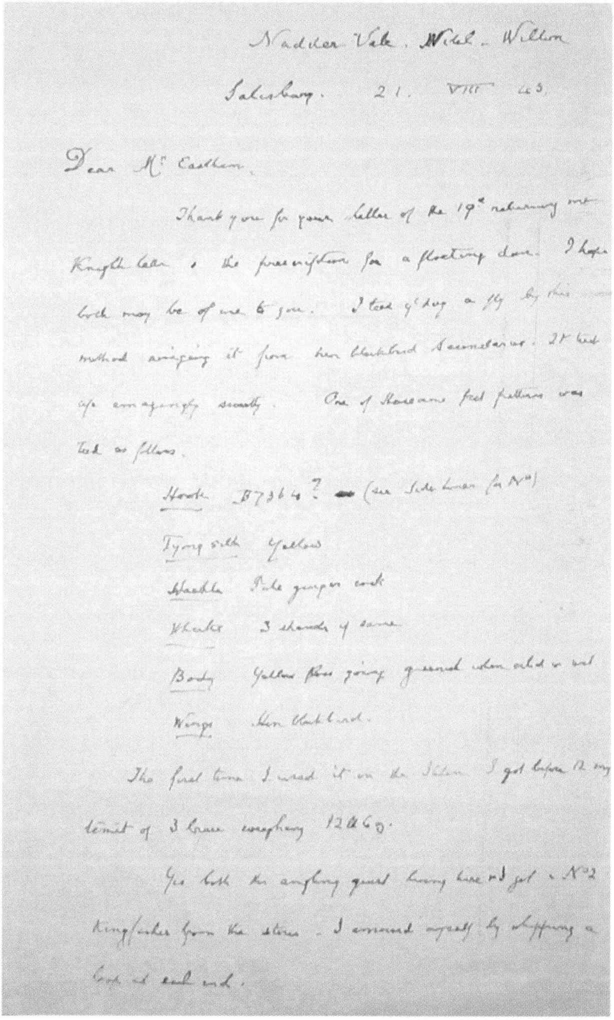

Part of a letter from G. E. M. Skues to Mr Eastham, a judge and founder of the A.C.A. (the Anglers' Conservation Association)

an argument against the practice on waters where the rules were less strict. Skues' comments suggest that the rules for the length of Itchen that he fished were not limited to the dry fly only so it does make one wonder why his fellow syndicate members were so against his use of the nymph. Skues did not 'think it necessary to pitch my case for fishing the artificial nymph to nymphing trout so high as to say that it revolutionises the entire practice of Hampshire trout fishing'. He further claimed that the nymph fisherman could approach nymphing fish with some certainty of success in bright weather and smooth water – conditions in which it had been thought to be impossible to catch fish – as well as catch a fish which might otherwise be hammered by a dry fly man or ignored completely by the 'understanding purist'.[5]

Although many of Skues' contributions to the *Salmon and Trout Magazine* were on fishing books and their authors and fly tying, he also wrote about nymph fishing, such as his article 'The Constant Nymph', published in the September 1933 issue. In that article he discussed the problems caused by up- and downstream winds and winds blowing across the stream. Cross-stream winds tended to blow the food against one bank of the river where the feeding trout were to be found. Nymphs were likely to be more numerous than floating duns and the bigger trout tended to force the smaller fish away from the food lanes and out into the mid-stream currents. He also wrote that it was important to fish the right pattern as a trout could see it more easily than a floating, dry fly, and, as a result, he fished the nymph successfully throughout the season.

The American Edward Ringwood Hewitt was invited to fish Skues' waters on the Itchen in 1925, although Skues was not able to join him. The next day Hewitt fished with John Waller Hills on the Houghton Club's waters on the Test. Although he fished with fourteen foot (4.26m) leaders (and in the USA he used leaders as long as eighteen feet (5.5m) in certain conditions), because the fish were scared so easily, he had a pretty torrid time. He described the Itchen as a 'great school for the fly fisherman'. Although he had caught fish on wet flies in the USA when fish were taking larvae on the bottom and nymphs were rising to the surface, he found the Test and Itchen fish to be the most difficult he had seen anywhere in the world. He was not helped by the fact that in his opinion there were no comparable rivers in the USA.

J. W. Hills, who had caught his first trout in 1875 and his first on a dry fly in 1890, was very fortunate to have fished with Skues a number of times on the Itchen as well as inviting him to fish on the Test. 'A more unselfish, humorous and sympathetic companion cannot be imaged.' was how he described him in his book *My Sporting Life*. Hills also described how Skues, when they were staying near the river, would go down to breakfast early and tie some flies for the day to come and, when necessary, even tying extra flies on the river bank, using a watchmaker's glass in his one good eye. He wrote that Skues was 'the begetter of the emancipated young woman, the nymph' and that he had shown that nymphs should be dressed sparsely, or continuing the nymph analogy 'the less clothes they put on, the more attractive they would be'.

Much of Hills' early fishing, certainly at the beginning of the twentieth century, was at a time when he described the dry fly purist as a despot and while he himself was fascinated by Skues' *Minor Tactics* 'it was received by the great ones not with interest but with fury'. Hills claimed to have seen a ray of light and knew that the orange partridge imitated the nymph of the blue winged olive which he saw 'in droves on warm July nights', but he did not persevere as he should have done. Sadly he admitted to the fact that he was not an originator. Hills wrote: 'The dry fly has fallen into its place in the great hierarchy and a high place it is, but a different one in the minds of most modern anglers from that which it occupied in 1886. Then it stood alone, unapproachable. Now the sunk fly, even in Hampshire, has its honoured usefulness.' According to Hills there had been no upstream, underwater fishing for individual fish on the Test since 1890. Fly fishermen had become set in their ways and totally inflexible – in a great part thanks to Halford – until Skues woke them up. During the first two decades of the twentieth century, there was 'revolution in pattern on the Test' when new patterns of dry fly were introduced, different in size and tying methods from earlier flies and spent-wing spinners which in their way were almost as revolutionary as nymphal patterns.

In 1917 he fished the Kennet at Ramsbury, during a holiday following his discharge from a French hospital, when he saw fish that he decided were nymphing but he did not know of the likely attraction of a sunk small red partridge.[7] On 27 July, 1914, just before the start of the First World War, Hills had fished a Skues' Tup sunk and caught fish on it. This was the first time that he had fished seriously with Skues' sunk patterns, tied for him by Strong of Carlisle to the instructions printed in *Minor Tactics*. It should be noted that at that time Hills was not in the habit of catching large numbers of fish but on this day he caught four fish, all on sunk flies, either a Tup or a Greenwell. Then on 2 August he used a sunk Greenwell, again with success, taking three fish that he would not have caught otherwise, before lunch. By now he knew that 'underwater fishing has made way slowly' and '. . . it demands different qualities' from dry fly fishing and '. . . the two best catchers of fish of my acquaintance both make it their predominant method. It is very ridiculous to condemn it, for it calls for the very highest watercraft.' (Could one of these 'two best catchers' have been Skues?) An example was when fishing with Skues on the Itchen when the master spotted that the trout were feeding just below the surface on nymphs, a 'supreme exercise of observation and experiment'. Hills observed that for all Skues' skills, he was updating – through the use of improved flies and tackle (interestingly Hills had a Leonard rod that he threw away) – a method that was at least two hundred years old, that of casting upstream to an individual fish and allowing the fly to sink. In *A Summer on The Test*, Hills goes into quite some detail about the history of fishing on the Test and records the names of those who were known to have fished upstream or up and across prior to about 1890.

Hills had rented the fishing on the Kennet at Ramsbury in 1902, and then fished it regularly with friends until 1914 when his brother had the water up to his death in 1922. The first time that he fished the Kennet was on the Association waters at Hungerford in 1900 and then in 1901 he took a ticket for a year for the sum of just £10. As well as fishing the Itchen with Skues, the Test for many years, he also fished the Driffield Beck and other Yorkshire chalk streams and had grown up on the rivers of Cumberland. Although fishing tackle was starting to be better made and designed, Hills had a problem with a new Leonard rod that he acquired in 1926. He had caught salmon with this rod and although it was good for fishing for salmon and sea trout (this would suggest that it was not a trout rod), Hills discarded it in favour of his Lennox rod, bought the year before. Was that the rod that William Lunn described as the best in the Houghton Club?

Although Hills was able to fish with the help of William Lunn, keeper of the Houghton Club's waters on the Test, when he was a member for five years from 1925 and had his first day as a member on 25 April of that year, Hills claimed that Lunn had not seen an artificial nymph until 1916 when he was shown a brown pattern by a member who fished it 'afloat and not sunk' to catch fish with it. Lunn had started tying flies in that year, when he was 54, and endeavoured to tie artificials which looked realistic to the trout. By 1919 Lunn had developed his 'little pink partridge nymph' although he was careful not to write too much about fishing with nymphs in his reports for *The Field* because many members objected to their being used. By 1929 Hills thought that it was essential to be able to fish nymphs if you were going to catch fish. Although he was still learning how, he felt that he had mastered the rudiments of the method (he said that William Lunn's son Alfred took two years to learn to fish the nymph) when he was elected to the Houghton Club, but he still did not try it frequently enough. During his years on the Test he learnt much including 'the distinction between a nympher and a bulger'. To fish nymphs successfully required – and still does – regular practice. Although the dry fly purists maintained that you should be able to see the fish to which you were casting, Hills maintained that at Stockbridge he rarely saw the fish he was after and was not averse to searching the water to catch a cruising fish. This lack of visual contact made it even more difficult to know when to set the hook. Hills' many early years' wet fly fishing the rivers of Cumberland and the Lake District proved to be a big help to him in mastering nymph fishing. 'It is a sixth

Top left: Lunn's Blue Winged Olive nymph *Top right:* Lunn's Greenwell nymph
Bottom left: Lunn's Pink nymph *Bottom right:* Lunn's Watery Dun nymph

sense, knowing when a fish has taken you.' In his private fishing diaries Hills recorded a good day with various nymphs proving successful on 14 July 1928 and then in August 1929 he tried a new Lunn nymph tied using brown seal's fur with gold tinsel, although this pattern is not included in the list of Lunn's forty patterns in Hills' book *River Keeper*. By 1936 he was using only one 'underwater' pattern that he had used in 1914 – the Dotterel Hackle. 'Lunn's Partridge Hackle and various nymphs have banished them.' Some of those nymphs, aside from Lunn's patterns, were Carter's Yellow nymph and his Brown nymph. He also urged readers of his books not to forget the truism that a sunk fly must sink and do so without hesitation. To help flies to sink quickly, and even deeply to fish lying deep, he recommended using some gold wire as a rib and noted that some fly dressers were starting to add a little lead foil to the hook. He also tried Skues' double hooks but rejected them as he felt that the bulk was likely to make them too difficult for trout to draw into their mouths without hindrance.

Skues was one of the first, if not the first, trout fishermen to produce an analysis of rise forms. Rise forms are, as we know today, often crucial to successful fly fishing. He wrote: 'A close study of the form of the rise may often give the observant angler a clue, otherwise lacking, to the type of fly which the trout is taking, and to the stage and condition in which he is taking it.' In Halford's day, fish were either rising and taking flies from the surface, or bulging and taking nymphs (there were tailing fish to be seen as well but that is almost the complete reverse of a rise). Halford advocated the use of field glasses to study fish seen to be rising, so that the angler could determine whether they were, in fact, feeding on floating flies or feeding below the surface on nymphs and other subaqueous food forms. By the late nineteen twenties, Hills knew the difference between nymphing fish and bulgers, no doubt based on Skues' writings, his own observations and lessons learnt when fishing with him. The chalk streams 'and rivers of quiet and even flow' were the ideal rivers on which to carry out a study of the rising habits of trout. Skues knew that it could be very difficult to determine from a visible rise whether the fish had taken an insect 'superaqueous, flush, or subaqueous'. This is not surprising as not all food items are big enough to be seen clearly by the naked eye.

Notes

1 Martin Mosely, who was a great friend of Halford's, was a fisherman, entomologist and a leading authority on Ephemeroptera.

2 Mosely, writing on 'The Ephermeridae', referred to the larva or nymph as one of the stages of the life of ephemera, in his little book *The Dry-Fly Fisherman's Entomology*. But later in the same book he wrote of the grannom as having both larval and nymphal stages.

3 Skues did know of Mottram's book as he stated in his own book, *The Way of a Trout With a Fly*, that Mottram had promoted 'an interesting method of nymph fishing' but that he had not tried his method or flies. He did not like Mottram's flies as he thought they were too rigid, dense and dull in colour and, more particularly, that they were fished 'dragging'. He also felt that because they had no hackles, they would have 'a tendency to fall heavily when cast' whereas the short, soft hackles on his own patterns were enough 'to help break the fall of the hook on the water'. Again Mottram was far ahead of his time as his flies looked forward to the hackle-less patterns of Sawyer and Kite with their quick entry and no encumbrance to sinking speedily.

4 In his long foreword to his friend Norman McCaskie's autobiography, *Fishing, My Life's Hobby*, Skues wrote from Beckenham in June 1949, that he had been a founder member of the Abbotts Barton syndicate in 1922, after Cox's death. He also referred to his meeting with 'Halford the Great' back in 1910. In Skues' view, his long-time friend and fishing companion, did not get the knack of hooking trout on nymphs until 26 June 1938, which was to be their last day fishing together on the Itchen. Although McCaskie was a highly experienced wet-fly man, nymph fishing did not have for him the same attraction as the dry fly and he found it difficult, particularly seeing what was happening underwater. But he did admit that when a trout was taking nymphs 'I think that it is the truest form of sport to fish for it with a nymph rather than trust to the fluke of taking it on a dry fly.'

5 This article was reprinted in the *Journal of The Flyfishers Club*, volume 20, number 77 of Spring 1931 at the suggestion of H. T. Sheringham, and Skues was happy to seek more publicity for it.

6 Eric Horsfall Turner put dry fly purism in its place when he wrote: 'True purism, moreover,

is based on the assumption that the clumsy creations of the hands of man can truly imitate the delicate upwinged flies of nature to the successful ultimate of real deception. I do not believe that.'

7   As one might expect from the use of the generic name partridge hackle, these flies were most probably North Country spiders. Hills' favourite was 'the old Cumberland pattern' the Orange Partridge followed by the Red Partridge. He found that they were most successful when tied on either very large or very small hooks: in between sizes were not popular with trout.

5 The art and practice of nymph fishing matures   1920 to *c*1960

'An artificial nymph can be used with deadly effect throughout the trout season, but I think it is only during the months of July and August that it can give the fisherman the highest degree of sport, and the knowledge that he is accomplishing something beyond the powers of the ordinary wet- or dry-fly enthusiast . . . Truly these are the days when the utmost enjoyment of nymph fishing can be obtained'

Frank Sawyer, *Nymphs and The Trout*, 1958

In his foreword to the first edition of *Minor Tactics of The Chalk Stream*, Skues maintained that a combination of Halford, his book *Dry-Fly Fishing, In Theory and Practice* and the dry-fly purists in bringing about 'the triumph of the dry fly, of which that work was the crown and consummation, [resulted in] the obliteration from the minds of men, in much less than a generation, of all wet-fly lore which had served many generations of chalk-stream anglers well.' He also looked back 'with some shame at the slowness to take a hint from experience' which was that day in September in 1892, and similar experiences two or three years later, when he still did not realise that he 'was on the edge of an adventure'. At this time, still relatively early in his fishing career, he was also quite prepared to fish the water and caught fish: 'That afternoon I killed two and a half brace of good fish with the wet fly fished into likely places without seeing a single rise.' In his early days favourite flies fished wet were a then-new pattern that he was to name the Tup's Indispensable and the Greenwell's Glory.

Skues attempted, in the main, to imitate inert, resting nymphs only. He was not that interested, it seems, in trying to catch fish feeding on nymphs in mid water. His interest in nymphs in or immediately below the surface film influenced the development of his many artificial nymph patterns and probably precluded him from ever developing techniques to give life to his artificials with what Oliver Kite christened the induced take. Skues first called nymph fishing a minor tactic. For him it seems to have always been an adjunct to the dry fly, a method to be used in certain circumstances when he decided, or realised, that the dry fly was either ineffective or could not be used to catch fish that were feeding sub-surface, probably on nymphs either hatching or about to hatch. It does not seem to have been a first or primary line of attack. Even in the mid 1920s he was still often reluctant to fish a nymph when, later, he knew he should have because he caught fish on nymphs that he had failed earlier to catch on dry flies. Is this why he did not develop deep-water nymph fishing and all that that entails, as demonstrated by others in the last years of his life and after his death? Although there have always been doubts as to how deep Skues did fish his nymphs, careful study of his writings suggest that he, and his fishing friends, did fish deeper than we might imagine. He dipped his nymphs in glycerine – 'filled up with glycerine' – to make them sink and also used glycerine on the last foot (300mm) of his cast (leader) the rest of which would have been treated with paraffin to help it to float. He also wrote how such flies as a wet Alder sank quickly and deep. We do know that he fished his nymphs at the depth at which fish were feeding as he referred to a trout

This photograph of Frank Sawyer was taken by Charles Ritz, probably in 1952, when he visited Sawyer and learnt to fish the upstream nymph

absorbing 'a nymph at a lower level' and that trout hovering in mid-water were likely to be feeding actively. As well as constructing artificial nymphs which would absorb water readily, he also helped them to sink by applying saliva to them and the end of his cast, or leader, glycerine as mentioned already and even cleaning the end of the leader with river mud or wet clay. These treatments would be renewed as and when necessary. He also felt that a nymph cast directly upstream would sink more rapidly than one cast up and across and, therefore, did not always have to be cast so far in front of a nymphing trout.

H. D. Turing, a long-time editor of *Trout and Salmon Magazine*, was very firmly of the opinion that nymph fishing, which had become known as a separate style of fishing was, in fact, 'part and parcel of dry-fly fishing'. When he was writing in about 1950 in his book *Fly Fishing*, he felt that if this classification had been accepted twenty years earlier, then there would have been 'less of the acrimonious, though often amusing, controversy over the use of a nymph in dry-fly waters'. Any suggestion that fishing a fly 'wet' – which would be received in horror by some – was simply wet fly fishing by another name was wrong as true wet fly fishing was not nymph fishing.

Turing divided the hatch of fly into four stages, the first of which was the rise of the nymph from the weed to the surface and it was this stage that was of interest to the nymph fisherman, although the second stage 'The time spent on the surface before the fly rids itself of its shuck' may be of interest at times. He knew that the rise could be almost at an end before the fish abandoned the nymph for the winged fly on the surface, so any angler who took 'the old advice to wait for trout to come on to the floating fly and ignore bulges' was likely to have very little sport. He felt that there was very little tactical difference between catching a fish that was feeding underwater compared to one that was feeding on the surface on floating flies. Although he felt that it was not necessary to fish very deep, it was important to use a fly that sank quickly to the required depth. Like Skues, he was also of the opinion that you could not buy a decent artificial nymph from a tackle shop. Commercially-tied nymphs were un-representative of the naturals and in Turing's opinion a good artificial nymph should have 'a slender body and a noticeably prominent thorax with only a single turn of hackle to represent the legs' with the tails represented by a few strands from a cock pheasant tail feather.

Skues obviously had a great influence on Turing's thoughts and practices about nymph fishing because he too agreed with Skues that a Half Stone, 'dressed with a rather sparse hackle' was a very good imitation of a nymph and that the hatching, or emerging, dun could be well represented by either a Gold-Ribbed Hare's Ear or a Tup's Indispensable, which were favourites of Skues. Turing's knowledge of nymphs and trout had gaps in it as he knew that trout fed on nymphs before they were ready to hatch 'since they are found in trouts' stomachs' but he felt that it was very unlikely that they were taken unless the trout was grubbing about in the weeds, or tailing, in which case it was very unlikely that such a fish could be caught 'unless an angler has the luck to cast a fly at the moment when the trout raises its head and can see it'. It is a shame that Turing was not, apparently, aware of Sawyer's writings on nymph fishing: 'The secret of success with an artificial nymph lies in placing the artificial just where the fish expects to see a natural and if the fish is feeding near the bottom it is useless to present your nymph in the surface', or, one might add, vice versa.

Another angler who had discovered that the nymph would give good sport during the 1938 season, and 'On several occasions sport was so good that the evening rise proper was in full swing before I had changed my nymph for the more orthodox dry fly or spent spinner, and, thinking it hardly worth while to make the change, I continued putting my nymph over rising fish' was T. J. Hanna in an article called 'The Floating Nymph' published in *Angling, A Quarterly for Every Angler*[1] in 1941. The 1938 season had been particularly bad for dry fly fishing so by August Hanna resorted to nymphing. The nymph quickly proved much more deadly and he found himself wishing that he had started using it earlier. He had good sport in the afternoons, 'using nymphs tied on the G. E. M. Skues principle' and continued to use the nymph later and later into the evening and then started to fish the evening rise deliberately with nymphs. 'Of course, I had some qualms. Fishing a nymph was all very well early in the day, when natural nymphs were struggling to the surface to emerge as duns, but what could justify its use when these same duns were falling on the water as spent spinners?' He pondered at length as to why this should be. He felt that the answer was that his artificial nymph was being taken as a spent spinner and not for a nymph. He decided that he 'ought to have legal advice on the matter and laid my case before Mr G. E. M. Skues.' Skues was of the opinion that trout would take a nymph for a spent spinner and surmised that a trout of two pounds that he had caught on the Itchen the year before might have fallen for such a nymph.

Hanna decided that some experimentation was needed to produce a nymph that he could fish very close to the surface or even in the surface film. He dressed some nymphs similar in shape and material to his usual patterns but with five or six fibres from a cock's spade feather as tails. He then greased these tails and the entire cast These flies 'floated surprisingly well' and if they did sink, they did not sink far but the fact that they did sink just below the surface at times did not seem to effect their performance. These flies with their long tails, slender, tapering bodies and a maximum of two turns of a 'tiny hackle suggesting the neuration of transparent wings' did not frighten fish when they sank in contrast, he felt, to a sunk dry fly which had a profile distinctly different from a nymph or spinner.

Major Oliver Kite attributed the development of nymph fishing upstream, the classic Netheravon style, to Frank Sawyer who was the river keeper for the Services Dry-fly Fishing Association on the Wiltshire Avon. Frank Sawyer was born in 1906 in a cottage in Bulford within sound of the river. He became keeper of the six and a half miles of the Avon stretching above Bulford in 1928, at the young age of twenty-two, when it was the Officer's Fishing Association waters (the name was changed in 1964). It was in 1928[2] that he saw his first fish, a grayling, caught on a nymph by Brigadier General H. E. Carey who had been re-appointed honorary secretary of the Officers' Fishing Association that year, a position he had held after the First World War. Brigadier Carey had read Skues' books and made his own nymphs and was responsible for getting the Association to change its rules to allow the use of the upstream nymph in 1928 on what had been dry fly-only water[3]. Most of Sawyer's nymph fishing in his early years was for grayling which provided him with very good schooling for when he went on to fish for trout. Sawyer published his first book, *Keeper of The Stream*, in 1952 when he had had twenty-four years of experience, as head keeper, of looking after and maintaining a chalk stream and its trout fishery. As Sidney Vines wrote in one of his linking chapters in *Frank Sawyer, Man of the Riverside:* 'All through these years he was looking into the water, studying the fish and insects, observing their life-cycle, and making careful notes.' It was these years spent not only by but *in* the river that were to influence his fishing and nymph fishing in particular, as well as his knowledge and understanding of trout and what they feed on.

The Pheasant Tail Red Spinner was Frank Sawyer's favourite dry fly and, when well chewed, the inspiration for his Pheasant Tail nymph

Frank Sawyer's name will be associated forever with his Pheasant Tail nymph. This intrinsically simple fly, along with the Gold-Ribbed Hare's Ear nymph, must be one of the most widely fished – and most successful – artificial flies of all time. It has caught fish from east to west, from north to south and from some of the highest rivers in the world to most of the lowest. In 1965 Sawyer revealed a little of the development of his famous nymph: 'The Pheasant Tail has been favourite with me since the time when I caught my

The river Avon near Netheravon, looking upstream towards where Frank Sawyer's ashes were scattered

first fish on it. This nymph was actually a follow-up of my Pheasant Tail Red Spinner which I found would take fish after it had lost all its hackles and sank.' Earlier he had mentioned in an article published in April 1957, fishing a representation of a red spinner when olives were on the surface.[4] Who would believe that such a famous nymph could have been developed from a much-chewed dry fly? When Oliver Kite wrote an article about Frank Sawyer as a fly tier, his article concentrated on Sawyer's dry flies and referred to his – Sawyer's – all-purpose Pheasant Tail Red Spinner which 'ranks with Lunn's Particular as one of the most effective artificials of its kind'. Sawyer's Pheasant Tail Red Spinner must have been based on the Pheasant Tail, first dressed by Payne Collier in 1901 in Devon, and the Red Spinner, as fished by Halford and William Senior in the 1890s, including one evening when Senior was eventually allowed by Halford, when they were fishing at Ramsbury, to fish one wet and down and proceeded to catch the only fish taken that day. R. B. Marston was doubtful that Payne Collier, who used the pen-name Pheasant Tail, did claim to have invented the fly. Sawyer's version had white tails (Collier's original dressing had two crimson whisks), body and thorax made from pheasant tail herls and a hackle a dark red Rhode Island shade. The fly was tied with red tying silk. Kite noted that the thorax was an essential feature of all Sawyer's patterns. Kite also fished the Pheasant Tail Red Spinner which he described

71

as a very effective all-round pattern. In his book *The Fly Fisher and The Trout's Point of View*, Colonel Harding included an illustration (one of his own) of a Pheasant Tail nymph with a body of ribbed pheasant tail fibres and a hackle at the head of the fly. Harding was concerned with the body of artificial nymphs which he felt was an important part of their make-up. He also advocated giving the nymph a twitch at the end of the cast, to attract a fish's attention with a sudden movement.

Even though it is one of the simplest of patterns, tied from just two materials – fibres from the centre tail feather of a cock pheasant and very fine, red-coloured copper wire – Sawyer's Pheasant Tail nymph has not been surpassed as a representative of olive nymphs when tied in different sizes. Sawyer admitted that it took him years before he 'dressed a nymph which could be deadly'. Although designed originally for use on rivers, it has proved to be equally effective on still waters. Fly tiers and fly fisherman have sought to tie many variations, some of which have lost the elegance of the original, but the original, as conceived by Frank Sawyer still proves to be the best. The Pheasant Tail nymph is a lasting memorial to a remarkable man.

Frank Sawyer was encouraged to write by Sir Grimwood Mears, a retired judge and a very keen fly fisherman, who lived nearby in a hotel in Amesbury. Sir Grimwood also arranged for Sawyer to meet his old friend G. E. M. Skues in 1945, just four years before the old man's death. They seem to have got on famously and corresponded at some length, for example on 22 January 1949, when Skues wrote to Sawyer to congratulate him on his 'admirable article on the Spurwings' in the *Salmon and Trout Magazine* of that month but of which he had only just seen a copy. Skues was also happy to encourage Sawyer as a writer and even introduced him to his publisher A. & C. Black which then published *Keeper of The Stream*. Skues was also instrumental in introducing Sawyer to R. L. Marston who was then editor of the *Fishing Gazette* which had been edited in Victorian times by his father, R. B. Marston, who founded The Flyfishers' Club. Sawyer had many articles published in the *Fishing Gazette* and Sir Grimwood sent some of them to Wilson Stephens who was the then editor of *The Field*. Wilson Stephens saw the potential for a book written by Sawyer and Sir Grimwood then negotiated a deal with A. & C. Black on Sawyer's behalf. As well as the many articles that he wrote, Sawyer published two books and his last serious piece of writing was his contribution, 'Nymphing in the Classic Style', to *The Masters on the Nymph* which was published in 1979, not long before his death the following year. He died on the afternoon of 18 April 1980, on the bank of the Avon when he was taking his dog for a walk. A plain wooden seat was erected to mark the spot.

For Frank Sawyer, 'Nymph fishing, when carried out as it should be, is, I think, the most fascinating of all kinds of angling.' And even in the heat of high summer when the light and low and clear water provided the best conditions for seeing fish in their feeding positions, it was 'the most difficult angling art'. Through his work as a river keeper he was to bring a completely new approach to nymph fishing, based on his acute observation of the habits and movements of nymphs in the water and the way that trout and grayling fed on them. Most of his findings were in contradiction of the experts, both so-called and genuine, who had gone before him. And he was not afraid to state his findings quite clearly and plainly.

Sawyer was a naturalist and very interested in fly life and what was going on around and particularly in his river. Many of his magazine articles were on these subjects and also made-up considerable parts of all his books. He was not just a river keeper and a fisherman. While watching nymphs to see how far downstream they would travel before hatching, Sawyer saw nymphs 'On their journeys down-stream many attempts were made by each nymph in an endeavour to hatch, swimming here and there, struggling to and fro, and at times drifting completely inert.' Sawyer's description here is in contrast to Mosely's earlier assertions on the behaviour of nymphs. He was also able to observe the difficulties nymphs can have in breaking through the surface film

Frank Sawyer on
the bank of the
Wiltshire Avon

of the water, at certain times of the year, to hatch. He was also quite happy to contradict earlier assertions that a nymph could, or even should, be fished in the same way as a dry fly. In his opinion that was quite wrong.

Frank Sawyer put nymphs and nymphing trout into two categories: nymphs that are still to be found deep down in the water but within a few days, or perhaps hours, of hatching, and hatching nymphs within the last minutes of their underwater life, that have risen from the river bed to in or just under the surface film. It was these latter nymphs that Skues represented and used to catch his fish. Skues maintained that such nymphs were inert, showing no movement. Sawyer disagreed with this judgement as he knew that nymphs about to hatch would float in the surface film for often quite considerable distances, and they would, frequently, make attempts to break free of their

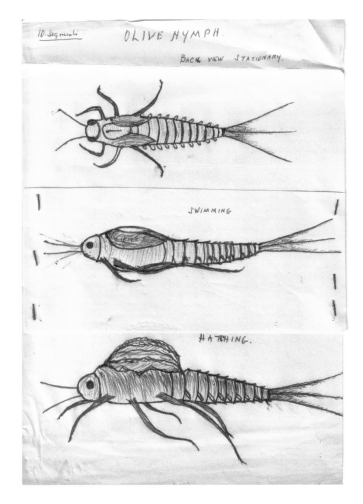

Frank Sawyer's drawing of an olive nymph. Note how its legs are close to its body when swimming (middle drawing) and the very pronounced bulge of its wings just before hatching

In Frank Sawyer's opinion high summer was the true occasion for practising the art of nymph fishing

nymphal husk. A suitable artificial that will float in or just under the surface film must be used to catch trout feeding on hatching nymphs. Sawyer liked to use a fly that appeared 'to be translucent and gives the effect of air beneath the nymphal shuck' and perhaps a few fibres to give the suggestion of moving legs and tails. Such a pattern should be cast with the accuracy and delicacy of a dry fly.

But Sawyer is best known for the development of the weighted nymph fished deep to represent nymphs moving about near the river bed and amongst weed beds. These nymphs are swimming nymphs, with their legs tucked in close to their bodies and with pronounced wing cases. Sawyer designed and tied his nymphs so that they had a quick entry into the water and then sank rapidly. To achieve these desirable characteristics he used no tying silk or thread and used fine copper wire to tie the fly and to add weight. General shape and colour, together with size, were the key points that Sawyer sought to represent, rather than exact imitation. 'I am in favour of exact representation for dry-fly or nymph, but when I use the word representation I try to carry it into effect. I want representation that is satisfactory from the trout's point of view. A correct imitation of the colouring and shape of an insect is not enough. To represent truly an insect, and successfully deceive a trout, the artificial must be offered at a time when he is taking, or likely to be taking, the natural from or beneath the surface of the water; offered in such a manner that it looks alive, or dead, or in a semi-inert stage, as natural ones are at the moment.' He used his Pheasant Tail pattern to represent dark nymphs and the Grey Goose to imitate lighter-coloured naturals. Sawyer claimed to have been the first to tie nymphs using only copper wire for 'base building, ballasting, and the tying in of the pheasant tail fibres, with fine copper wires'. It is interesting to note that Sawyer did not make this claim in the first edition of *Nymphs and The Trout* but it does appear in the second edition, published eleven years later in 1969.

In September, 1993, the American magazine *Fly Fisherman* published an article entitled 'Sawyer Nymphing', written by Mike Griffiths who knew and fished with Frank Sawyer on the Avon. Mike Griffiths wrote that, at first, Sawyer's new Pheasant Tail nymph was not well received. He quoted Sawyer as saying: "They saw it as a lure and a poaching instrument and many refused to speak to me about it.' In *The New Encyclopaedia of Fly Fishing* Conrad Voss Bark wrote that Sawyer met similar opposition to his weighted nymphs as had Skues to his unweighted patterns, 'In some cases opposition was even more bitter and contemptuous, for Sawyer was a water-keeper and did not [at that time] have the skill to argue with his critics in the way that Skues could.' But through persistence and demonstrating his patterns and his technique to many anglers, he managed to convert them. This process must have been made easier once he started to write.

Another of Sawyer's famous flies was the Grayling Bug which was later named the Killer Bug by the well-known American fly fisherman Lee Wulff. Sawyer once described this pattern as 'a miserable concoction of wire and wool, a thing anybody could make in less than a minute, and which to the human eye has not the slightest resemblance to any living creature.' This pattern was very successful for taking grayling on the Avon, in mistake for shrimps, and for lake trout which possibly took it for a hatching sedge when

Frank Sawyer landing a fish on the Wiltshire Avon

Frank Sawyer's daughter Pat nets a fish for
him

'moved by the rod tip in a slow and even draw to make it swim upwards'. This artificial was developed at a time when it was thought to be a good thing for a river, and trout fishing, to catch and kill between sixty and seventy grayling at time. Opinion on the harm done by grayling has now changed dramatically in England although the grayling is still not seen with quite the same fervour and high regard as in Europe and Scandinavia. Sawyer first tied this pattern with fuse wire[5], 'the wool over the silver-coloured fuse wire, has a certain translucency', but later changed to red-coloured wire. While the choice of wire colour may not have been critical, for Sawyer the choice of wool was. The wool he used was Chadwick's 477 and although he tried other wools, none was as successful as the 477 colour[6].

Sawyer developed his original patterns for nymph fishing after mid summer which he felt was the most sporting time of the season for this method. This meant that there were many ephemeroptera that he did not need to represent and that it was the swimming group of nymphs that were of primary interest to trout. He sought to represent three species of olives, pale wateries and the spurwings. His Pheasant Tail nymph represented the olives, when tied in different sizes, and he had an artificial to represent the pale wateries which did not survive into the second edition of his book. That fly was tied on a size 0 hook only with plain copper-coloured wire. He used four or five fibres from a ginger cock hackle for the tails and the body was 'fawny-pink darning wool'. Although he did not say so, one can assume, from the description, that this

Frank Sawyer keeping low and back from the water while stalking a big fish nymphing in mid stream

would have been Chadwick's 477. He used a third of a strand, spun round the wire in the manner of the pheasant tail fibres used for the Pheasant Tail nymph, tied from hook bend to eye. He made the wing case from a section cut from the dark edge of a wood pigeon primary feather, tied backwards and then forwards over the thorax area and tied-off behind the eye.

Another pattern that did not stand the test of time was his original Spurwing nymph. This was tied in two sizes, 00 and 1, with the same red-coloured copper wire used for the pheasant tail. The tails and body were three fibres from a condor wing feather with a browny-yellow colour. They were tied on in exactly the same way to just behind the hook eye. In an unusual departure, the copper wire was tied-off and replaced by gold wire which was used to complete the thorax. The condor fibres were then lapped back and forward to make the wing case and the fly was finished by making about a dozen turns of the gold wire behind the hook eye. These two patterns of nymph changed colour when wet and also had a translucent effect.

Although he learnt the majority of everything that he knew on his beloved Avon, he enjoyed fishing overseas where he learnt much too. Bavaria and its fishing continued to play an important part in the lives of nymph fishermen during the twentieth century. Skues before him had fished in Bavaria and the leading American trout angler Ernest Schwiebert was to fish there after Sawyer did, in 1962. Frank Sawyer had been invited to fish as a guest of Prince Paul von Quadt at Isny. As a river keeper Sawyer approached his visit to Bavaria in a different way from Skues and much of what he wrote about his visit concerned the fly life that he discovered in the river Argen in early July. He found Mayflies and Mayfly nymphs, although hatches were never big enough to interest the trout, and many stone flies and was fortunate enough to see some laying eggs. All the flies that he knew from chalk streams were present plus one that he had never seen before. He spotted one of these unknown flies floating down the river but before he could get hold of it, a trout rose and took it. So Sawyer retrieved his rod and caught the trout on a nymph. When he gutted it he was able to retrieve the specimen that he was after and he identified it as a late March Brown. He found a fast-flowing river that rose in the mountains that was surprisingly full of fly life as well as a few crayfish, big bullheads and burbot.

One day he gave a demonstration of nymph fishing to a German teacher who fished a pool full of refugee rainbow trout that had been washed out of the lake above, on the understanding that he returned the fish he caught to the lake. Sawyer, using a nymph, proceeded to catch fish after fish and eventually called a halt when he had caught twenty. The river was full of brown trout, grayling and various coarse fish and the biggest trout were to be found in the rapids.

Charles Ritz, of the Ritz hotel group fame, benefited from a nymph fishing demonstration by Frank Sawyer on his home waters of the Avon at

Charles Ritz giving a casting demonstration from a footbridge over the river Avon when he stayed with Frank Sawyer and learnt how to fish the upstream nymph in the Netheravon style

Netheravon, on 10 July1952. When fishing for one particular fish in water about four feet (1.2 m) deep, Ritz wrote that Sawyer tightened his line slightly – when he thought that his nymph had passed by the fish without being taken – 'to give animation to the lure'. The result of this induced take was a hooked fish.

Ritz had read about and tried fishing nymphs without any consistent success until he watched Sawyer's demonstration. He wrote: 'Most of the time the theoretical knowledge derived from my reading became mere chaos when on the water.' Ritz had fished with the American A. J. McClane in Normandy in 1948. McLane caught a fish on an American artificial nymph with a black back and a yellow-striped underneath. That pattern was one of a selection of grey, brown and black nymphs. Ritz went on to introduce Sawyer's method to French anglers.

When in England, Ritz learned the necessity for accurate casting – as accurate as if fishing a dry fly – fishing at the same depth as the fish and the need for a sixth sense when detecting the take as well as being aware of the indications given by the leader and the movement of the target fish, when visible. Ritz wrote: 'I shall never forget that afternoon, my excitement and satisfaction of having discovered and learned something really new in the practice of fishing. I am eternally grateful to Sawyer who revealed his secrets to me with joy and enthusiasm.' Ritz then went on to try to prove that Sawyer's method could be adopted to most rivers that contained salmonids. He had learnt enough from watching Frank Sawyer to be able to demonstrate the technique to friends in Germany and Austria where he was able to catch both trout and grayling. He considered nymph fishing to be 'the acme of the art of fly fishing'.

Frank Sawyer casting to a nymphing fish on the Syrencote House stretch of the Avon

The original caption for this photograph started 'The crucial stage in the fight'. Frank Sawyer has stopped the fish from passing under the foot bridge

Two years after Sawyer's death, Barry Lloyd wrote, in *Trout and Salmon*, 'Perhaps what I remember best about Frank, apart from his quiet sense of humour and country-style gentlemanly manners, was his ability to stimulate me to learn for myself more about different aspects of fishing . . . One of his greatest contributions to fly-fishing was to point many beginners in the right direction, intervening only if a gentle nudge were needed to keep them to the right path. It was truly the sign of a great teacher, and this pupil, at least, will always be grateful for the knowledge gained from the master of the nymph.'

Brigadier Carey paid a warm tribute to Sawyer for his 'skilful and untiring work' in the Conclusion to his book *One River* about his life spent on the banks of the Avon from the early to mid-1920s. How much he was influenced by his association with Frank Sawyer is not entirely clear but he used nymphs that were constructed to sink quickly and used heavy nymphs to tailing fish. It was, of course, Carey who had introduced Sawyer to nymph fishing and also showed him how to tie Skues-style nymphs. When Carey wrote about his 'modern' fisherman using but few dry fly patterns and being even more conservative when it came to nymphs: 'his own patterns are few in number', he could have been writing about Sawyer. The two had many informative 'chats and rambles by the river-side'. He wrote about the attractiveness of different types of river weed to nymphs and was intimately involved in the Association changing its rules from dry fly only to permitting upstream nymph fishing. Commenting on this rule change, he stated: 'the introduction of nymph fishing has opened up a fresh branch of the art, or perhaps has

81

resulted in a more sportsmanlike revival of older methods: for, provided that nymph fishing is kept within the confines that Mr Skues, its chief advocate, lays down, I think it is quite a fair branch of the art, and it is certainly as difficult as dry fly: in fact I think more so.' Later he wrote: 'It appars (*sic*) nonsense, and also bad for the fishery, that the angler should be expected to continue to scare fish with floaters while on the other hand he has a reasonable chance of outwitting them with a well-presented nymph.' He knew from personal experience how very difficult it was to acquire 'that extra sense which marks the expert nymph fisher' and he was of the opinion that many gave up trying to master the art after initial failures. He never considered that a dry fly man would give up using the dry fly if the fishery rules allowed the use of the nymph. Rather 'all he asks for is to be allowed to use the nymph when he knows it is a better representation of the food the trout is looking for than is the floating fly.' The use of the nymph inferred 'that the quarry must be selected, and stalked, and the nymph presented, in practically the same way as the floater; only that it comes to the trout submerged.'

Another very interesting and perceptive observation that he made was that the blue winged olive when hatching 'sits on its shuck longer than other small ephemeroptera. It might be worthwhile to tie a pattern with an imitation of the shuck adhering to a partly emerged dun.' How many years were to pass before we started tying and fishing emergers with trailing shucks?

Frank Sawyer despaired of ever teaching Brigadier Carey and a fellow officer friend, Colonel Sharp, to fish his nymphs successfully. They could both catch fish on nymphs when fish took them close to the surface but neither had the eyesight or appreciation of what was happening when fish took nymphs fished much deeper. They could not see a fish take a nymph and missed many good fish by not responding quickly enough. In Brigadier Carey's case this is not that surprising as he was an elderly man who was to die in 1944. But Brigadier Carey did encourage Sawyer to collect and identify natural nymphs and he, Carey, attempted to tie imitations. Sawyer followed his methods and ideas but realised quite soon that they would not sink quickly enough. He had seen Carey use lead to weight his flies but he felt that this spoiled the appearance of the finished article. So Sawyer hit on the idea of using fine copper wire to both weight the hook and build up a base of the right shape. He then dispensed with any tying silk. He showed his nymphs to Carey and Colonel Sharp but neither was impressed and although they both tried them they failed to catch any fish. Sawyer knew why but held his counsel.

For Oliver Kite the true Netheravon style of nymph fishing was characterised by the use of artificial nymphs with a complete absence of hackle which were meant to deceive, and not lures (nymphs with hackles) which were designed to attract trout. He maintained that Sawyer developed the modern technique of upstream nymph fishing at Netheravon, based on Skues' discoveries and experiments. Kite had his own very high standards, amongst his own admitted idiosyncrasies, such as not using hooks larger than size 1 (15 in today's sizes) and rarely bigger than size 0 (size 16 today) except when fishing deep pools for grayling or fast, rough waters for trout. In his view 'an artificial nymph is a reasonably close representation in size and general appearance of a natural nymph. I have not yet seen a natural nymph with wings. Winged artificials may be effective, indeed we know they are, but they are not nymphs. They may be conveniently thought of and fairly described as wet flies. With regard to hackled nymphs, if the rules of the water permit the use of hackled nymphs, it is up to the individual to employ these patterns if he so wishes.' Later in the same book, *Nymph Fishing in Practice*, he likened nymph fishing to deer stalking: 'The cast, like the actual shot, should be no more than the coup de grace. The hard work, both the physical effort involved in the approach and the mental preparation which precedes it, is mostly done beforehand. The

Oliver Kite deep in thought on the bank of the river Avon

nymph fisher, however, has one great advantage over the stalker. Whereas the latter's hands are tied, in that his shot must take one particular trajectory, and one only, from the point at which it is fired, the nymph fisher can put his artificial within reasonable reach of the trout and persuade his quarry to come and get it.

'This, indeed, is the very foundation of the Netheravon creed. It postulates the simple hypothesis that if you show a trout an artificial, vaguely similar in size and form to a natural but above all behaving like a natural nymph, the fish will take it as such, if you present it when it is feeding on natural nymphs of like size . . . The craft of the nymph fisher takes time to acquire, however, for you must know when your nymph is taken and set the hook in the fish's jaw in the brief moment in which this is possible. The foundation of this craft is informed anticipation and this I stress again.'

In the Introduction to his book, Kite described how he caught his first trout on a nymph, one tied by Frank Sawyer. It was one day in 1957 which was his second season on the Avon. Frank Sawyer suggested to Kite that, as things were quiet on the river i.e. no fish rising, that he tried higher up and with a nymph. Kite had some shop nymphs which he did not consider to be worth using and so was happy to accept a couple of Sawyer's small Pheasant Tail nymphs. He went up to Choulston to the Court Reach at Netheravon, and just below Haxton bridge he saw 'a good trout swinging to and fro in a streamy current where it emerged from between two clumps of starwort.

'The trout refused various dry-flies. I put on one of the small nymphs I had been given, casting it accurately a few feet ahead of the trout. As it passed the fish's head without being taken, I raised the tip of my rod to withdraw it. As I did so I saw the trout turn, so I stayed my hand momentarily then, as the trout turned back, I struck. And that was how I caught my first trout on the artificial nymph.' That was to be the inspiration for what he described as his nymph-fishing technique which he was to develop, modify, test and practise regularly for ten or so seasons right up until his early death in 1968.

Kite felt that it was very important that nymph fishermen should ask themselves just what they are trying to do. If it is simply to catch fish, then use a net, but if the object is to catch fish with rod and line, then use worms or maggots. But if the objective is to catch trout and grayling, feeding underwater, by deceiving them into taking an artificial nymph pattern, the angler must decide for him- or herself what constitutes a nymph. The angler is free to formulate his own ideas and limits, within the rules of the water to be fished.

Both Kite and Sawyer demonstrated their nymph fishing abilities at home and overseas and in so doing spread the doctrine of the Netheravon style to Europe and Scandinavia. Kite wrote in an article in *Trout and Salmon* in January 1963 that the Netheravon style of nymph fishing was practised and

Oliver Kite tying on a fly one spring day on the bank of the Avon which looks in fine fettle

understood in Normandy where a number of local anglers had learnt the art from Frank Sawyer either in Netheravon or on Sawyer's visit to Normandy. In Normandy nymph fishing was practised mostly in the summer after the end of the Mayfly season. This accords with Kite's observation that no Mayfly *(E. Danica)* nymphs should ever be used and that when the Mayfly was hatching, then the dry fly was obligatory. Kite fished extensively in Denmark in June 1964 (when he stayed with Preben Torp Jacobsen whose wife was quite taken by the red flannel night shirt that Oliver Kite wore) and also in Swedish Lapland with Nils Färnström, the founder and editor of the Swedish fishing magazine *Sportfiskaren*.

Writing about fishing for grayling in November 1960 *(Trout and Salmon)* Kite made an interesting reference to 'the old nymph-fishing style' with reference to fishing for and catching active grayling in mid-water or just below the surface. But Kite noted that the better fish would be found 'well down' and to catch them the angler would need to know how to get his nymph down to them 'and then on his skill at making it behave like a natural nymph.' If these two requirements were met, Kite felt that the pattern of artificial was un-important. There should be no slack in the line between the rod tip and the point where the un-greased line dipped below the surface. 'An immediate reaction is necessary to set the hook in the fish's jaw when a slight check is noticed.

'When the nymph is being fished deep and slight lift is being imparted with the rod to attract a large fish, the angler's movement is usually followed by a very slight pause before the cast dips sharply with a pronounced tug.'

Another technique he used, particularly for grayling, was the swing-drift to achieve an induced take when grayling were lying on the far side of a river. The technique was to cast a yard or two beyond the fish's lie and a similar distance upstream. 'Then, by the time it approaches the grayling, and has sunk to its approximate depth, the current, acting on the extended line, will cause the nymph to lift in the water, so triggering off the take. You may even feel it, which you never do in orthodox, upstream nymph fishing.'

Kite even went so far as to maintain that trout could be caught on a bare hook 'if a little fine copper wire is spun round the shank to provide the necessary sinking power.' He continued 'If this is augmented with a few pheasant tail fibres, it results in the best dressing I've ever come across and one which yields me hundreds of fish every year.' These comments would suggest that what is now known as the Bare Hook nymph was, originally, intended to be just that – a bare hook – but he appreciated that a little weight was needed to get a bare hook to sink to the required depth. He repeated this assertion in *Trout*

Oliver Kite fishing in either Devon or Cornwall

86

and Salmon in another article on grayling fishing in October 1965 when he wrote of 'the effectiveness of bare hooks, wired to sink and realistically handled in the water'. Kite's original intention for this 'pattern' is at variance with comments made after his death by Frank Sawyer in a letter published in *Trout and Salmon*. In that letter about what he called 'this bare hook business', Sawyer wrote: 'The so-called bare-hook nymph which was used by Oliver Kite at times, is a hook wound about and shaped nymph-like with fine copper wire. This gives it weight to sink quickly and deeply . . . He found, even as I had told him, that fish would take these artificials readily when most, and sometimes all, of the dressing covering the wire base had worn off by constant fishing, and in the mouths of fish.' (The reference to a nymph with the dressing worn off would, no doubt, be a Pheasant Tail nymph.) In his book *Nymph Fishing in Practice* (published in 1963), Kite made only fleeting references to his Bare Hook nymph such as that a trout will take his offer 'even if it is little more than a bare 0 hook' and 'as near a bare hook as you've got'. He also found that he continued to catch both trout and grayling the more worn his nymphs became 'provided that the basic structural outline with its humped thorax remains.' Kite's later writings suggest that he made much more use of the Bare Hook nymph than Sawyer would have us believe. In *Trout and Salmon* (November 1966) Kite published his catch statistics for the years 1957 to 1965. He wrote: 'The nymph, in most cases, was a Pheasant-tail, size 0 or 1, but in recent years would have been a bare hook, wired to sink'. Some of those 'recent years' would have been after publication of his book three years earlier. Kite used his Bare Hook nymph for catching still water rainbows as well as brown trout and grayling in rivers.

Oliver Kite tied Frank Sawyer's Pheasant Tail nymph and Grey Goose nymph a little bulkier than Sawyer and with tails about three eighths of an inch (10mm) long rather than Sawyer's one eighth of an inch (3mm). To both Kite and Sawyer, the size and construction of the artificial so that it imitated the general appearance of the natural nymph was critical. The artificials must sink quickly too. (This characteristic is very important to the design and tying of Czech nymphs as they do not all rely solely on added lead to make them sink quickly.) Kite would place his own and other people's nymphs on the surface of a glass of water. If they failed to sink immediately, they were no good 'for nymph fishing in the modern style.' The nymph fisherman should aim to imitate nymphs at all stages of their existence, not just when they are sub-surface in their last minutes of nymphs (before hatching into duns) which is what he maintained that Skues did. Throughout his life, Kite used but two of his own nymph patterns and these two patterns of Frank Sawyer. This was possible because of his way of fishing depended on the manner in which the artificial was fished and not the pattern.

Oliver Kite was a very different character compared to Frank Sawyer. He was a powerful man who used quite a lot of brute force in his fishing (he fished with a six weight line compared to Sawyer's four weight) and a brilliant communicator, both on television and in his work for the Army re-writing training manuals. He was a superb performer for television and made a number of series of programmes including *In Kite's Country* which started on 27 September 1965. Edward Channell who filmed Kite over a period of four years, initially once a month and then weekly, described Kite as having a military bearing, someone who did not suffer fools gladly – but took care to avoid them – very precise in his fishing and a natural in front of the camera. Edward Channell said that he wasted very little film as when Kite said that he was going to catch a fish, he did! He said Kite had great respect for Frank Sawyer and although their relationship was uneasy, he never had a cross word to say about him.

A contemporary, Major Sidney Vines, attended one of his fishing courses in 1962 and was to meet him on many occasions when they were both collecting daughters from parties. Major Vines recalls that Kite was extremely good company and a charmer with a fund of good stories. Another contemporary, a photographer for *Shooting Times*, was John Marchington whose photographic sessions soon extended to days spent on the river fishing, as they got to know each other. John Marchington described Oliver Kite as being a

Oliver Kite netting a trout on the river Avon. His utilitarian landing net, creel with no lid and old fibre glass rod can all be seen very clearly

genuine, warm, sincere, wholesome and good man. Even though carbon fibre, or graphite, rods were available he still preferred to fish with a rather tatty old glass fibre rod. Marchington described another of his party tricks (the best known being catching grayling with a blindfold over his eyes). On meeting a fellow angler for the first time he would take him into his study in Netheravon, put a hook in his fly-tying vice and pluck a lump of wool from the carpet, or from the sweater he was wearing, and then tie it to the hook as a simple thorax. With an exclamation of 'that'll do' it was off to the river where fish would be caught on the 'carpet' or 'sweater' nymph. It is generally accepted that Kite learnt all he knew about nymph fishing from Frank Sawyer although one 'supporter' and friend of Kite's maintained that he was the complete, finished nymph fisherman by 1960, just two years after he and Sawyer met. Kite was an interpreter of other people's, primarily Sawyer's, ideas rather than an original thinker. His best known fly invention was his Kite's Imperial dry fly.

Oliver Kite was to fish in northern Sweden with the late Nils Färnström in 1963, four years after Sawyer had also fished in Sweden with Färnström. Färnström was very cagey about where he took his friends fishing and, I understand, often did not tell them the real names of the rivers and lakes that they fished. After a number of months of detective work I eventually managed to track down where the two of them went. It was an area called Suorkejokke. But where exactly was it? It was Kite's old Danish friend Preben Torp Jacobsen who was able to pin-point the location of Kite's expedition and send me a map showing where he believed that they had pitched their camp.

Nils Färnström, who was born in 1914, was a very important figure in the development of fly fishing in Sweden. He was a very good journalist and writer, a good fisherman too, and as well as taking leading English anglers fishing in Sweden, he had fished in England and at Netheravon. He was a fisherman and jazz lover for forty years and edited and published the Swedish magazine *Sportfiskaren* from the first issue in 1935 until 1964, with the exception of one year. He wrote many fishing books, including *Streamer mot Strömmen* which included a chapter on his expedition to Swedish Lapland with Kite, fishing articles for newspapers as well as articles on stamps and travel. He seems to have had access to rivers and places that were out of bounds to others as well as not wanting hordes of fellow anglers visiting his favourite places. According to Kite he was responsible for introducing to Sweden the American fan-wing Royal Coachman fly, which soon became a very popular pattern. Färnström died in 1975.

Oliver Kite wrote about his experiences in a series of articles in *Trout and Salmon* in January and February 1964. He described the twenty-three mile length of glacial lakes and connecting rivers in a very remote and mountainous area of Swedish Lapland as virtually unfished, or even visited, and how they had little idea what to expect in the way of fishing and what they might catch.

The first fish that Oliver Kite caught in Swedish Lapland was an Arctic char

He arrived in Kiruna in July to be greeted by a bitter wind and driving rain and a temperature of only about four degrees Celcius. Conditions were too severe for the party to take-off by float plane from a nearby lake until the next evening. They flew over mountains and ravines and landed on a long, narrow lake lying between snow-capped peaks after an hour's flight. They went ashore and set-up their camp and as midnight approached they set off to fish. This was the start of what was to be for Oliver Kite an unforgettable experience in 'this strange and beautiful northern land', fishing beneath the midnight sun.

Fortunately the wind had died and Kite saw in 'the strange, fiery light from the midnight sun (was) reflected in the smooth waters of the lake' signs of fish moving. Kite was to catch his first fish, an Arctic char, on a nymph. He described that fish as having a 'flaming belly, as startling as the northern sky'. This was the first of six char that he caught that night. The wind rose during the rest of the night and they suffered from heavy rain and snow on two occasions over the next eight days. Because of a lack of dry clothing, he ended up cooking the daily meal of rice and fish in chest waders and a sweater, which, he wrote, did little to keep out the all-pervading cold. Kite had taken responsibility for cooking duties so that Färnström's wife, Britta, could act as 'quartermaster and film cameraman' for the film that Kite made of his adventure. Thanks to the rain and snow they found the water levels were so high as to make the rivers almost unfishable. They caught char in the lakes – but no trout or grayling – and Kite caught a brace of trout on his second day in one of the rivers.

Kite restricted himself to fishing waters where his preferred methods would be rewarded, such as wide pools. He caught most of his fish on nymphs (some of which he had tied on the train from Stockholm to Kiruna), particularly a pattern that he called the Reindeer and Red. This consisted of some red wool 'such as the Lapps use for the big pompon on their traditional headgear' which he used to camouflage the copper wire and a tuft of reindeer hair for the thorax tuft. While he found that the char would take his flies voluntarily, he caught a number on the Reindeer and Red using the induced take.

When I arrived at Suorkejokke forty years after Kite, the weather was similar but fortunately nothing like as cold. When the temperature started to rise, we soon had biting mosquitoes and swarms of little black flies called knots filling the air. Kite too, had experienced vast hatches of heather flies *(Bibio pomonae)* when the temperature rose for the last two days of his stay. He enjoyed superb sport with the dry fly during these prolific hatches. The knot is a particularly unpleasant little fly as it is small enough to get into your mouth and up your nose. Knots are a very important source of food for fish in these high, northern latitudes and hatch in their millions.

Even forty years ago, Sweden was one of the leaders in producing hydro-electricity and this has resulted in massive dams across some of the country's largest rivers many of which have been lost to salmon fishing. These dams and

The mountain in the background featured prominently in a number of Nils Färnström's photographs of Oliver Kite when they fished at Suorkejokke in 1963

power stations need regular maintenance and the summer of 2003 was no exception. Work on one of the biggest rivers nearby meant that water was being diverted into the Suorkejokke river system. The result of this was that the water temperature was low – thirteen degrees Celsius – the water level was exceptionally high and probably very similar to the levels Kite had experienced. But for today's fisherman levels were higher than the year-round average, and exceptionally high for summer. This meant that access to good fishing areas was limited and it proved difficult to locate areas where fish – brown trout and Arctic char – could be found. In places the water was two or three feet above the vegetation marking the normal water level.

In the first chapter of *Streamer mot Strömmen*, 'Lapplandsröding' (Lapland char), which was his account of their two week visit, Färnström described how Oliver Kite arrived with no more than a dozen ready-tied flies but a complete fly tying kit which he used to tie superb flies every morning, to match those that were hatching or on the wing. Kite was not that keen on wet fly fishing and when the possibility of spinning was suggested, it was rejected out of hand! Färnström may have suggested this because, it seems, the waters had been recommended to him by a spin fishermen and they were finding that because of the power of the river, the good places for fly fishing were few and far between and that the river might have been better suited to spinning. The best fish of their trip was a five pound (2.26 kg) trout that was caught in a big pool

Late evening at Suorkejokke in 2003

between the lakes. Färnström caught this fish on a dry fly while Kite was back at the camp on the shore of the lake.

Kite was reported by Färnström to have been very taken with nymph fishing for char in the lakes, where he caught many fish and some over two pounds (just under one kilogram) in weight. He was happy to sit and enjoy the scenery while drinking a cup of coffee with his rod close to hand. As soon as fish started to rise, he was on the water. On the first or second afternoon, after twelve fish had fallen to his nymph, he was quite happy to stop fishing as he felt he had no need to catch more or anything to prove. Some of these and other char and one trout were put into a pool they made in the rocks beside the river, as an experiment to see how they would recover after being caught and 'released'. Apparently the char were still alive after twelve days and the only casualty was the small trout.

Frank Sawyer had been invited to Sweden to fish with Färnström to see if his method of nymph fishing 'could be used to obtain more sport in some of the waters in Sweden.' In his first article written for *Trout and Salmon*, in December 1959, Sawyer wrote that if he had known before he left 'the class of country' into which he was to go, he was doubtful if he would have accepted the invitation. Where he went was a place 'high in the mountains near to the borders of Norway and Lapland.' From Sawyer's description it was similar to where

Kite enjoyed nymph fishing for char in the lakes

Frank Sawyer was invited to fish in Sweden to see if nymph fishing would be successful in some Swedish waters

Oliver Kite went, but on a smaller scale and with more wildlife such as elk, reindeer, otter, bear and osprey to be seen[7]. Like Kite, Sawyer was also quite happy to sit and absorb the beauty of the place. He also made a promise not to disclose the exact location, for fear that it might be desecrated by too many visitors, 'But somehow I don't think this will ever happen. Only those who love nature and the catching of really wild fish, could withstand the privation and endurance necessary on such a trip.'

Although he caught his first fish on a size 0 Pheasant Tail nymph, he was unsure as to how successful his methods would prove on the lakes and the inter-linking rivers and streams. He records that the first fish of any size that he caught, a brown trout of two and a quarter pounds (1kg) took seventy yards (65m) of line and backing off his reel. It was during this visit that Sawyer developed his Grey Goose nymph and he used it to good effect in large sizes of the equivalent to a size twelve or fourteen hook. This nymph accounted for trout up to four pounds (nearly 2kg). Later that day he went to meet Färnström who was also able to put the new Grey Goose nymph through its paces with great success.

The weather in July 1959 was very much better than that experienced by Oliver Kite. Photographs show Sawyer fishing in shirt sleeves and there were the most prolific hatches of fly and 'a congregation of spinners such as I have

DATE	WHERE CAUGHT	RIVER	RODS	FLY	FISH	WEIGHT Lbs. Ozs.	TOTAL	REMARKS
11 July	Figheldean Bridge Lavington	Avon		P.T. Nymph	Trout	2. 4	1.	
15 July	Lavington Beat 2 Lavington Beat 1	Avon		Fav.	Chub.	2 4/1.3/4	2	
24 July		Avon		Coypu Curp.	Perch. Chub.	1/2 lbs.	2	
17th Aug	Broadlands	Test		Hays & Spoon.	Chub.	4 1/2	1	
Aug 19th	Chew Valley Lake	Lake		Funk	1 Brown 1 Rainbow	2. 10. 1. 10.	2	
24 Aug	Figheldean 2 Choulston	Avon		Nymph Spin.	Trout.	1. 2.	3	
30 Aug	Netheravon	Avon		Nymph.	Grayling.	11 1/2" 12"	13.	
28th	Somerley	Avon		Red Spinner	Trout	11 1/2 - 12 1/2	2	

A page from one of Frank Sawyer's fishing diaries that recorded when Nils Färnström caught his first English trout, below Figheldean bridge, on a pheasant tail nymph. Note also the use of a Grayling bug and Red Spinner.

never seen before, or, I think, am ever likely to see again.' As Sawyer's new nymph continued to prove its worth, Färnström suggested renaming it the Sawyer Swedish, to which the inventor agreed, but suggested that they abbreviate it to SS. It was not until his return to England that he discovered that the natural it was designed to imitate was the *Siphlonurus spinosus*. It could not have been named better! He credited his success with his new pattern to his knowledge of entomology, time spent studying what was happening underwater and examining the stomachs of trout that he had caught. Sawyer made no mention of using a marrow spoon while in Sweden. He referred to examining the stomach contents of trout that he had caught in his first article for *Trout and Salmon* which was published in December 1956. For someone who had met and corresponded with Skues in the last years of the latter's life, it seems strange that Sawyer had not adopted the use of a marrow spoon which, after all, had transformed Skues' fishing all those years before.

The following year Färnström fished the Avon with Frank Sawyer and caught his first trout in England on 11 July 1960, by Figheldean bridge on 'A rough sort of day but the fish rose well' was how Sawyer recorded it in his fishing diary.

It was a mark of the calibre of the man, and the respect in which he was held by his contemporaries, that so many notable anglers fished with him on his beloved Avon and invited him to fish abroad. Major Vines met Sawyer in 1959 but it was some five years before Vines felt that he had gained Sawyer's trust – he had the traditional countryman's reserve. Major Vines is fulsome in his praise and respect for Frank Sawyer, describing him as a great man, a creative and original thinker who extended the frontiers of human knowledge. Sawyer was wary of being used – as he was by Kite who he ignored for the last five years of his life – was sensitive, by his own account, and if a discussion with fellow fishermen started to get heated, he would walk away. Sawyer sought recognition for who he was and felt that he was shown little respect by the small salary that he was paid and from some of the officers of the SDFFA, as when the chairman at an AGM said: 'Sawyer, go and see if the tea is ready.' This may have been the way Army officers addressed each other and other ranks, but it was not the way Sawyer liked to be spoken to. Sidney Vines produced a biography of Sawyer (published in 1984) after his death with the full co-operation of his wife Margaret.

Oliver Kite was famous for the development of the induced take used when a fish 'disregards the artificial until attention is drawn to it by some deliberate action of the angler'. Whether or not he was influenced by James Leisenring and his lift – which was, perhaps, more of a complete style of fishing compared to the induced take – is not recorded anywhere. Who invented the induced take? Sawyer or Kite? Sawyer did write of the importance of 'control in the water' of your nymph and giving it 'just that little something to simulate life'.

That 'little something' he described as a 'slight lift of the rod gives a movement and a lift to the nymph and this immediately attracts the eyes of the fish'.
The lift should be made just when the fish is expected to take the artificial and
can be used 'to make him take it'. To achieve an effective movement or lift, it
is essential to eliminate all slack from the fly line so that the angler has direct
communication with their fly. Charles Ritz noted when watching Sawyer
demonstrate how to fish a nymph that he suddenly raised the point of his rod
very slightly. He quoted Sawyer as saying afterwards: 'When I thought that
my nymph had passed the fish without being token I slightly tightened my line
to give animation to the lure, which often incites a fish to take.'

Compared to the Leisenring lift, Kite's induced take involved much smaller
rod movements, either upwards to simulate a nymph rising up through the
water or, sideways and upwards smartly to suggest the rapid dart of nymphs,
found in deep waters, such as the slow-water olive or small spurwing. Using
either method, the artificial should move about a foot (30cm) through the
water, moved by the tip of the rod. If the position and timing of the movement
of the nymph are both correct, the nymph should be taken by the trout. As he
wrote in *Elements of Nymph Fishing* 'You must therefore be keyed up, ready in
all respects to react in turn, and set your hook in the jaws of the fish at the
moment of take you have so artfully induced.' Like so many things in fly
fishing, it is very easy to describe how to perform the induced take but quite
a different matter to put it into practice successfully. The keys to a successful
induced take are being able to see the fish you wish to catch and knowing
where your nymph is so that you can move it at just the right time. But done
well the satisfaction can be immense. The induced take can also be used when
fish are nymphing in mid-water, to simulate a nymph darting from one clump
of weed to another perhaps. Kite also used the induced take when fishing to
a fish in a known lie, but invisible to the angler, from where he is fishing, but
where he can see into the water to one side of the fish or the other. He used
the induced take to lure the fish across to where it could be seen and it would
then be easier to see if the fish took the nymph.

Another crucial aspect of nymph fishing that still bedevils many anglers is
knowing when a fish has taken your artificial nymph. Skues wrote about how
you could see the wink or flash of white of the inside of a trout's mouth as it
turned, opened its mouth and grabbed a passing nymph or the angler's artificial. But for Kite the most important indicator of a take was close observation
of what he called the dipping point. This is the point at which the ungreased
point or tippet pierces the surface of the water. Kite maintained that it paid
'to grease the thicker links of the cast . . . so to act as a float to give you some
indication of the whereabouts of your artificial'. Greasing the butt of the leader
up to the dipping point, also helps to emphasise takes. Trout taking nymphs
often move forward to intercept them and when the nymph taken is the

angler's artificial, the forward movement of the fish will 'cause a slight tug to be imparted to the floating part of the cast which is duly registered at the dipping point.' Detecting takes and setting the hook successfully and consistently when fishing for nymphing trout takes close and careful observation and much practice. Other writers have commented on good nymph fishermen seeming to have a sixth sense and to tighten their line for no apparent reason other than a feeling, it would seem, that a fish has taken their nymph. This sixth sense can be developed with patient practice. Fishing a gin-clear river where you can see every fish does make life very much easier.

Another of Kite's legacies was his classification of the different nymphs into six main groups: bottom burrowers (*ephemerids*), silt crawlers (*caenids*), moss creepers (*ephemerellids*), two classes of stone clingers (*ecdyonurids* and *potamanthids*), laboured swimmers (*leptophlebiids*) and agile darters, again in two classes (large *siphlonurids* and small *baetids*), in contrast to Sawyer's earlier classification into four groups namely swimming nymphs, crawling nymphs, flat nymphs and burrowing nymphs.

Most fishermen probably carry with them far more tackle than is necessary. Kite was one who took the practice of fishing with the bare minimum to an extreme, usually setting out with nothing but an often-troublesome landing net, a spool of tippet material, tin of line grease and a box of a few dry flies and nymphs, in addition to rod, reel and line. But he was quite happy to tie flies by the river when necessary often 'over a glass of ale', including the Imperial, his favourite dry fly and his New Forest nymph when he was advised that a black fly was required. He caught both salmon and sea trout on nymphs, including one artificial that sounded suspiciously like his Reindeer and Red nymph developed in northern Sweden for Arctic char. His waterside lunches were often as spartan as his tackle: a bunch of fresh-picked water cress 'with a hunk of my wife's fresh-baked bread, a few sardines and a stoop of ale'.

His writings for his column, Fisherman's Diary, in *Shooting Times & Country Magazine*, brought out his character and the human side of him much more than his book. Yes, he lost flies and leaders in bushes, broke hooks in fish and had a particularly awkward landing net that often failed to open at the crucial moment. These writings suggest that he was, in practice, not as strict at following his own rules as laid down in *Nymph Fishing in Practice*. For example he wrote of casting a prodigious number of times to certain fish before catching them, sometimes sixty, seventy or even more times. He would chuck a nymph into a likely lie and on another occasion when he spotted a rising fish, he 'couldn't be bothered to fiddle about tying on an Imperial, so I slung the bare hook far upstream . . . I saw a bow wave as the fish turned out when I induced, judged when he might make contact, and fortuitously put the hook in.' Another interesting point was his use of the word 'induce'. Instead of using the induced technique when all dead-drift offers have been refused, Kite seemed to have set out to induce a fish from his first cast. He seemed happy to do this on a fairly regular basis.

Although Kite is best-known and remembered for his exploits as a nymph fisherman – and his only book was on the subject – he was very happy to fish dry flies and, in fact, often caught more fish on them than on nymphs during particular times of the season. 'Tolerably easy dry-fly fishing and the less easy nymph fishing' was his summation of the two methods. Kite earned his living as a professional fly fisherman often fishing for over twenty days a month, teaching fishing, as a writer, film-maker and broadcaster. He was once reported to have remarked that his accuracy and reflexes would suffer if he missed a couple of days on the river. As a boy he had fished for roach and eels with an old bamboo rod and bread paste for bait. He was always catholic in his fishing tastes and would happily fish for any fish that swam at home or abroad with the Army, perhaps with the exception of salmon of which he only ever caught two. He had learnt upstream worming for beck trout in Lancashire around 1937and started fishing the chalk streams for the first time in 1956 when he had a half Rod on the Officers' Fishing Association waters. He is known to have read enthusiastically which helped him to get to terms with the Wiltshire chalk streams.

What have been the major influences on the development of nymph fishing since the days of Sawyer and Kite? One significant influence has been the change in social and other conditions and attitudes that has resulted in far less restrictive rules on most waters and the general acceptance of nymph fishing. Changing attitudes have led, in turn, to an appreciation of the need to fish the water and likely lies with the nymph which had been frowned on for many years although chalk stream anglers had been allowed to fish the water with dry flies for decades. Although it is still possible to see and only fish for feeding fish on chalk streams, not every river has perfect water clarity and so sensible 'fishing the water' is often the only way for an angler to have some sport.

The regular use of lead for weighting nymphs to produce artificials that can be fished deeper and sink quicker is another notable development. Both round and square lead wire is freely available and other sources of suitable lead include capsules of wine bottles and even dental X-ray lead foils. Lead is also available in self-adhesive sheets, which can be cut into strips of the required width, and heavier materials such as Tungsten are now available in forms suitable for fly dressing. Various anglers had experimented with lead ballast for nymphs in the 1920s though it was not taken up by many of their fellow anglers. Another important development has been the extraordinary explosion in the range and availability of modern fly tying materials, primarily synthetic but also some natural such as tying nymphs using CDC feathers.

Now there is an ever-increasing range of hooks: different shank lengths, different weights of wire from light to very heavy, wide range of bend shapes and styles, continuous bend for tying shrimps and hooks with moulded lead bodies for producing very heavy Czech-style patterns.

John Goddard and Brian Clarke developed a sensible modern philosophy for nymph fishing in their book *The Trout and the Fly, A New Approach*. 'We *do* believe that the nymph should be fished selectively, to specific fish that can either be seen in the water, or that by means of water displacement betray the certainty of their presence at particular places in the water. We are as concerned as any purist going back to Halford himself not to spook unseen fish, not to injure or alarm undersized fish and not to spoil the chances of the man coming up behind, by casting at random about the river.' As well as a practical, modern approach to nymph fishing, the two of them developed a technique of using a heavily-weighted artificial shrimp and suitably long leaders for fishing for deep-lying fish such as might be found in deep runs of rivers, hatch and weir pools, and a technique that they called 'the plop' whereby a weighted nymph would be cast close to a fish so that it made an audible plop as it hit the water. The resulting disturbance was often enough to attract the attention of a fish and draw it from the cover of an inaccessible lie under an over-hanging branch or a bridge for example. To be effective the technique must be used with control and 'wit and skill to execute well'. Such a technique can also be used, again with discretion and modesty, to waken a slumbering fish. Brian Clarke's deep nymphing technique uses a heavily-leaded shrimp pattern and a very long leader, perhaps twenty feet or six metres, cast to fish that can be seen feeding in very deep chalk stream hatch pools and other deep stretches of water. The long leader is required to allow the nymph to sink far enough and quickly enough to reach the depth at which the fish is seen to be lying. Leaders of such length are associated more usually with still water fishing but they do have their time and place on rivers.

Other developments such as the extraordinary improvements that have been made in the design and manufacture of fly lines and tippet material have played their part. Today floating lines do just that and better than any of their predecessors. Modern leaders and tippet material allow leaders to be fished with very fine, but still strong, points and, when tied with the correct knots, they are very unlikely to fail at a crucial time. Weighted nymphs and fast-sinking tippet materials mean that it is no longer necessary to limit the number of false casts for fear of drying a nymph enough to prevent it from sinking, as was the case in Skues' day.

Although there are more fly patterns available than anyone could want, it is remarkable how a few old favourites continue to catch fish around the world. Such flies must include Sawyer's Pheasant Tail nymph and the Gold-Ribbed Hare's Ear nymph. With the addition of 'modern' encumbrances such as gold or copper bead heads and in the case of the GRHE more or less weight, these two patterns will cover almost every eventuality.

Notes

1 This issue contained a letter from G. E. M. Skues about the mayfly on the Nadder in 1940.
2 In the first edition *of Nymphs and The Trout* he gave this date as 1927.
3 I was interested to read in one of Frank Sawyer's articles in *Trout and Salmon* how he felt that it was permissible to fish downstream when conditions were against fishing upstream. On the October day in question he was using 'a four ounce rod and a No 1 line' which he considered were not up to casting against the wind. He wrote that his only chance of getting a fish was to cast with the wind and 'Rules for upstream fishing with dry fly or nymph could not possibly apply on a day like this.'
4 I was able to confirm this, through correspondence with Sidney Vines, and then Colonel Charles Tarver, who first fished the 'services water' in 1967 and on through the 1970s when Army postings permitted, and learnt much from Frank Sawyer. Colonel Tarver confirmed that Frank told him that the Pheasant Tail Red Spinner was almost the only dry fly that he used, whatever the fly on the water, and it was effective in larger sizes when Mayfly were hatching. Colonel Tarver found, too, that the fly was often at its best when somewhat bedraggled and sitting down in the water. It was then a matter of having the imagination and understanding to transform the remains of a well-used dry fly into what was to become probably the world's most successful nymph.
5 John Veniard, in his *Fly Dresser's Guide*, first published in 1952, advocated a base of fuse wire to weight nymphs which were required to sink quickly as he felt that it was easier to use than lead wire.
6 Frank Sawyer is also remembered for another fly, the Bow Tie Buzzer designed primarily for use on still waters. See chapter eight.
7 Nils Färnström wrote a little booklet in the *Fritidsfiskarnas 'Special'* series, number seven, which was called 'Fiske Med Nymf' In this booklet he wrote about Frank Sawyer's methods for fishing nymphs and then fishing with him in Sweden on the Storån in Dalarna. The area that they fished was, certainly, very near the Norwegian border but it is a long way south of the Arctic Circle. In the book *Frank Sawyer, Man of The Riverside*, Sawyer wrote: 'Few places in the world can be more beautiful than this setting in the mountains of northern Sweden, more than 200 miles from Stockholm, beyond Grovelsjon.' Grövelsjön (to give it its correct spelling), is someway to the south of the Storån. Two hundred miles does not get you very far from Stockholm and certainly not very close to the Arctic Circle.

6 English techniques developed to suit local conditions

'In retrospect, the first cast I made with a nymph instead of a dry fly on my leader was a turning point in my angling pursuits'
E. H. 'Polly' Rosborough, *Tying and Fishing the Fuzzy Nymphs*, 1988

The history of nymph fishing in the USA, and many other countries, is one of taking English flies and techniques and developing both to suit local conditions. Particularly in America, artificial nymphs were developed to match the multitude of insects found in the many and varied rivers and streams and, similarly, English nymph fishing techniques were modified to suit local rivers which were often much bigger and faster flowing than their English counterparts. Anglers in the USA have developed techniques, particularly for fishing the big powerful western rivers, that may seem very crude compared to the simplicity of the typical upstream nymphing technique as practised on the gentle English chalk streams. But many American techniques can be used on similar streams and rivers from Swedish Lapland to the foothills of the Andes in Chile and Argentina. Short line and high sticking have similarities with techniques used by the Poles and Czechs. Fishing a nymph as a dropper tied to the hook of a dry fly, sometimes known as a trailer, has been adapted by New Zealand anglers. Two nymphs, one large and heavy, can be fished in a similar manner with the second one, smaller and more likely to catch a fish, tied as the trailer. Some methods that require the use of a large indicator that is big enough to suspend a weighted nymph, or even a weighted nymph plus extra weight such as split shot[1], may be too near to float fishing for some people. US nymph fishing has got an unfortunate reputation of, to quote John Gierach, simply 'chucking lead'. In his book *Good Flies*, he questioned the morality of using lots of weight to catch trout lying deep where they are perhaps resting and recovering from being caught and released or hiding from fishing pressure. But no one is saying that you have got to use, or even try, methods that do not appeal and may seem out of place on a particular stretch of water.

Development of suitable nymph patterns did go down some blind alleys, such as the American hard-bodied flat nymphs. Ernest Schwiebert wrote in his seminal work *Nymphs, A Complete Guide to Naturals and Imitations*, 'The nymphs in our fly boxes were strange creations. Some had been tied in England and looked good, but we had little real faith in them. American nymphs were fanciful patterns that usually had no counterparts in aquatic entomology.

'Except for the odd fish on some dark British pattern and a few small nymphs I had copied in the flat-bodied Hewitt style of dressing, most of my nymph fishing had proved relatively unproductive.' He also blamed American anglers' pre-occupation with the dry fly for hindering the development of nymph fishing

According to Chauncy Lively, wet fly fishing was very much the order of the day during the nineteenth century and early years of the twentieth and it was not until word of the 'new dry fly drifted across the Atlantic', to be received with enthusiasm, that American anglers started to fish the dry fly and then the nymph. Eugene V. Connett wrote to the editor of the *Journal of The Flyfishers Club* in April 1939 and in his letter confirmed that at that time American nymph fishing was, in effect, wet-fly fishing but using an artificial nymph which would be cast and fished across and down or downstream. American fishermen were less bound down by tradition than their English counterparts and quickly realised the need to adapt classic English styles and patterns to match American flies and to make them more suitable for fishing American rivers and streams.

Americans, in particular as well as others, have never been so wedded to fishing upstream – whether with a nymph or a dry fly – as English fishermen and are happy to fish across and down and even straight downstream if they feel that it will result in a more effective cast and drift. Mottram, and others,

Americans have never been so wedded to fishing only upstream as English anglers

also appreciated the need to fish from angles other than straight upstream although Skues was less than approving.

Skues' book *Minor Tactics of the Chalk Stream* played a part in introducing nymph fishing to the USA and Theodore Gordon, who is acknowledged as the father of dry-fly fishing in the USA, corresponded with Skues about nymph fishing. Gordon had also corresponded with Halford, Marston and others. According to Ernest Schwiebert, Gordon also fished nymph-like patterns to fish feeding below the surface. Schwiebert was also very well aware that in the early days worn flies such as the Hare's Ear and Greenwell's Glory caught fish as 'they imitated emerging nymphs and pupae'.

Theodore Gordon was born in 1854 and died in 1915. His first article on fishing was published in the late nineteenth century in the *Fishing Gazette* in England; he became the magazine's American correspondent in 1890 and produced a series of 'American Notes'. He also contributed to the American magazine *Forest and Stream* from 1903. Strangely for a very knowledgeable and prolific fly fisherman and writer, he never wrote a book on the subject. In a piece for *Forest and Stream*, dated 31 May 1913, Theodore Gordon wrote about F. M. Halford's latest work, *The Dry-Fly Man's Handbook*. Gordon was very well aware of the 'purists and ultra-purists' in England as well as 'Of recent years a school of anglers has sprung up in England who are experts with the dry fly, yet not entirely wedded to it. When trout are feeding upon nymphs coming up to hatch upon the surface, "bulging" it is called, or "tailing"; that is, rooting in weeds or shallows for larvae, shrimps and snails, these men imitate the nymph or larva and cast upstream to these feeding fish which are usually diffi-cult to catch. The flies they use are certainly wet, but many fishermen consider it fine sport, as this method enables them to take a few good trout on days when the dry fly is useless. As one of the masters of the wet and dry fly remarks, "I should always instinctively fish the dry [fly] if my intelligence did not often tell me that the wet is the sounder method at the moment." This point of view will be approved by many American anglers, but we quite understand Mr Halford's position and opinions formed upon waters which command a high rental, and which are stocked, nursed into fine condition, and protected in order that they may afford the best of fishing for large trout and the very best sport with the dry fly only.' Gordon continued in the same piece about how he had persisted in fishing with a dry fly even though he knew that it would be more profitable to change to a wet fly, or flies, but he loved 'to see the tiny fly dancing with its little wings "cocked"' as it floated towards him. He admitted in an article in 1914 (9 May), on the death of Halford, that he had been given the dry fly fever in 1890 having read Halford's first and second books.

The major subject of most, if not nearly all, Gordon's letters to Skues was fly tying and fly tying materials. He wrote, in his first letter in 1905, 'We labor under many disadvantages over here in getting good materials for fly making', and in other letters he mentioned buying materials by post from Bainbridge of Eton. The first reference to nymphs did not appear until a letter written on 8 February 1912, after the publication of Skues' first book which Gordon had not yet read. Gordon wrote 'Would not small feathers from butt or inside of wings of a number of birds be useful for your nymphs?' Then on 10 March 1912, he wrote about trying his hand at nymphs. 'Think I would use quills for ½ or ⅓ of body if I had the correct colours. That new-skin idea is fine but I do not think that it would work well over seal's fur.' In a letter of 24 April in the same year he was very critical of Halford's enthusiasm for the 'wholesale adoption of the dye pot (it seems to me) is objectionable and should not have been necessary'. Halford's use of so many dyed materials and his reliance on having his flies tied by professionals, Holland and Son, was, Gordon felt, likely to be detrimental to the pleasure to be afforded to the amateur fly tier in attempting to find the right 'self-coloured materials' to imitate the natural fly.

Gordon soon realised when he received examples of English fly patterns that they would be of limited use in the USA, where the local flies were different species, and the rivers and streams were often faster flowing. But he knew that he could adapt some of them for local use and learn from the way that they had been tied when he designed his own patterns.

It was not until 23 June that we hear about fish feeding on nymphs or emergers being caught. The fish were feeding on a fly called the dark grass worm and Gordon tied some wet flies 'the color of the larva or nymphs, detestable work, as the little soft hackles are miserably weak' for a friend. Then: 'It was evident from what he said that the trout were taking the insect on its way up to hatch, or at the instant of transformation. Well! He thanked me for the flies, and then began a discourse upon the dry fly. You would have imagined that I had assailed dry fly fishing, whereas my only wish was to help him to a bit of sport, when the floating fly was almost useless. This annoyed me.' We now know that there were dry fly pedants on both sides of the Atlantic as long ago as 1912. By the end of 1912 Gordon was buying commercially-tied Skues' nymphs although many of them were not to his liking.

In a letter written on 1 May 1913, Gordon wrote: 'Mr Halford is like many another. He has become an authority on a dry-fly fishing and has been tempted in *Ethics of the Dry Fly* to speak authoritatively on a subject (wet fly fishing) of which he knows nothing. How any man can be such an unmitigated ass as to "flog" a slow clear river like the Test or Itchen downstream, I cannot imagine. It seems such a brainless performance. But to crawl up and present a tiny wet fly to a bulging or rising fish is quite another matter. A good angler would not scare any more fish with the wet than with the dry fly.' He finished this letter with a plea with which we can all sympathise: 'How I wish Marryat had written a book. Even H. (Halford) calls him "Master".' Gordon had expressed similar concerns about Halford's lack of knowledge of wet fly fishing and attempts to paralyse original thinking in an earlier letter of 4 April also penned from Neversink, New York.

Although Gordon had fished the dry fly since 1890 – 'because it was more interesting and effective' (than wet fly fishing) and seems to have caught most of his fish in this way, he was only too aware of the need to fish the nymph for nymphing or bulging fish when, as he wrote, the floating fly would be useless.

As well as developing flies and techniques, Gordon was also influential in the development of fly rods. He wrote about 'the light yet powerful American dry-fly [rod]': '. . . the American rod is usually quick and nervous in action, it has wonderful life and resiliency, and is built to suit American methods and temperaments, yet many English dry-fly men prefer our Leonard rods.' Skues was one of the first anglers in England to use a Leonard rod at the start of the twentieth century and continued to use Leonard rods for the rest of his days.

Skues never met nor fished with Gordon but he fished with another American, George Benson Stewart and became good friends with W. D. Coggeshall[2], also an American, but who lived in England. Stewart was born in Canada but grew up in the USA. Skues described him as being a 'first-rate fly fisher' and as well as fishing together, the two tied flies and Stewart was associated with working on the development of some of Skues' early nymphal patterns and how to dress them. Stewart's was the second method illustrated in Skues' book, *The Way of a Trout with a Fly* .

Ray Ovington described the nymph as 'the most constant and varied all-season food readily available to the trout' and also wrote about how he had observed through a pair of binoculars fish taking nymphs and that this had 'sold [him] once and for all on the sport of nymph fishing.' He, like Gordon, promoted an American approach rather than simply following English ideas and techniques.

Another important angler in the development of wet fly and nymph fishing in the USA was James Leisenring who was born in Allentown, Pennsylvania in 1878 and died in 1951. He is best remembered for his flymphs – a cross between a true artificial nymph and a traditional spider wet fly – and the Leisenring lift but he should also be better known for developing the dubbing brush or dubbing loop. Vernon S. 'Pete' Hidy described how 'Leisenring developed and perfected his lift technique by trying to please trout swirling and feeding just beneath the surface or, quite often, by teasing and coaxing trout to feed in a lull.' Charles Brooks described the Leisenring lift – when used properly – 'as the deadliest of all nymph techniques . . . for taking larger trout'. In his opinion the choice of fly is not critical but the technique works best when an artificial bears some resemblance to the natural particularly if the naturals are caddis which often ascend to the surface in a rising arc. Leisenring used his lift technique when casting to fish that he could see at quite short distances or when fishing known and specific lies. He raised his rod tip from water level to fully overhead in a smooth even lift – a more extreme rod movement than Oliver Kite's induced take. The lift makes the fly become what he described as 'deadly' as the soft hackle fibres and the fur of the body quivered and moved as the fly approached a fish, rising to the surface and possibly escaping the jaws of a hungry fish. Leisenring based his 'lift' technique on the traditional English way of fishing wet flies. He took the slack out of the line immediately after casting and would use the lift to make the fly swing and rise – like a nymph swimming towards the surface – immediately in front of a fish that he could see, or in a likely lie. This is a technique that can be very effective during the pre-emergence stage of a hatch. A lift could also be achieved by checking the rod as it followed the flies, before the end of the cast was reached, when the flies would lift-up in the water as the line tightened.

Leisenring developed his flymphs, along with Hidy, as described in his book *The Art of Tying The Wet Fly*. This was published originally in 1941 and then reissued later in an expanded form as *The Art of Tying The Wet Fly & Fishing the Flymph* in 1971 after Leisenring's death. The book was based on what Leisenring had learnt from fishing the streams of both eastern and western states every season from 1910 to 1940. A flymph is a fly that represented the emerging stage between the nymph and the fully-emerged dun. Leisenring and Hidy developed flymphs, and nymphal patterns, at a time when hard-bodied artificial were very common. His wingless hackled flies were said to 'simulate the hatching nymphs of mayfly, caddis fly, or other aquatic insects' as they reached the surface or drifted suspended just under or in the surface film.

The Danish fisherman and fly tier, the late Preben Torp Jacobsen, wrote in an article in *Trout and Salmon* of December 1974 about how an artificial when thoroughly wet and then dried would trap air in the dubbing which would appear as small bubbles. 'Now, not many air bubbles are adhered to the fly, but one single big one located on the back. After a while it loosens its connection with the fly and rises to the surface, but another, a little smaller air bubble, is now formed in the same place, and this last one stays for a long time.

'A parallel to the process of squeezing and blowing (to dry the fly) takes place during our false-casts. The only things we have to do, is (*sic*) to wet the fly beforehand – not with saliva – and then, after a few false casts, deliver the fly so that it immediately goes under water.

'The father of this discovery is the American, Vernon S. Hidy. He found it when he worked with the problems connected with his efforts to walk further in the footsteps of Skues and create imitations of the dayflies in the moment when they change from nymph to fly, named by Hidy as "flymphs".'

Gary LaFontaine was to write about his attempts to simulate the bubbles created by emerging sedge pupa in his book *Challenge of The Trout* in 1976. He should have read Preben Torp Jacobsen's article as it included instructions on tying a Finnish sedge pupa pattern, Simo Lumme's Sedge Pupa, the name given to it by Jacobsen.

In the introduction to Hidy's contribution to *The Masters on the Nymph*, he is quoted as saying when asked to comment on fly fishing techniques: 'Try to become a versatile fly-fisherman, try to please the trout and, above all, be kind to dry-fly purists.' For Hidy the tying and fishing of flymphs which imitate *hatching* nymphs had been developed by anglers such as T. E. Pritt, Skues and his fellow-American collaborator Leisenring of Pennsylvania where Hidy learnt much of his trout fishing on the streams of the Pocono and Catskill mountains. Hidy's technique was based on his knowledge of 'the changing appearance of the insects during their brief but dramatic metamorphosis – as the trout see them.

'Here is what the trout sees: first, each hatching mayfly nymph and mature caddis pupa is shedding its nymphal shuck, and there is a thin film of air beneath the shuck that creates a subtle translucence. Second, the new, unfolded wings have a hydrofuge (water resistance) that creates a film or a small bubble of air . . .

'When properly tied, such flymphs mimic the film of air and/or the bubble of air that trout see during the insect's metamorphosis.' Hidy's flymphs added mimicry to the list of desirable qualities that an artificial fly might have and is attractive to trout.

Light tippets were crucial when fishing his flymphs with their soft, translucent bodies of fur or wool that blended with the under-colour of the tying thread when wet, and the hackles were activated by the current to suggest a living nymph. In Hidy's opinion natural furs – preferably fresh – were the only materials to use for flymph bodies. Synthetics were fine for dry flies but lacked the right texture and subtle colours of natural fur and also the water resistance that contributes to the hydrofuge. (This is based on what Hidy wrote in about 1979 and synthetic materials have developed out of all recognition since then.)

A number of different techniques for making dubbed fur bodies for nymphs have been developed over the years. Interestingly Halford was one of the first fly tiers to use a technique similar to the modern dubbing brush. Halford hung a length of tying thread over a nail, applied the fur to one of the two strands and then locked the fur in place with the second strand. He then spun the two strands together to make a long hackle brush. He used this method to make hair hackles rather than bodies. But it was Leisenring, and a friend of his called Richard Clark, who perfected the technique. Leisenring originally used only his fingers but Clark developed a small block of wood with a cut in one end, into which one end of a length of waxed tying silk was trapped, the silk was then taken between two pairs of pegs and round another peg opposite the slot. Another slot, or cut, in the side of the block was used to hold the other end of the thread under tension. Fur was spread on the long, taut length of thread and then trapped in place with the other end of the thread. As with Halford's method, the thread and fur were twisted into a rope which was then used for making nymph bodies. Leisenring use this method to produce a number of bodies at a time, in different colours, to match the natural insects that he had observed in the streams that he fished. He then stored the ready-made bodies on pieces of oblong card with notches cut in the long sides. As long as the silk was waxed, he found that the bodies did not unravel if left for a few days.

In the 1930s in the USA, artificial nymphs had round bodies whereas natural nymphs have, in fact, flat bodies although this was a somewhat narrow view of the cornucopia of natural flies in the United States. Although the science behind this was not very good, it did move developments in the right direction. Wet flies, particularly traditional patterns when well chewed and fished in the right way would catch fish feeding on nymphs which these flies imitated acceptably well.

John Alden Knight worked with Edward Ringwood Hewitt in support of the latter's experiments to produce satisfactory American nymph patterns in the summer of 1931. Hewitt bought all the nymph patterns that he could from England and then developed his own patterns based on his local insects. Charles E. Brooks, in *Nymph Fishing For Larger Trout*, is somewhat dismissive of Hewitt for being dogmatic, inconsistent, contradicting himself and making mistakes in his various books. So it is perhaps not surprising that his patterns have not survived. Hewitt's nymphs had flat bodies, not the round bodies of nymphs that had been tried to that date. He used mink fur coated in celluloid varnish and then flattened with pliers when nearly dry. Hackles were trimmed top and bottom to leave legs sticking out either side. Gary LaFontaine wrote that Hewitt's flat-bodied nymphs failed because they represented the least-important factor: accurate, exact imitation. They fished badly and flip-flopped showing the dark back and light under body in a most unnatural way. According to Brooks, Hewitt preferred to fish his nymphs in the style of Skues but my research suggested that he also felt that fishing across and down in riffles, particularly in the USA, resulted in his nymphs swimming at a more natural angle, not the head-down attitude he experienced when fishing upstream. Perhaps this is a good example of his inconsistency and how he changed his mind over time. No doubt some of his enthusiasm for fishing in the Skues' style was due to the fact that he fished both the Itchen, unfortunately without Skues, and the Test in 1925, as well as two other English rivers. He was certainly right to base his artificial nymphs on local nymphs and he also advocated the use of long fine leaders which he thought were essential to successful nymph fishing. Another American who made hard-bodied nymphs was Wendle 'Tom' Collins who also made soft-body nymphs which he flattened with pliers. Collins used fuse wire of between one and a half and four amps to weight his nymphs.

In his little pamphlet, *Hewitt's Nymph Fly Fishing*, published in 1934, Hewitt included a very good, if slightly wordy, definition of nymph fishing 'Nymph Fly Fishing is a conscious attempt to imitate with an artificial fly the under water insect life of stream insects which live in the nymph stage before they hatch out into adult winged flies.'

Knight recommended fishing deep in the spring, when the water is cold, and used fuse wire twisted round his leader to sink his flies. Later in the season he would treat his line and leader so that he could fish from six inches to twelve inches (15 to 30cm) below the surface. For Knight a nymph was a 'suggestion' of an insect, not an imitation. And he was also well aware that sub-surface drag could be as harmful and difficult to deal with as surface drag.

In *New Lines for Fly-Fishers*, W. B. Sturgis described how to tie nymphs with flat bodies. They were tied with bodies of either wool or cotton dubbing, 'made very soft and compressible'. The body was then saturated in lacquer and dried on the outside by applying heat from a light bulb. When the outside was dry but still soft inside, the artificial was shaped by compressing the body with special pliers with grooves cut in the jaws. Any cracks that resulted from squeezing the body into shape could be covered in another lay of lacquer. Different colours of lacquer could be used to produce two-tone nymphs.

The Americans were not alone in going down the blind alley of hard-bodied nymphs. In England, in his 1927 catalogue Percy Wadham made great play of his 'Nature' water nymphs designed to be 'lifelike' and 'made in seven fancy and six natural patterns'. These nymphs were made with bodies of celluloid, using a process developed and patented by R. B. Marston, editor of *The Fishing Gazette* magazine.

In contrast, in the early 1930s Lee Wulff tied his version of the Nondescript nymph (which 'Polly' Rosborough attributes to Jim 'Red' Chase who lived on the Williamson before retiring to Portland, Oregon), on size 10 hooks with a grey angora wool body – as on his Gray Wulff dry fly – and a few turns of peacock herl at the head 'to dress it up a bit'. But he couldn't sell them as they did not look like anything that his fellow anglers thought would catch a trout. In his book *Trout on a Fly*, Wulff wrote that he discovered that Frank Sawyer had the same problem. Wulff sat next to Frank Sawyer at one of Charles Ritz's Fario Club dinners in 1972. Sawyer asked Wulff what fly he thought that he caught most of his fish on. Wulff said a grey nymph, whereupon Sawyer produced 'simple gray-bodied nymphs tied on #12 hooks'. From another box he produced similar nymphs but with a gold rib and 'a bit of dark material at the head'.[3] He, Sawyer, said: 'I have to dress them up like this to sell them.' Who would disagree with Wulff when he wrote: 'It is apparent that most anglers buy flies for their own enjoyment rather than that of the fish'?

Ernest Schwiebert followed in Skues' footsteps when he fished in Bavaria, Germany, in the 1950s and learnt much about nymph fishing. In Germany

Ernest Schwiebert
playing a trout on the
Test at Longparish

Schwiebert found a German river keeper whose artificials suggested the colour, configuration and size of the naturals and the keeper 'insisted that his nymphs be fished to duplicate their movements in the river'. This technique was different from the straightforward dead drift or hand-twist retrieve which could be used to produce a swimming motion. This can be a critical factor when fishing nymphs in slow-flowing rivers. Schwiebert also pointed out a common error made by the dry fly man which is to assume that a rise is always to a floating fly by a surface-feeding fish when it was very likely that the fish was taking nymphs instead. For Schwiebert learning that to imitate the behaviour of the natural nymph would result in a good basket of fish was 'a revelation after a diet of Hewitt and Bergman'.

Schwiebert credited Ray Bergman with introducing nymphs and nymph fishing to a complete generation of American fly fishermen. Ray Bergman's first nymphs were tied in England and were 'nothing more than bodies of flies made a bit thick near the head, with a few turns of hackle constituting the feelers'. As he found them to be less effective than winged wet flies with the wings cut off, he stopped using them. He had used these modified wet flies as early as 1918. Bergman often used a 'hand twist' retrieve which he used to impart some action to the fly and created interest in the fish. But he maintained that undue motion or a noticeable change in the speed of the retrieve would frighten fish. Getting the timing and speed of the hand twist was critical as could be the size of artificial being fished. Although Bergman wrote that a size 14 was usually as small as you would need to fish, there were times when hook sizes 16 and 18 and even smaller were essential to catch trout feeding on the myriad of tiny nymphs and larvae to be found in most rivers and streams.

As well as soaking his nymphs before casting to a fish, so that they would sink immediately, Bergman fished 'a dry-fly dropper on the leader above the nymph' as this helped to float the nymph correctly as well as acting as an indicator for what was happening under the surface. In his book *Trout*, Bergman recounted an interesting story about fishing with A. W. Miller – better known as Sparse Grey Hackle – when he introduced him to nymph fishing for the first time. Sparse Grey Hackle, who was a real dry fly purist, 'became a more efficient dry-fly fisherman because the use of the nymph taught him some things that the dry fly could not.'. He, like Bergman, had experienced the fact that there are times when fish cannot be caught on dry flies and so a nymph should be used, and just as important, that there are times when the nymph will not catch fish.

Another important influence in the development of nymph fishing in the USA was A. J. McClane who fished widely in the States and also the Traun river in Austria. He used a nymph to search the river bed for feeding fish. Although a 'dead' nymph, fished slowly along the bottom will catch fish, particularly early in the season when the water is cold, he also recommended casting and letting the nymph drift before working it with short, delicate pulls to simulate an active nymph rising from the river or stream bed. He also fished floating nymphs to imitate the emergers and sub-surface nymphs being taken by bulging fish. McClane wrote in *The Practical Fly Fisherman* that the appearance of an artificial nymph depended on how it was tied. 'It should be almost translucent, so that the trout's view is of an insect with legs tucked in close to the body, a conspicuous bulge where its wing cases are breaking through, and pinpoints of light where air is forcing the nymphal shuck from the emerging fly.' Frank Sawyer would have agreed with much of this description of a swimming nymph McClane also made 'it a rule to give the trout as little as possible to find fault with – just present something that could be mistaken for food' and that smaller flies fished and floated more naturally, although they might not represent large stoneflies and similar big nymphs.

Charles E. Brooks came to fly fishing via fly tying in 1930, when he was but nine years old and started fishing the following spring. It was not until after the Second World War, when working as a ranger in Yosemite National Park, that he saw his first artificial nymph, a cased caddis belonging to a visiting angler from Pennsylvania. Over the next few years as and when US Air Force postings allowed, he developed his skills as a nymph fisherman, concentrating particularly on learning all that he could about trout and trout streams and the nymphs in them. In 1961 he turned his research to finding out what went on under water, using a face mask. This allowed him to see how nymphs behaved under water and the action of artificials when his wife drifted them down to him. He retired to Montana in 1964 at the age of forty-three with the intention of coming to know his local streams and the nymphs and insects in them. By about 1968 or 1969 he realised that he would have to narrow his field of research into just the most important nymphs in his rivers. It was on this extensive and all-consuming research that he based his nymph fishing techniques, specifically the Brooks' Method.

The Brooks' Method was developed for fishing the fast, deep runs, between the fast, shallow riffles and rapids, on Brooks' local rivers in Montana. The technique requires a powerful rod, fast sinking line, short leader and a heavy nymph. As Brooks described casting such an outfit as 'a form of Russian roulette with eyes and ears as takes', he used a rod 'with enough backbone to raise thirty feet of deeply sunken line and a weighted nymph and hurl it back upstream without false casting'. Fish sheltering in deep water and behind or in front of big boulders are unlikely to move far unless they think they are going to get a good mouthful, hence Brooks' use of big nymphs. As well as ensuring that the fly is down where the trout will see it – and stays down – the angler must be in contact with his fly so that he can set the hook the minute a trout takes. When the fish leaves his sheltered resting place to pursue a passing food item, it will feel the full power of the river and want to return back upstream to shelter as quickly as possible. The take is likely to be hard and fierce and must be met with a quick response if the fish is not to be lost. Brooks used leaders of between four and six feet (1.20 and 1.80m) in length and a tippet of between 0.010 and 0.012 inches (0.25 to 0.3mm) in diameter. Fly sizes were from size 4, 4X long to size 8, 3X long. As his underwater studies had shown him that nymphs stay the right way up whether drifting or swimming, he preferred artificials with no distinctive top or bottom and an all-round hackle rather than one trimmed to replicate legs sticking out sideways.

In the Brooks' Method the cast is made upstream but is fished downstream. Casting upstream gives the nymph enough time to sink to the required depth when the angler takes control and starts fishing it. He would cast a short line – 10 feet (3m) – up an across and as the fly reached a position directly opposite where he was standing, perhaps just six feet (1.80m) away, the slack would be gathered up and the fly, which should be on the bottom, taken under control. As the fly and line move downstream, the rod tip is kept high and directly over the line where it enters the water, with just a slight droop between rod tip and water. With a short cast the length of line will be such that the rod will not need to be lifted much above waist height to take control of the slack. But for a long cast it may be necessary to point the rod straight in the air at the end of an out-stretched arm. The actual fishing phase of the cast is from just downstream of straight across the river or run until the fly is directly downstream. As the fly swims downstream, the angler turns and lowers and swings his rod to keep it over the line where it enters the water. Some slack must be maintained in the line to prevent the fly from being lifted up through the water column, but too much slack will result in missed strikes. No line is retrieved by the line hand during a cast. At the end of each cast, the fly must be left in the water so that the bow in the line is taken out. That bow is caused by the fly travelling in slower water near the bottom of the river and the line and leader cutting through the fast surface current.

Brooks would fish a stretch by casting up to five times without lengthening his line. He would then lengthen his line by about five feet (1.5m) and make another series of three to five casts, each one further towards the middle of the river. He would continue casting, from the same position, until he had extended his line to its maximum manageable length. Then he would retrieve his line and move down stream and start another series of casts, ensuring that he covered the water thoroughly. He developed his own specialised casting technique which saved him energy and was safer than any other method. For both normal and off-the-shoulder casts (depending on which way the current is flowing and where the angler is standing), he used a powerful horizontal swinging cast, with the rod parallel to the water, and a strip or single haul.

When *Selective Trout* by Doug Swisher and Carl Richards was published in 1971, the authors had decided that a fur body was an essential requirement for artificial nymphs. Once again their choice was based on what the artificial looked like when wet. They tried other materials such as quills, floss, wool and various plastics which may look good out of the water but, to them, had a decidedly unnatural appearance when wet. (The authors also recommended wetting an artificial when placing it against a natural nymph found in a river as a result of using a seine net, as it is the colour and appearance of a wet artificial that is crucial.) They recommended a variety of different furs including rabbit, muskrat, opossum, fox, mole and beaver. Swisher and Richards used feathers from wood duck, mallard and partridge, dyed to the correct colour when necessary, for tails and legs, a few of which should be tied facing forward but the majority tied facing backwards. Their observations of nymphs swimming in an aquarium led them to develop extended body and hinged-body wiggle nymphs in an attempt to match the undulations of swimming nymphs.

Their extended body nymphs had the abdomen tied on a piece of wire, tied to the hook shank, which could then be bent in the required direction, giving the artificial what they felt to be a more realistic appearance. The wiggle nymph took this idea one stage further by attaching the extended body to the hook with a loop hinge so that the extension would wiggle as the artificial is fished. As well as being very effective when used to match a hatch, both nymphs can be fished as attractors.

For Swisher and Richards imitations of emerging nymphs were the most effective and would catch fish all season long. They tied artificials with short wings on heavy hooks, which could be fished deep, and on medium-weight hooks with longer wings for use during the early stages of a hatch. They also used emergers tied on fine wire hooks, treated with floatant if necessary, throughout a hatch. Their emerger patterns are the same as nymphs but the emergers have wings instead of wing cases. This approach harks back to some of Skues' patterns fifty or so years earlier. Emergers can be fished on the surface, in the surface film or just sub-surface, again as did Skues.

Swisher and Richards sought to develop and tie a realistic imitation 'that would gull the trout into thinking it is a natural insect'. This is a very different approach from that of Frank Sawyer who was much more interested in representing key characteristics of nymphs such as their swollen thoraxes just before hatching. Imitations of the emerging nymph are probably the most deadly and effective pattern of all and they tied emergers on different weights of hook so that they could be fished at different depths, from deep down to right in the surface film. They tied their emergers in the same ways as nymphs but replaced the wing case with wings, short for deep patterns and longer by degree for patterns to be fished nearer the surface. Emergers can be fished at different depths, depending on the weight of hook that they are tied on and whether or not they are treated with floatant, which makes them very versatile flies for the fly fisherman to have in a fly box. Swisher and Richards seem to have been influenced in the design of their nymph patterns by the traditional soft-hackled wet flies in that they continued to tie legs on their patterns, even for their extended-body and wiggle nymphs.

While *Selective Trout* was concerned primarily with upwing or mayflies, someone who has taken the development of tying and fishing artificial midge and caddis pupae to a new level is Don Holbrook, sometimes in association with Ed Koch. Don Holbrook had a similar experience in the early 1970s to that of Skues nearly one hundred years earlier. Holbrook caught a trout late in the evening and when he shone a torch on it so that he could see to unhook it, he was astonished to see that its mouth was full of tiny twinkling and glistening nymphs, between five and ten millimetres (approximately a quarter to half and inch) long. When he gutted it at home, its stomach was full of the same nymphs as its mouth. Holbrook acted immediately and tied a dozen nymphs on size 18 hooks with six different body colours, all dubbed rabbit fur starting around the bend of the hook and wrapped forward to the eye where he finished them off with an oval head or collar.

Ed Koch described in the Preface to *Midge Magic* how the next night Holbrook was back on the Big Spring Creek, near Newville, Pennsylvania, to test his new creations. He caught fish on his grey, cream, tan and olive patterns. He fished at least twice a week for the rest of the season and the next two seasons and found that his new patterns produced fish consistently, from mid-summer, through the autumn and even into the winter. At that time anglers were allowed to kill one fish over fourteen inches (35cm) and Holbrook took just four fish a season and used their stomach contents to check their diets. He found that the size of midge larvae remained the same but there were many colour variations. He then started to experiment with a wide range of tying materials, some of which were successful and many were not. He started to make real, significant progress when he discovered an advertisement for cross stitch yarns for sale at a local craft shop. The nymphs, with smooth bodies ribbed with yarn, that he tied using these yarns out-fished his fur-bodied patterns. He then tried tying some with fine gold or silver ribs which worked

Ted Trueblood netting a fish sometime in the nineteen forties

as well as the yarn-ribbed patterns. His book, written with Ed Koch, is a living testimony to a continuing obsession with tiny flies imitating tiny natural midge larvae, containing as it does hatch charts and recipes for many different patterns and variations as well as tiny shrimps, top water patterns and Elk River 32s.

Another early pioneer of nymph fishing in the USA was the famous outdoorsman and writer, Ted Trueblood. Trueblood was born in Idaho in 1913, on his family's farm in Boise. His name, 'so perfect for an outdoor writer' caused controversy as many thought that it was a pseudonym. But it was his real name. When he started writing for *Field & Stream* in 1937 or 1938, his name was the cause of great debate on the letters pages of the magazine. He wrote for the magazine for over forty years up to his death in 1982. Trueblood was a passionate angler who helped fly fishing get to where it is today. He was a product tester for Scientific Anglers and was involved in developing modern synthetic fly lines. He helped to develop the company's first sink tip line and also field tested some early carbon fibre (graphite) fly rods. Towards the end of his life, while still fishing editor of *Field & Stream*, he fished in New Zealand with Rex Forrester on the Tongariro. (This was one of a number of interesting snippets and nuggets of information that I found in John Parsons' and Bryn Hammond's book *One Hundred Years Of Trout Fishing in New Zealand*.)

Trueblood fished leaders of at least nine feet (2.75m) to give his nymph a chance to swim and drift as naturally as possible. In low water he would fish a leader up to twenty feet (6m) long. He also fished deep as so many different types of nymph inhabit the bottom of rivers and streams. He believed that 'An angler's imagination is his most valuable asset in fishing a wet fly or nymph' as he may not always be able to see what his fly is doing under the surface but he can imagine what may be happening to it. He also suggested using a large

One of Ted Trueblood's nymphs

and very visible dry fly as an indicator, tied on near the butt of the leader. Such a fly indicates takes by moving slightly. He was also convinced 'that most of the time the way in which a fly is fished is much more important than its color or size.' Yet he was only too well aware that there can be times when only one fly 'fished in one particular way' will catch trout. He wrote that the best nymph fishing was most likely to be just before a hatch but a properly fished nymph would catch fish at other times as well. He preached the importance and benefits to be gained by studying and understanding the life cycles of the various mayfly and stonefly nymphs and caddis pupa that trout feed on so avidly so that the angler knows why and how to fish the different artificials.

Although Trueblood was an advocate of fishing all-purpose nymphs with fuzzy, dubbed bodies in shades from light tan to nearly black, he did develop some specific patterns such as the Otter Shrimp fly, on rivers and lakes near Sun Valley, Idaho, in the late 1940s. He wrote about the fly in *Field & Stream* in 1956. The fly was the result of many years of experiments to devise a pattern that trout would take when feeding on shrimps. This was at a time when there were very few 'good' commercially-tied nymph patterns available in American tackle shops: 'I have yet to be in any fishing-tackle sales room where there was a good assortment' of nymphs. The fly has a body of dubbed tan otter belly fur, but dubbed in a special way. Trueblood coated a length of tying thread with drying shellac varnish – so that it was sticky – spread out the fur dubbing and then pressed the sticky thread on to it. The thread picked-up the fur which he then rolled between the palms of his hands. He made the body tapered at both ends and did not roll it too firmly. The result was similar to the noodles made by E. H. 'Polly' Rosborough. The noodle was tied on at the tail end of the fly and wrapped forward to just behind the eye where a brownish partridge hackle completed the tying.

E. H. 'Polly' Rosborough was a contemporary of Ted Trueblood, who wrote the Foreword to *Tying and Fishing the Fuzzy Nymphs*, which was first published in 1965. Rosborough started fishing for trout in 1922 in northern California, where he fished a small, winding creek, well stocked with 'smart' trout with many weighing up to four pounds (1.8kg). (He returned to southern Oregon in 1936.) Although he caught some of these big fish at certain times on dry mayflies and terrestrials, many were the days when he caught only the little fish. He then 'sensed that this strange behaviour called for something entirely different in both method and patterns.' He decided to abandon dry flies altogether and fish with nymphs. Fortunately for him he had little outside influence on his first attempts at tying nymphs he had seen in mail order catalogues.[4] The first material he used was seal's fur (blue dun and natural cream) but he had to work out just how to tie flies with it. He had never spun a fly body nor had he seen anyone else do so either. But he was an inventive man and he 'spread out a couple of inches of the [natural cream] fur a quarter of

E. H. 'Polly' Rosborough
fishing the Williamson River
in Oregon in September
1982 on his eightieth
birthday

E. H. 'Polly' Rosborough at a fly tying
fair

an inch wide and gave it a thin coat of waterproof cement.' He allowed the cement to dry until it was tacky when he lifted the fur with a knife blade and then rolled it into a cylinder the size of a match stick. He tapered both ends and when his 'noodle' was thoroughly dry, he tied in the thinnest end at the bend of a hook. Rosborough used the word noodle to describe all the fur body cylinders that he prepared in advance. He took hold of the loose end of the noodle with a pair of hackle pliers and twisted it into as tight a rope as he dared without breaking it. When wound forward in a close spiral, the result was a naturally segmented fur body. He finished the fly with a few hackle flues on the bottom, to represent legs. He wrote: 'It didn't look like much, but as it turned out I had unknowingly created a fair simulation of a caddis larva . . . That first fuzzy nymph was a killer.'

The first time that he fished his new pattern around 1927, he landed five brown trout of one to three pounds (0.5 to 1.5kg) in an hour and 'was keenly aware that here was a new and very exciting fly-fishing idea'. Although he admitted that the way he first fished this nymph was entirely unconventional, he caught a lot of fish over the next few years, during which time he was always questioning why this or that happened and wondering if the early nymph fishermen had gone far enough. Eventually he arrived at a series of conclusions, first that during a hatch the larger fish preferred nymphs and nymphs were deadliest when fished 'rather shallow', particularly to bulging fish at the start of a hatch; the second was that artificial shrimps and scuds had to be fished deep and on the bottom where they live. Although he had probably never heard of him, 'Polly' Rosborough was following directly in the footsteps of Skues as they both fished the top of the water with their nymphs. Rosborough's first fuzzy nymph pattern was followed by his second original pattern, the Black Drake nymph, which over the next forty-five years was to be the most effective pattern on the West Coast. The Black Drake nymph came into being around 1933 and eleven years or so after he caught his first trout on a fly.

When tying his new nymphs Rosborough wanted them to have fuzzy bodies and match the natural insect in size, shape and colour; there were to be simulations and not imitations. His Near Enough nymph is a good example, representing, as it does, most of the greyish swimming nymphs. Over the next ten or twelve years he developed many new patterns, each of which went through many evolutions before he arrived at the final version of a full complement of twenty-five nymphs. Sometime in either 1945 or 1946 he stumbled upon what was to be his then revolutionary tying technique. He sheared the fur off the belly of a muskrat skin and put it in a pan of hot soapy water and stirred it with his fingers. He then tipped the fur into a sieve and put it under the hot water tap to remove the soap before drying it with towels and spreading it out to finish drying, 'The end result was a well-matted or felted mass that now suggested possibilities far beyond anything I had been using.' He took a very small wad of fur and teased it out and then rolled it into a noodle with tapered ends. The noodle is tied-in at the bend of the hook and then spun into a loop of tying thread coated in cement. He also applied the same cement to the hook shank, for added durability. He roughed up the body of the fly with a piece of fine-toothed hacksaw blade. Although he tied his first few patterns with noodles made from one fur, he much preferred to use a blend of two or three materials to produce the desired colour as the colours of natural nymphs are always a mixture of shades of the basic colour.

Polly Rosborough was a bamboo rod man who liked slow-action but very sensitive rods 'so sensitive one can almost feel the fish before it strikes'. He selected the length of rod according to the size of river to be fished: a long rod for big rivers and when wading deep and a short rod for fishing small streams from the bank. Although he preferred to fish a floating line on smaller streams, he also used a sink-tip for larger nymphs and when fishing during high spring runoffs. He did not use leaders of extreme length but was careful to match the weight of the tippet to the size of fly. He used longer – nine foot (2.75m) – leaders when lake fishing. On the winding meadow streams that he fished for much of his life, Rosborough often fished a nymph very much like a dry fly, often casting so his fly landed on bankside vegetation – particularly when fishing an undercut bank – and could then be given a tweak so that it dropped into the water. He would fish upstream, up and across and downstream as conditions dictated although he knew that it was easier to hook fish when fishing upstream.

Given his inquisitive and enquiring mind, an innovative approach to designing and tying flies it is surprising that Rosborough is not better known today. The final sentence of his book is a good memorial to him: 'I want to start you thinking, to do more examining of facts.' His lifetime of fly fishing

'Polly' Rosborough's
Black Drake nymph

121

and fly tying was based on research and trial and error methods. Although he did play around, in later years, with some of the hard lacquered bodied nymphs that were the rage during his early days, he rejected them for the very reason that trout rejected them: they were too hard and felt unnatural. His patterns with their soft bodies felt more natural so a trout would hold it in its mouth a fraction longer, often giving the angler enough time to set the hook before the fish could eject the fly.

American nymph fishermen will often use an indicator in an effort to obtain a drag-free drift which, particularly in faster streams and rivers, cannot be achieved when a tight line is relied on to tell the angler when a fish has taken his nymph. A floating strike indicator can be used to control depth even when using heavily-weighted nymphs or split shot, signal a take and provide a drag-free drift. Indicators come in all shapes and sizes from a tiny piece of fluorescent-coloured floating synthetic dough pinched on to the leader to pieces of foam and a bunch of polypropylene floating yarn that is almost a true float and would not be appreciated on an English chalk stream! Some indicators are big and unsubtle but this does not mean that by simply using the biggest indicator that you can find that you will, automatically, catch more fish. Different waters require different types – and sizes – of indicator but all indicators have one thing in common: they amplify and telegraph any underwater movement of an artificial nymph, some of which may be caused by a fish. Because you can see more indications of what is happening underwater, the use of an indicator may allow you to fish at greater distances than can be achieved by simply relying on watching the dipping point of the leader. When fishing with an indicator the hook should be set every time there is what seems to be an unnatural movement or hesitation of the indicator. A dough, yarn or CDC indicator can be used as just that – an indicator of sudden or unexpected movement – without it having any other perhaps unwanted effects.

One way to fish with an indicator is to fish the indicator itself as though it is a dry fly by, for example, mending the line to prevent drag when casting and fishing across variable currents. Although it will not be visible, these currents will cause the nymph to drag and underwater drag is just as harmful as is surface drag to the dry fly. As one American wrote: 'Floating indicators bring nymphing into the realm of the visible'. A dry fly is often fished as an indicator with the nymph on a dropper. The nymph can be tied to a dropper to either the eye of the dry fly hook or the bend of the hook, as a 'trailer'. Fishing with a nymph for fish lying well down in deep water is nearly always going to be made more difficult by the variation in speed of flow at the surface and at the depth at which the fish is lying. Using a large, foam indicator that will 'turn over' can be one answer to this problem. To make an indicator turn over, it must be cast upstream of the nymph itself as this allows the nymph to sink to the required depth and when the indicator catches up with and overtakes the nymph, it will turn over. As this happens, the slower-moving nymph will start dragging as it is being pulled by the faster surface current acting on the line and indicator. As the indicator reaches the turn over point, concentrate hard as a take is very likely.

One American technique that seems to have stayed 'at home' is right-angle nymphing. This technique was developed for nymph fishing in rivers with a relatively slow and constant flow and depth. A large yarn indicator is tied to the end of a relatively short and heavy leader and a level tippet, which should be about a twelve inches (30cm) longer than the depth of the river, is tied, with a slip knot, to the end of the leader. The whole leader will float on the surface and the nymph, usually well weighted, hangs straight down at ninety degrees to the leader. A buoyant, bushy indicator will telegraph every touch by a fish. Each upstream cast should be followed by an upstream mend to position the indicator upstream from the fly: this will allow the fly to reach fishing depth unhindered.

Ed Engle wrote an article, 'Freestyle Nymphing' (*Fly Fishing & Tying*, Winter 2003) promoting a much simpler and purer form of nymph fishing – much closer to English upstream nymphing – as a reaction to the all-prevalent US rig of two nymphs, split shot or other forms of added weight and often large indicators – as favoured by John Gierach's lead chuckers. American anglers tend to add weight to the leader to get their flies to sink, in preference – and often in addition to – using weighted flies. 'What I like most about freestyle nymphing,' he wrote 'is that in its purest form it's as visual as it gets – pure trout hunting.' Fishing in clear water the fish can often be seen taking the fly and no indicator is needed. He recommended using heavy hooks and water absorbing materials so that the flies would sink quickly, particularly in slow water. When fishing deeper water he advocated the use of the tuck cast to give time for the artificial to sink, as well as using weighted flies, and also when fishing faster waters. He found that stalking and casting to sighted fish, rather than fishing the water dead-drift style, was much more challenging and would bring much greater rewards in the number, size and quality of fish caught.

As we know, Skues had witnessed the efficiency of fishing with a short fixed line in Bosnia in September 1897 when he and a companion first saw a Turk fishing 'the dazzling blue waters of Bosnian Pliva' with 'a wand of some eight or nine feet, and casting among the cascades a short but accurate line'. Other 'Turkish sportsmen of the peasant class' were seen casting 'pre-Waltonian flies towards the river's edge', often fished on a cast of four flies. Rods were one piece and made from 'a singularly hard type of wood' and they did not use a reel or winder, nor a running line. The casts were made of very fine and strong horse – actually pony – hair and the flies favoured by the locals had wings 'of soft wild goose' or feathers from under the wings of geese, owls or eagles, no

Concentration is very important when fishing nymphs, whether upstream in the conventional style or short line as here in the Czech Republic. The use of an orange leader as an indicator can be seen

legs and bodies made of raw silk. Skues did not say if they were weighted or not. 'With these flies fished down stream I have seen the natives yank a three-quarter pound grayling from the water and catch it in the left hand.' Although these anglers were fishing downstream, their flies cannot have sunk very deep – because of the speed of the current and the short line – and so many of them must have been taken as nymphs or emergers. Skues spent sixteen days in Bosnia, around the area of what is known as Bosnia Hezergovina and Croatia today, and he found all 'the natives', even on different rivers, were using much the same tackle and technique. What he saw was similar to today's various short-line nymphing techniques.

One of the best-known short-line techniques is the 'short nymph' method that was developed by Polish anglers in the 1970s on the Dunajec river. The key to the technique is controlling the flies under water. It was developed for fishing fast, deep waters and particularly for grayling which in such rivers are less timid than trout and so the angler can get closer to them and catch them with a short line. And it is most effective when used in fast, turbulent or slightly-coloured water where the fish cannot see so clearly and any drag caused by leading the flies through the water is masked by the turbulence and less than

Short line nymphing is a very effective way of catching grayling which are not usually as shy as trout

125

Fish on! Short line nymphing in the Czech Republic

perfect visibility. Equally, the technique becomes less effective in slower and shallower rivers and streams.

The Poles use their technique to search water very thoroughly, fishing with a very short line and fishing over only a very short stretch of water at each 'cast'. At a competition between two Polish teams, a team from the GDR (the former East Germany) and the former Czechoslovakia on the Dunajec river in Poland in 1984, the Polish competitors used this short line technique with a length of monofilament (instead of a fly line which most of them did not own as it was difficult then to buy good quality fishing tackle in Poland). Their flies were imitations of caddis larvae, hydropsyche with bodies of hare fur and rhyacophylia with a green body and tail. Both patterns had backs made from peacock fibres and hooks were either straight or with a gentle bend. The Polish team won the world championship on their home waters in 1985, with the Czechs second.

The development of the Polish short nymph technique[5] has not been an unqualified success, largely due to its extraordinary effectiveness, resulting in the death of often large quantities of fish at a time when fish stocks were under pressure from pollution and a reduction in natural reproduction. Fishing with leaded nymphs was banned on some rivers. But these problems have had a beneficial effect that has seen increases in size limits, reductions in catch numbers and the introduction of catch and release regulations.

While the Czechs were still discovering the secrets and learning the tech-

126

nique in the years 1985 to about 1987, developments were being made in materials used to tie the flies, particularly the strip over the back of the flies. Materials tried included sausage skin and the skin from catfish and eels. The use of very thin lead wire brought about very much slimmer nymphs tied on a gammarus hook called Admiral (a suitable substitute is the Kamasan B100) compared to the early fat nymphs which were known as Bobesh nymphs. Natural skin for the backs was replaced by strips cut from latex surgical gloves which proved to be much more durable, easier to tie and more transparent. Latex was, in turn, replaced by special plastic foil backs which are available in a wide range of colours and some printed in bright colours or even glitter. As well as using hare's ear and rabbit fur for the bodies, seal's fur was used and this started further innovations and experiments with all sorts of exotic animal furs. Great strides were made in developing new hook shapes and hooks with lead bodies which meant that flatter bodies could be tied on such hooks. The early tapered leaders, which did not sink very well, were replaced by straight leaders made from one diameter of new leader materials. As Czech and Polish fishermen travelled abroad to fish in the world championship, they were introduced to new materials and the short nymph technique was adopted by anglers from other countries.

Polish woven nymphs and subsequently Czech nymphs hit the fly fishing headlines in 1990 when the Czechs won the World championship in Wales and again in 1994 in Norway and 1996 in Czesky Krumlov. A Czech, Vladimir Sedivy won the individual World championship in Sweden in 2001.

The perfection of the method of tying woven Polish nymphs was a significant contribution to the recent development of fly fishing

Playing a Czech grayling

A fine Czech
grayling

The technique was explained to the English team in 1996 and that explanation resulted in the publication of a number of articles. The short nymph technique relies on registering the maximum number of delicate takes and fishing the nymphs with a dead drift. A fine leader, longer than the water depth, is used so that the flies will sink quickly and they are fished under the rod tip, with no line on the water. Polish nymph fishermen take care to balance the weight of the fly with the strength of the current so that the artificial nymph will fish close to the river bed but without fouling it too frequently. Lead wire is used to weight heavy patterns but copper wire is also used, for lighter weighted nymphs.

To use this style most effectively you need to be able to read and understand a river and its pattern of major and minor currents and the effects that they will have on a fish's position and the likely food lanes. It is a technique that can produce fish from the most unlikely looking places too. Places that look to be far too turbulent to hold fish. But even in some of the most turbulent water there will be back currents and eddies that afford a suitable lie for a fish.

Polish fishermen often stand sideways to the current and cast up stream, laying the line on the water briefly to allow the nymphs to sink before lifting the line clear of the water. It is now vital to keep in touch with the nymphs by leading them down stream under the tip of the rod, allowing them to drift as naturally as possible, with the leader kept straight. How high the rod tip is held depends on the length of line and the depth of water being fished. Leading the flies at the correct speed is a major contributor to the effectiveness of the technique. A firm strike is made as the cast is fished out, before the next cast. As a cast may be fished for no more than two or three metres/yards, it is often that final strike that sets the hook in a fish. Every movement or hesitation of the leader as the flies are being lead down stream should trigger a response

A selection of Czech nymphs

from the angler. The rod is held in one hand with the fly line trapped against the rod handle by the index finger. A small loop of line can be left between the reel and the finger to provide a little slack should a fish make a first rush. Care must be taken to lead the flies smoothly although a jerk which causes the flies to move unnaturally and erratically can be effective.

Everything is done to get the flies, usually two but sometimes three (only two flies are allowed in Poland), down deep as quickly as possible. This is why Polish and Czech nymphs tend to have very smooth profiles with very little hackle which might delay the sink speed. Although heavily-weighted hooks are available with moulded lead bodies, less heavily-weighted flies are often used that sink quickly because of the way that they are designed, have been tied and the materials used in their manufacture. It is not unusual to use an unweighted fly on the dropper with a weighted fly on the end of the leader. Shrimp patterns are often heavily-weighted so that they will fish close to the bottom, where feeding trout and grayling would expect to find them.

Although there is no normal casting involved as only a short length of line is extended beyond the top rod ring, a fast-action, fairly stiff rod is required. Rod length (and line weight) can be changed to suit the size of river or stream being fished: a longer rod for bigger rivers and a shorter one for small streams. The design of the leader is very important. It is untapered (as no traditional casting is involved) and made out of a length of mono of a suitable breaking strain, based on size of fish likely to be caught and the character of the river bottom. You need mono that is strong enough not to break if you hook the bottom or a rock. The dropper or droppers are usually twenty inches (51cm) apart and are always the lower end of the upper length of mono. The overall length of the leader should be a little more than the depth of water and it can be attached to the line using a coloured braided loop.

At the end of each cast, let your flies hang on the dangle for a few seconds and tighten the line, or strike, before lifting leader and flies out of the water. You can often tighten and find that a fish grabs a fly. Then, quickly and simply, describe an upstream arc with the end of your rod and project your flies a bit further out into the river or stream. The minute your flies land in the water, you must watch the end of a line for the slightest movement, hesitation, dip or check that indicates a take. Raise the rod at the slightest of indications of a fish.

Success with this method depends on locating fish in the river as you are not fishing to rising or visible feeding fish and not every likely spot will hold fish and equally, places that are difficult to fish may hold a lot of fish; you must know where your flies are in the water and, finally – as in all nymph fishing – you must know when to set the hook, before a fish ejects the fly.

The early days of the nymph fishing in New Zealand were based on English practices for many years. Although Mottram fished successfully with nymphs in 1911, it was to be nearly fifty years before nymph fishing started to gain real popularity although it is reasonable to suppose that other visiting anglers fished with nymphs too. Upstream nymphing, as opposed to wet fly fishing across and down, is thought to have started on the middle and upper reaches of the Tongariro river in the mid to late 1960s. But since the 1960s New Zealand has made its own contribution to nymph fishing. That contribution is the method of attaching a nymph on a dropper so that you can fish with two nymphs at a time. John Parsons came across this method sometime between 1985 and 1994 when he was fishing the Tongariro river on the North Island. He met an angler who fished with 'a size 8, heavily weighted something-or-other with a size 12, unweighted, black-headed white caddis on a link of tippet looped to the bend of the larger hook. It was the small caddis wavering in the current that did the damage'. This method must have been in use before 1985 – when John Parsons might have first encountered it – as John Goddard had written about it – or at least seen it in practice – before 1984. He had also seen a dry fly fished with a trailer nymph on the South Island in the early 1980s. When a fly is fished as a trailer, the tippet needs to be long enough to keep the two flies far enough apart so that if you miss a fish on the first fly, when you try to set the hook, you will not foul hook the fish on the second or trailing fly. Both variations can be used with sizes of fly appropriate to the size and type of water being fished. Fast, turbulent rivers will require bigger flies than a chalk stream or pellucid meadow creek.

Which fly is the point fly and which is the dropper? Ian Neale, in an article in *Trout and Salmon*, described this method and wrote that the dropper fly was tied to the end of the leader and the point fly was attached by a half-metre length of tippet material to the bend of the hook on the end of the leader, using a half blood knot. Personally I think that the dropper is the fly attached to the bend of the hook of the fly tied to the end of the leader. The names of the flies are not important but it is a technique that works. This technique is sometimes known as Tongariro nymphing, after the Tongariro river on New Zealand's North Island. Here a twelve feet (3.5m) straight mono leader is used with a very heavy nymph tied to the end. A Trilene knot is then used to knot an eighteen inch (45cm) length of mono to the bend of the hook and another, lighter nymph tied on. The weight of the two nymphs is proportional to the

The New Zealand set-up with two nymphs, one fished as a trailer tied to the bend of the hook of the fly on the end of the leader

depth and speed of water to be fished: the flies need to reach the bottom but not fish so deep that they keep getting caught on rocks and so on. A yarn indicator, heavily saturated with floatant, completes the set-up. The flies are cast up stream at an angle of about sixty degrees and the lines is mended as necessary, to produce the longest drift possible. If the indicator bobs or plunges, tighten as quickly as possible and there should be a fish on one of the flies. According to John Goddard a group of visiting Americans introduced strike indicators to New Zealand in about 1982; Goddard had never seen such devices before.

Much of the trout fishing in the early days in New Zealand seems to have been with bait, spinning, trolling in lakes, minnows, and dry and wet fly fishing, often with salmon flies and heavy tackle. In *Where the Rainbows Rise!* G. W. Johns mentioned nymphs in the early 1930s, when fly fishing was growing in popularity and his Atiamuru Lodge on the Waikato river had some of the very best fly fishing, both dry fly and wet on 'beautiful dry pools, [and] glorious wet fly reaches'. Johns wrote about the heavy sedge hatches: '. . . during the late evening, the angler presenting his imitation sedge or nymph in the correct manner may return home well rewarded for his efforts'. A friend of C. T. Hand-Newton caught a six pound (2.75kg) trout on a nymph sometime during the Second World War, on the Halswell near Christchurch. By the 1970s many anglers were fishing and catching trout on nymphs. Even in New Zealand there were, what seem today, somewhat bizarre restrictions, such as only unweighted nymphs being legal on the Taupo fishery and the realisation in 1976 that an upstream nymph fished on a floating line would catch as many or more fish than a traditional wet fly fished downstream which had been the order of the day since the early to mid nineteen thirties, according to Robert Bragg[6] the English fly dresser and angler who made his home in New Zealand. The Taupo Fly-Fishers' Club managed to have local regulations changed to allow weight to be added to lures of up to a size 10 hook but it was not until 1978 that the use of weighted nymphs was permitted. This put Taupo nymph fishermen on the same footing as the weighted nymph fishermen of Rotorua. Sadly these relaxations lead to some anglers abusing the rules by fishing with globugs and muppets and other monstrosities, often suspended from plastic or polystyrene floats masquerading as indicators. These practices gave New Zealand nymph fishing and fishermen an unwanted reputation.

An angler who played an important role in the development of fly fishing in Australia was Richard Henry Wigram who had been born in England on 25 February 1903. As a teenager he had the good fortune to fish, and poach, the Itchen at Abbots Barton where Skues fished. Skues referred to him in an article, 'The Rising Generation', published in the *Journal of The Flyfishers Club* in 1918. Skues wrote: 'Young Dick – another fourteen-year-old-is going to be a mighty angler before the Lord. Already he ties trout flies with quite a professional touch in them.' (He was to become one of Australia's first professional and, indeed, most proficient fly tiers and ran adult education fly tying classes for many years.) Wigram's uncle took him with him when he went to fish the Itchen with Skues one lovely May day. Wigram fished with 'a little nine-foot American split cane'. He caught a fish – 'a good two pounds' – on a hackled Alder of his own tying. Later he caught another fish on a yellow dun of Skues but lost the fish when he fell into a hole which allowed the fish to gain refuge in a patch of weed. Skues recorded his 'regret about that young man is that I shall not be here to see how he shapes when in his prime.' Wigram was to write many years later that he knew when he fished with Skues, even as a school boy, that he had been watching 'fishing magic'. When he was twenty-one years old Dick Wigram and his brother John emigrated to Australia where he fished in New South Wales and Victoria. His great uncle, Money Wigram, had been instrumental in introducing brown trout to Tasmania in 1864, shipping trout ova on a ship called the *Norfolk*. In 1925, a year after Wigram arrived in Australia, a brown trout of twenty pounds (9 kg) was caught. His first season fishing in Tasmania was that of 1926-27. According to his book *The Fly*, in 1928 the average size of brown trout caught in the Great Lake was nine pounds (4kg) and that of rainbow trout just over five and a half pounds (2.5kg). As a professional fly tier, Wigram needed to be able to tie at least eighteen flies in an hour to be able to make a profit, but he still managed to fish almost everyday, particularly on the Macquarie river, which was his favourite, and the South Esk. He wrote that 'a grounding in coarse fishing is the best approach to the art of fly-fishing, [as] it teaches the habits of fish and the playing and landing of them'. He had his first fly rod, an ancient greenheart rod, when he was seven and slept with it at the foot of his bed and the reel and line under his pillow.

He returned to England in 1946 when he heard of the death of a member of his family in the hope of claiming his share of the family estate. Once in England he discovered that he had been left nothing and was unable to return to Tasmania until a friend there sent him the funds for his return passage. Contemporary accounts suggest that he lived most of his life pretty close to poverty. In 1955 Dick and his second wife Sheelah decided to retire to England when he rented a cottage on the Avon. While in England he tied flies for Ogden Smiths and Farlows, 'who ordered three or four hundred dozen at a time', and other English companies. He met and fished with Frank Sawyer[7] on the Avon during this stay and on his return to Tasmania took with him information on how Sawyer tied and fished his nymphs. On his return voyage to Australia he met Ken Ross and his wife Jean, and together they opened a tackle shop, Wigram and Ross, that was financed by Jean who had private

R. H. 'Dick' Wigram was a highly-talented professional fly tier who had a great impact on the development of artificial flies in Australia

funds although the venture nearly bankrupted her. Wigram's last years were more comfortable as a local businessman provided him and his wife with a home and car and kept on eye on them. He wrote a number of books between 1938 and 1953, contributed regular fishing columns to local newspapers and wrote many magazine articles both in Australia and England. Wigram died after a car accident on 30 April 1970, aged sixty-seven. His last work, *The Fly*, was published posthumously in 2002.

Wigram was responsible for Tasmania's most famous nymph – and his most effective fish-getter – Wigram's Brown nymph which he developed between 1931 and 1935. I have read suggestions that Wigram based his nymph on a brown nymph that found its way from England to Tasmania possibly through a friend of Wigram's from Devon, Major B. W. Powlett[8], who visited Tasmania a number of times between 1929 and 1939 and was to have quite an influence on local fly tiers and the development of Tasmanian fly patterns. Could that nymph have been Carter's Brown nymph? Wigram's Brown nymph was later known as the Pot Scrubber nymph because of the inclusion of a strand of flat copper from a pot or pan scrubber, instead of the original rib of fine gold wire. Wigram tied his nymphs with a mixture of seal's fur and wool as he felt that the slightest movement of a fur-bodied fly would cause the ends of the fur fibres to move in a life-like way. He mixed wool with fur as it

An illustration of
Wigram's famous
Brown or Pot
Scrubber nymph

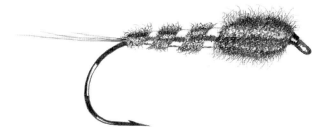

helped bind the fur together and made it more secure when dubbed on a hook. What was crucial to the success of the fly was dying the mixed seal's fur and unspun white wool, in equal quantities, to exactly the right shade which he described as 'rather red chocolate colour'. He used a brand of dye called Dolly Dye and mixed together five packets of nigger (*sic*) brown, half a packet of pillar box red and one third of a teaspoon of black, with a tablespoon full of vinegar in half a pint of water. He described the dry strands, when held up to the light, as showing a 'definite reddish tint but without the strong light background it should look a darkish chocolate brown'. The original dressing was tied with either brown or black gossamer silk, with a dozen strands from

An elderly R. H. 'Dick' Wigram with a fine trout

135

Date	NAME	Dressing ~~ADDRESS~~	REMARKS
'X'X'	RIFFLE BEETLE	Body. Peacock only. Carapace is made from a piece of Crow feather from outside wing covert. A bright shiny black.	On the rivers in Oct + Nov in Tasmania. Size 0000 or 000. not a good floater but fur will take floating or Sink. A heavy sunk fly.
	BROWN NYMPH.	Body Brown fur made from seals fur + unspun wool wool mixed. Rather more fur than wool. Tail few strands dark R.I.R feather. Rib feather R.I.R. flat copper.	Size 2,3 or 4. The Dye (Sally) of 'Riffel Brown' 3 Packet, 1 Jewel Leadfoan Pillar Box red. But need a primer I think to look. Do not work the fur in detergent, leave to soak in algebrata + examine coarsest portion in fresh water its for correct col. Colours for fur.

A page from one of Dick Wigram's diaries

A page from **R. H. 'Dick' Wigram**'s fishing diary, with the original dressing for his **Brown nymph** and a sample of the mix of dyed seal's fur and white wool of the correct colour a hackle of a Rhode Island Red for a short tail, the dyed seal's fur/wool mix for the abdomen and thorax (with the thorax twice as thick as the body) and a rib of flat copper wire from a copper pot or pan scrubber. He finished the fly with an extra pinch of the fur/wool mix at the head. An early version of his nymph had two turns of hackle at the head to represent legs, no doubt an influence from Skues, and the body was fully-ribbed with no thorax. The head hackle was probably dropped when he added a thorax to the design. Towards the end of his life he tied all his nymphs weighted with copper wire and he added it to his famous Brown nymph. He wrote how this fly killed fish all over Australia, Tasmania and New Zealand and that many English anglers had been converted to it after he had caught difficult trout on the Colne at Bibury and 'a great many trout and grayling in both the Bristol and Hampshire Avons and the Test on small sizes of this fly'.

A fishing friend of Wigram, one Frank Wadley, is reputed to have tied a giant nymph, also ribbed with a strip of copper wire from a copper pot scrubber, which he called a Pot Scrubber nymph. The story goes that Wigram immediately saw the commercial value of this name and added a pot scrubber rib to his own Brown nymph which was then known as Wigram's Pot Scrubber nymph. Should a new or used pot scrubber be used to supply the rib material? Again no one seems to know but it's not unreasonable, I think, to suggest that it would, in all probability, be a used scrubber.

As well as his Brown nymph Wigram developed the Cob nymph that had a dark grouse feather 'tied Skues fashion' to represent legs and he also tried making nymphs with flat bodies. Wigram put nymphs of interest to the angler into three categories, namely flat larvae that lived under stones; round swimming larvae; and crawling larvae covered in spines. His attempts to represent flat nymphs, by applying varnish to the seal's fur body, were to be abandoned as he felt that 'the ordinary round ties seem to lure fish just as well' and was also much easier (and quicker) to tie. He had a list of six essential nymphs which he stated must be 'correct in colour and shape' – these were the patterns that caught the big fish – where as the 'near enough' patterns would, in general, catch only the smaller trout. He sought suggestion in his artificial nymph patterns, rather than exact imitation. He encouraged anglers, through his writing, to spend time watching nymphs when hatching to learn how they swam and moved.

Wigram was an exceptional angler and enjoyed nymph fishing which he described a 'most fascinating method' but one which, for him, had 'proved very much easier than the usual methods of wet and dry fly'. In the nineteen-thirties nymph fishing in Tasmania was still not very popular although, in Wigram's opinion, the rivers were very suitable. Although it was not a new method, it was a method that had been ignored by both anglers and angling writers. It was a method that would catch fish when flies were not hatching and would catch larger fish than with wet or dry flies. His experience was in notable contrast to the early English anglers who condemned nymph fishing for being responsible for catching undersized fish. Wigram was one of the few anglers who thought that drag could be used to good effect when nymph fishing. He wrote that a nymph 'HELPED' (his capitals) by drag, deliberate drag will catch fish 'time and time again'. When casting and fishing upstream, he liked to 'work' his fly slightly and to make his fly travel slightly faster than the current. He also developed another technique which he called the oiled nymph and used at the right time – when nymphs were held just under the surface film and hatching seemed to be delayed perhaps due to a change in atmospheric pressure – was 'one of great joy to the angler'. He fished a nymph, well oiled with fly oil or floatant, on an ungreased cast, or leader, so that he could cast his fly well above a feeding fish, pull it under and because the fly was oiled, it would bob-up and float in the surface film. Although the floatant he used was often washed off after a couple of casts, he maintained that if the first cast was accurate, a second was rarely needed. He poured a drop or two of oil on to the eye of the hook so that it would then soak well into the body of the fly. Any surplus oil could be squeezed from the fly with a thumb and finger. The fly was then ready for action.

Wigram certainly made his mark on fly fishing and the development of local

R. H. 'Dick' Wigram on the river

fly patterns in Australia and Tasmania, as Skues had anticipated all those years ago, and achieved a more-lasting legacy than Skues.

Notes

1 Anglers fishing with Clyde-style nymphs, which were normally tied unweighted, were often advised to fish them with small split shot when fishing a cast of three flies, with one shot above the tail or point fly and one between the first and second droppers.

2 Walter Durfee Coggeshall played a very important role in introducing lightweight American-style fly rods to the UK from about 1902 and also the development of fly lines and line dressings.

3 There does not appear to be any such nymph – with a gold rib – in any of Sawyer's writings.

4 Edward R. Hewitt's book on nymphs was one of the few books available at the time but Rosborough did not read it for some years.

5 For some strange reason – certainly in England and probably other English-speaking countries – the Polish short nymph method is known as Czech nymphing. For a time it was known, incorrectly, as the rolled nymph. It is likely that the success that the Czechs had with this method at fly fishing championships enabled them to hi-jack the name of the method.

6 Robert Bragg self-published a very interesting, unusual and somewhat eccentric book, *Introduction to Fishing in the British Isles and Overseas, 1915 – 1939*, limited to but three copies. A quick glance at it will show that there were not many countries where he had not fished. As a fly dresser he did develop some nymph patterns such as his Dragonfly nymph, Cased Caddis larva and tied Skues' Blue Dun nymph. His father had a fishing holiday in New Zealand in 1907.

7 Wigram referred to Sawyer's Pheasant Tail nymph and also mentioned that Oliver Kite 'who, I think, fishes the same water' believed that the pheasant herls were unnecessary and that a successful nymph could be tied with copper wire only, his bare hook nymph. He wrote 'Such a hook would rely entirely on shape and stimulated movement.' He then went on to deal with another of Kite's 'tricks': 'This gentleman says that he has demonstrated upstream nymph fishing when blindfolded, it is, of course, not difficult provided you have a delicate sense of touch. Most of us prefer to fish with our eyes open.'

8 According to Wigram, Major Powlett was a pioneer of nymph fishing on the river Usk and invented many patterns used on Devon rivers and streams. He died in Ottery St Mary on 19 April 1953, aged eighty-one. Although Wigram – and others – referred to him as Major W. B. Powlett, his correct name was Major Barton William-Powlett.

7 An introduction to upstream nymphing

'All trout take more of their food from below the surface of the water than from upon it; and it is for this reason that the ability to fish the nymph is such an important weapon in the angler's armoury.'
Brian Clarke and John Goddard, *The Trout and the Fly, A New Approach*, 1980

There are still many anglers who do not appreciate what they are missing by either not fishing nymphs or not developing the skills to fish nymphs successfully. Dry fly anglers claim that there is nothing to beat casting a fly to a rising fish, seeing the fish rise and take their floating fly. When there are rising fish, few anglers will deny that there is little to beat dry fly fishing the traditional way. But is it not equally – if not more – exciting to stalk a fish feeding underwater, particularly in clear water, cast to it and see (perhaps) a flash of white as it opens its mouth and takes your nymph? And is it not better, both from a practical and ethical point of view, to offer a fish feeding sub-surface an artificial imitation of what we think that it is feeding on, rather than hammering away at it with a dry fly?

Although Skues, Sawyer, Kite and many others have written complete books on nymph fishing, it does not have to be complicated. In essence it is a very simple and straightforward way to catch fish. But that is not to deny that there is much to be learnt and that there can be many more difficult days on the river than easy ones. It is a method of fishing that will appeal to the thoughtful angler who enjoys rising to and meeting a challenge.

Fishing an upstream nymph is more difficult than fishing a dry fly as it is fishing in three dimensions. It involves judgement of how far upstream – and thus in front of a fish – to cast, which side to cast (rather than straight over a fish and risk frightening it with your line), and, crucially, how deep to fish your fly. How far upstream, or in front of the fish, to cast is subject to many variables including the speed of flow of the river, the depth at which the feeding fish is holding and whether or not there are obstacles in the way such as weed beds. Surface and unseen underwater currents can both contrive to sweep your nymph past a fish and out of sight or range. The depth at which an artificial nymph is fished is achieved and controlled by weight (or lack of) of the artificial, the length and diameter of tippet and how much of the leader is greased to make it float.

Upstream nymphing requires good, consistent presentation and accurate casting. Usually the nymph must be cast and placed very accurately to get a reaction but sometimes a fish will move perhaps two feet (61 cm) or more to take a nymph. Upstream nymphing relies on achieving a dead drift over as much of your cast as possible. In certain conditions you will achieve a satis-factorily long perfect dead drift; in other conditions the perfect dead drift may last for only a few feet. This may be because of invisible drag caused by the subtle differences in speed between the surface of the water and nearer the bottom of the river where the flow is usually slower. In faster water this is not usually a problem. But fishing in slow water, when the fish have more time to inspect your offering, subtle drag can frighten trout. If you are sure that your nymph has not been subject to unseen drag but has been ignored by your target fish, try a cast to the other side of the fish, a closer cast or varying the depth of your fly. When you cast, watch for the tell-tale splash to see where your nymph landed as this will show you where it is in relation to your fish. Good eyesight, clear water and Polaroid or Polarised sunglasses will help you to follow your fly as it drifts downstream and thus increase your chances of taking a fish. Accurate casting is particularly important in high summer when water levels are at their lowest and the sun is high in the sky: a line will throw a shadow that can clear all fish from a stretch of water. A stealthy approach,

Upstream nymphing requires good, consistent presentation and accurate casting

delicate and accurate presentation and a long, fine leader can all help. Only cast as close to a fish as you think you need and do try to keep the end of the line behind the fish so that it is out of sight. Try to keep casts as short as possible consistent with not getting so close to a fish that you frighten it.

Frank Sawyer animated his nymph by raising his rod tip to make his nymph rise in the water, making the trout think that the nymph was about to escape. Oliver Kite is credited, by Sawyer, with coming up with the phrase 'induced take' and he would often use an induced take first cast. Kite wrote that 'Successful nymph fishing is primarily dependent on the life-like employment of the artificial by the angler.' To induce a fish to take your nymph, by making it rise in the water, requires that you know and can see where your artificial is in relation to the fish. Again water clarity makes a big difference. The tyro nympher may find that a small, subtle bite indicator will make life easier.[1] When you cannot see your nymph reasonably clearly, or the fish, or at worse neither, then making a good induced take is much more of a challenge. You can make it speculatively and sometimes be rewarded by connecting with a fish but more often find nothing on the end of your leader. A short line will help make an induced take easier to execute as there will be less slack line to be removed before the raised rod tip has an effect on the artificial. The lift should be smooth and even as you are trying to make your nymph look as though it is gliding towards the surface to hatch. It must be remembered that natural nymphs can move only slowly, under their own steam, and not very far in one way. So they must pause on their way to hatch, before making another 'push' towards the surface. Even when they are swimming, they will be at the mercy of the current, less so in slower water than fast water. Like so much of successful nymph fishing, practice is required because it is very much easier to describe how to make an induced take than to perform one.

Many nymphs and shrimps live on or near the bottom of rivers and streams and your artificial needs to fish near the bottom, where feeding fish will expect to find food items. When fishing a deep, well-weighted nymph check your hook regularly for weed. Although it is annoying to keep catching weed, it does tell you that your fly is getting down to the bottom of the stream. If you can see your nymph and it looks to be getting too near the bottom, a little lift with your rod tip (like an induced take) will make the fly rise up in the water and keep clear of weed and may even induce an unseen fish to grab your fly before it disappears from sight.

Fish that are bulging and taking nymphs that are hatching or about to hatch will be interested in artificials that are fished at the same depth at which they are feeding, typically in or just under the surface film. To achieve this use an artificial that has less weight or grease the tippet nearly up to the fly or a combination. This is one time when the use of an unleaded nymph may be called for. To ensure that an un-weighted nymph does penetrate the water surface spit on it well and make sure that the last few inches of your tippet are quite grease free. This is less necessary with a nymph with a sparsely-dressed body like a Pheasant Tail, but for nymphs with hairier bodies, such as a Gold-Ribbed Hare's Ear, then spitting on it will help to make sure that it sinks, rather than floats on the surface.

The same rod and floating line that would be used for fishing a dry fly can be used for nymph fishing. Rod length is not critical but a short rod can make line control on the water more difficult, particularly if it is necessary to mend line or there is a lot of bank-side vegetation. A floating line is all that will be needed and also floating leader as you are unlikely to be fishing water deep enough to need a sinking line or leader. The floating leader plays an important role in controlling the depth of your fly and detecting takes. You can adjust the depth of drift of your nymph by modifying the length of tippet and greasing more or less of it. For a fish lying deep, you will not grease any of the tippet but for a fish feeding just under the surface, you will have to grease all but the last few inches.

Fly size is important. Remember that both Frank Sawyer and Oliver Kite fished flies tied on sizes 16 and 18 hooks – sometimes smaller – and hardly ever bigger than size 14. Most nymphs are small, with notable exceptions such as some stoneflies, and are best represented by artificials tied on small hooks. Even when fishing nymphs near the bottom in deep water it is not always necessary to fish large flies. Small flies can be tied with extra weight to ensure that they sink deep enough. If that extra weight results in an exaggerated thorax, that is no bad thing. But not many anglers would have Oliver Kite's complete faith in his Bare Hook nymph, even if it started life as a Pheasant Tail that had been well chewed, to the virtual exclusion of all other patterns. It is, however, worth noting that Kite claimed to carry a basic tying kit in the boot of his car so that he had hooks, vice, fine copper wire and a selection of suitable feathers; he could then tie some nymphs to match the local hatch. Whatever other patterns of fly there are in the nymph fisher's fly box, it must contain Sawyer Pheasant Tail nymphs and Gold-Ribbed Hare's Ear nymphs, both in a range of sizes. The Gold-Ribbed Hare's Ears can be tied with different amounts of weight and today, both patterns are tied with the addition of gold or copper bead heads.

When you have identified a feeding fish in an approachable lie the objective is to cast your nymph up and across the stream and to allow it to follow a dead drift, at the same speed as the current, back down towards the fish. You should always endeavour to get into a position so that you can cast up and across at an angle – this is the basic approach which keeps your line and leader away from the fish. Casting straight upstream and alongside a fish is an easy way to scare it, particularly on a sunny day in low water conditions. But with a fish lying under your own bank, unless you can wade into a better position or mount an attack from the opposite bank, there may be no other way than to cast straight upstream and hope that you can achieve a shepherd's crook cast, so that the fly is in-line with the fish and your line well to one side. Before making that first cast, spend a few moments watching your fish and observe the movements it makes, or does not make as the case may be. You may find that it has a preference to move to one side rather than the other, or to move up and down in response to approaching nymphs.

Having made your cast you need to retrieve line as the nymph floats downstream towards you. In fast water this can happen very quickly. The figure of eight retrieve, used typically by still water anglers and which is designed to impart movement to a nymph, is not needed on a river. What is needed is a longer, flowing continuous retrieve, particularly when fishing faster waters. Such a retrieve can be achieved by taking hold of the line, as soon as you have cast, near the stripping ring and pulling your hand as far behind and away from you as possible. Keep the coil of line in your hand and reach up to the stripping ring again and retrieve another length of line. Always hold the line between the index finger of your rod hand and the handle as this allows you to trap the line when you need to tighten into a fish. In very slow water simply retrieve line straight into your hand. But whichever method you use, always make sure that you have as little slack as possible between the end of the rod and the fly. Too much slack can make tightening on a fish impossible. Always

Having made your cast you need to retrieve line as the nymph floats downstream back towards you, in a flowing continuous retrieve, the speed of which is dictated by the speed of flow of the river

keep the tip of your rod low and pointing down the line towards the fly. The only time that you will want to raise your rod tip is when making an induced take or at the end of a cast.

When you lift off and cast again will depend on whether or not your nymph may be seen by other fish but, to ensure that you will always fish upstream and not downstream, you must lift off when your nymph is still in front of you. There are occasions when you will only want a short drift and your line may be at an angle of forty-five degrees across the river and on other occasions you will want to fish out the cast to the bitter end by raising your rod so that only the leader is on the water. Particularly when wading it can be very effective to raise the rod when you have retrieved all but enough line to be able to cast again and fish out the cast by raising the rod and then using a roll pick-up followed by one false cast to extend your line further and then completing your cast. The roll pick-up helps load the rod when you have but a short length of line beyond the top ring.

A trout can take a nymph with great delicacy and expel one from its mouth with equal expediency. There is what you will come to recognise as an exqui-site, heart-stopping moment when the downstream drift of your leader is checked and it 'draws' under. You raise your rod and tighten, unsure whether you have hooked a fish or your nymph has snagged weed. Almost before you have time to think, a brown trout explodes into action and you know it was a fish and not weed. At least that time! How do you recognise a take? Sometimes it can seem almost impossible. A sixth sense tells you that you have a fish on the end of the line. Sometimes a shallow feeding fish will make it easy by taking your nymph as it hits the water. Although you are endeavouring to cast to a fish that you can see or one that has betrayed its presence with a bulging rise form, it is not always possible to see the fish. When wading, your range of vision into the water is limited and so you do need to be able to detect a take. Two keys to success are watching the fish and concentrating hard on the end of the leader which mast float. There are times when it can be helpful to fish with a small 'strike' indicator which gives you something to focus on. If your fish turns, rolls or opens it mouth – look out for the white flash of the inside of a fish's mouth as it draws in your nymph – tighten straight away. If you cannot see the fish and the end of your leader seems to stop, is drawn under water or moves in some other way, again tighten straight away. If you have got it right, you should have a fish on the end of your line firmly hooked in the scissors. Sometimes you will find that you have tightened into the bottom or a lump of weed will fly past your ear or you may think that you have hooked the bottom and it turns out to be a fish. By the time you have realised it is a fish, it can be too late to tighten into it properly.

Keeping the leader well greased and watching the dipping point (as advo-cated by Oliver Kite) where the ungreased length of leader penetrates the surface film, is vitally important. The automatic reaction to any unexpected movement or hesitation of the leader at the dipping point should be to tighten the line immediately. As I have said already, not every movement or hesitation will be a fish but enough will turn out to be fish that would not have been hooked had it not be for setting the hook every time.

Another very good reason for casting to fish that you can see and watching that fish all the time is the frustration of seeing a swirl of a fish as you lift off to cast again: this could be 'your' fish which followed your nymph downstream and decided to make a grab for it just as it was about to disappear, or, another fish that you had not seen. Once you have committed yourself to lifting off and casting again, it can be impossible to stop even if you spot the following fish. A fish following your nymph downstream can, I believe, be the reason for seemingly missing fish. For example you cast upstream to a bulging fish, your fly passes the spot where you think the fish is lying and then your leader checks. When you tighten there is nothing there. What may have happened is that the fish turned and took your nymph facing downstream and as you tightened you simply plucked the fly out of its mouth.

If there are no fish rising or obviously feeding, how do you decide which fish to cast to? If there is a choice of fish, go for the one that is highest in the water and nearest the surface. Such a fish is more likely to be feeding or at least showing interest in food. As mentioned before, you may see a flash of white as it opens its mouth or it may move to one side to intercept a passing nymph. Fish that are lying very close to the bottom, hardly moving, can be caught but they may need waking up before they are prepared to take your nymph.

Some fish may be 'on the fin' and taking nymphs. Other fish may be bulging and taking nymphs just below the surface and the tell-tale bulge will give away their position. Sometimes a fish will move about chasing nymphs, making it difficult to know just where to cast. If you fish blind or fish the water in the hope of intercepting a fish, you run the risk of frightening fish that you have not seen or do not know are there. If local rales allow the use of two flies at a time, when fish are taking both nymphs and duns, fishing a nymph on a short dropper tied to the bend of the dry fly New Zealand style, can give you the best of both worlds. Another advantage of this system is that it is very quick and easy to add a nymph on a dropper, rather than cutting-off the dry and then tying on a nymph. When you want to go back to a dry fly only, simply slip the dropper off the hook.

Notes

1 For those anglers who consider the use of a bite indicator on a par with float fishing, some indicators – particularly the large ones – are nothing more than floats, designed to prevent a heavy nymph from sinking too deeply or keep it at a set depth. Small indicators, made from a little pinch of floating putty or a short tuft of floating yarn tied to the end of the leader when

attaching the point or tippet, can be very useful as the indicator shows you where the leader is and gives you something to concentrate on. Readers who are interested in finding out more about the morality, or otherwise, of using indicators should read The Indicator Papers by James R. Babb and published in his book *Crosscurrents, A Fly Fisher's Progress*.

8 Nymph fishing on still waters

'Fishing a nymph on reservoirs is a highly sophisticated and fascinating technique, which has it addicts who will fish little else.'

Conrad Voss Bark, *The Encyclopaedia of Fly Fishing*, 1986

The explosion in fly fishing, and more specifically on lakes, ponds and reservoirs and other still waters in the UK, can be attributed to the development of much-needed drinking water reservoirs and the opening of Pitsford reservoir, followed by the 1570 acres (635ha) of Grafham Water on 1 June 1966, although there were other reservoirs, such as Ravensthorpe, opened in 1893, which had been fished regularly by trout anglers since the late 1940s and early 1950s. It was public policy to stock the new reservoirs with trout for fishing. The creation of these reservoirs was followed by private fisheries on lakes and flooded gravel pits. But this was not the start of nymph fishing on still waters: Mottram[1] had fished Blagdon Lake in 1910 – and possibly earlier as it was opened for fishing in 1904 – and knew that it could be very effective to fish nymphs when fish were taking duns on the surface as they would take nymphs as well whereas the angler fishing a dry fly was unlikely to catch any fish feeding on nymphs. He also developed a series of suitable patterns including caddis nymph, diptera larvae and pupae, midge larvae and a smut. Mottram's midge larva, with its black and white striped body, was the forerunner of Geoffrey Bucknall's Footballer pattern. Also on Blagdon, Dr Bell developed his Amber nymph, Grenadier and Blagdon Green Midge which were the forerunners of today's sedge pupae and buzzers.

Blagdon Lake, 430 acres (174ha) was built by the then Bristol Waterworks Company to supply water for the increasing population of Bristol. Construction started in 1891 with the building of a dam across the river Yeo at Blagdon and, eight years later, the new Yeo Reservoir as it was known then, started to fill. The lake reached its top level in 1903 and the first bank fishing permits (a maximum of eight per day) were sold on 21 May 1904. Fly fishing only was allowed from boats but any method from the bank; worm fishing and ledgering were banned in 1905. Permits cost ten shillings (50p) and a boat and boatman for the day cost all of £2. Although only 102 brown trout were caught during the first season, they had an average weight of four pounds thirteen ounces (2.25kg) and the heaviest weighed nine pounds and two

ounces (4kg). It was the extraordinary size of trout in the lake that was responsible for establishing Blagdon's reputation in its early days.

Dr Howard Alexander Bell (1888 – 1974) will be associated forever with
Blagdon Lake and the flies that he developed, based on countless post-
mortems of fish caught there, and his method of fishing his flies. He had fished
at Blagdon from 1920 and then in 1935 he bought a medical practice in
Wrington, Somerset, and later opened a surgery at the neighbouring village
of Blagdon. He fished on Fridays (except during his annual holiday on the
river Spey) when his patients were not allowed to be ill as he held a short
morning surgery only for the most urgent of cases. He ran what would seem
by today's standards to have been a pleasantly eccentric, rural medical practice. He hated and never sought publicity and was reputed never to have
written anything about fly fishing although notes for an unpublished article,
dated 1941, were published in *The Buzzer* in 2003. Bell had read Skues and
followed his example of using a marrow spoon to examine the contents of the
stomachs of all the trout that he caught. He found that most fish contained
nothing but small larvae and pupae including the pupae of the black midge.
Thus he saw that the natural food of the trout bore no resemblance to the flies
then in common use, typically traditional sea trout and low water salmon flies.
Dr Bell then started to create and tie his own patterns to imitate the larvae
and pupae in the trout. Success was, it seems, pretty immediate. He fished
small, unweighted patterns and fished from the bank casting only as far as was
comfortable and allowing the flies to sink slowly until the point fly was just
clear of the bottom. He used the knot on the end of his greased line as a bite
indicator. He made a point of fishing where there were underwater features
such as drowned hedges, old ditches and streams which would be both attractive to trout and a good source of food items. Fishing similar features brought
success to the early anglers at Grafham Water and do so to this day wherever
new reservoirs are made. As *The Field's* obituary writer wrote, Dr Bell revolu-
tionised bank fishing at Blagdon. His revolution was the basis for the success
of a new generation of stillwater anglers.

One of Bell's longest-enduring flies was the Amber nymph which is still used
today. According to his notes published in *The Buzzer*, Bell first saw this nymph
some six or seven years earlier. He was wading Rugmore shallows when he
saw one on the surface that then tried to crawl up his waders. A trout that he
caught on a corixa had amber nymphs in it when he opened it up. Bell said
that the 'nymph' was the stage between caddis pupa and a small, light brown
sedge fly. He thought that it hatched in fairly deep water before swimming up
towards the surface where it continued swimming along just below the surface.
He tied his artificial on a size 12 (old scale) hook and painted the shank with
white paint, after J. W. Dunne, to produce a translucent effect. The body, thick
and tapered bluntly at the rear, was tied from a mix of white floss silk and fine

black horse hair. The fly was finished, using orange silk, with a turn or two of bright ginger hackle at the shoulder, with all but five or six fibres left on each side after pulling off the fibres on the back and front of the fly. The floss was covered with amber varnish to produce a long-lasting translucent body. If the correct colour of silk was used to tie the fly, this last procedure was not necessary.

Bell fished the fly by casting between rising fish, if possible, and letting them fight for it as a bit of competition was always helpful, or to one side of isolated rises. He used a greased line and allowed his flies to sink without any movement for ten or twenty seconds, depending on the depth of water. The flies should then be retrieved 'maddeningly slow – about two inches in a second'. He did admit that that was not easy, particularly when big fish were swirling on either side. The urge to cast again should be resisted at all costs.

While Bell was developing new flies at Blagdon, in Scotland R. C. Bridgett M.A., B.Sc., was doing much the same. Unlike Bell, Bridgett was happy to promote his ideas and wrote a series of influential articles for the *Glasgow Herald* newspaper which were later compiled to become one of his books, *Loch Fishing in Theory and Practice*, published in 1924 and then *Tight Lines*, published two years later, in which he quoted Mottram at some length in a piece entitled 'Fisherman and Flies'. His first book was published around the same time that Skues was bemoaning the lack of any scientific investigation or research into still water fishing. Bridgett knew that there was more to fishing on lochs than with a simple cast of traditional wet flies and although he was not an entomologist, he identified a range of olives, sedges and midges, in their various stages of development, in the many Scottish lochs that he fished. He stated that a sunk lure should represent food including 'nymphs of aquatic flies'. Bridgett argued that the tail fly was the most important of a cast of two or more flies and should, therefore, represent a nymph, larva or shrimp. He wrote about how, when and why to fish nymphs on rivers too.

One of his first designs was a representation of a bright green beetle that he found on Loch Leven in early June. He tied his fly with a green wool body and small red hackle and when he found that it caught fish on lochs where there were no bright green beetles, he decided that it must be an acceptable representation of the green midge. He then modified his dressing and called the fly the Green nymph. Later he was to discover that his fly was very similar to the Blagdon Green Midge of Dr Bell. Based on the success of his first pattern, he developed an olive version and black nymph which he recommended for early in the season when blue and black midges were on the water. Although he had success with nymphs of all sorts and developed his own way to present them to nymphing loch trout, spiders were still the best fly patterns as far as he was concerned.

Another very important still water fishery was Alex Behrendt's famous Two

Lakes fishery which opened near Romsey in Hampshire in 1951. This was one of the first small commercial fisheries in the UK and Behrendt soon established a reputation for the size and quality of his fish due to his good water management. Alex Behrendt, who was the son of an eastern European carp farmer, was conscripted into the German army in the Second World War and brought to England as a prisoner of war. He transformed an overgrown waste with two lakes, into a successful and viable trout fishery, over a period of four years. His original plan for the lakes was a carp farm but that idea was abandoned when he found out that the English do not eat carp. Oliver Kite was a regular visitor, as was Conrad Voss Bark and many others.

Both Kite and Sawyer fished still waters and, of course, Frank Sawyer developed his SS nymph on the lakes of the Storån river system in Sweden and the Bow Tie Buzzer on home waters. And he created Corfe End Lakes to provide still water fishing for members of the Services Dry-fly Fishing Association. His first use of his Pheasant Tail nymph on still water was on one of a series of gravel pits near Andover, Hampshire, in the 1950s when he succeeded in catching two fine trout, to the amazement of the owner of the pits. A year or two later, he fished Blagdon in early October, with Harry Hiscock, but had no success fishing a Pheasant Tail nymph from a boat although he was confident that using a nymph, based on his experience near Andover, would prove profitable. He wrote that there were few fish feeding where nymphs would attract them. Initially Frank Sawyer was an infrequent visitor to still waters and lakes and it was not until about 1957 that he really began to see and understand the attraction of the sport offered at places such as Blagdon and Chew Valley. In fact he fished at Chew Valley four times before he caught his first trout there, on a Killer Bug which he thought the fish took as a hatching sedge.

Sawyer fished still waters with light quick-actioned tackle and usually only one nymph or Killer Bug. He could reach all the feeding fish that he wanted to without the need for a long, heavy-line rod or a shooting head. He stalked the fish feeding in the shallows and around weed beds and other features attractive to trout. His view was that his method of nymphing for trout in lakes was more akin to dry fly fishing than fishing wet flies and stripping lures at speed. He placed his nymph carefully and precisely and knew that he must fish his nymph very, very slowly if it was going to be attractive to a hunting, feeding fish.

Oliver Kite advocated the use of a nymph on a still water in places and at times when a trout might be expected to be aware of the presence of active natural nymphs nearby. For him the use of a nymph on still waters could be an 'artistic method' of catching fish. Kite found the use of a nymph to be most effective on smaller waters, preferably with some shelter, containing some weed even if the weed should be confined to bays and shallower areas, and likely to support a population of natural nymphs such as representatives of the cloeon, procloeon and spurwing families. When weed starts to grow well, it will make a good home for natural nymphs. He found Sawyer's Killer Bug to be an effective still water pattern.

When Frank Sawyer fished in Sweden in July 1959, he fished a series of lakes from as small as four acres (1.6ha) up to as much as thirty acres (12.1ha). These lakes contained brown trout, often very large and some char. Sawyer fished the lakes and interlinking rivers and streams. His first trout fell to a Pheasant Tail nymph dressed on a size 1 hook (14). Sawyer examined the contents of the stomach of the first sizeable trout that he caught and found in it caddis and nymphs of a variety that he had never seen before and much larger than his size 1 fly. He felt that a hook size number 3 or 4 would be needed to match the size of the natural nymph. These nymphs were fast swimmers and moved freely through the water. Sawyer tied his artificials with fibres from the wing feather of a grey farmyard goose that he had in his fly tying kit. He was soon to catch four fine trout of up to four pounds (1.8kg) on his new Grey Goose nymph. He then gave some nymphs to his host, Nils Färnström, to try. And Färnström was soon catching fish on these nymphs.

Frank Sawyer's Bow Tie Buzzer was named by a friend, possibly Harry Hiscock. Sawyer had been using this fly for a number of years before he felt that it was proven enough to start promoting it. It seems to have been his last creation and dates from between 1958 and 1969, so he must have tied and fished the first examples in the early 1960s. Sawyer was only too well aware of the importance of buzzers in the diet of lake trout and the problems to be overcome in producing successful imitations. These problems were two: deception could not be aided by moving the rod and line as is the case with most swimming nymphs as buzzers cannot swim in that sense and move to and from the surface in a vertical plane, and the second is that most buzzers hang vertically in mid water and at the surface. His novel solution to these problems was to make his fly in two parts. The white fringe, or celia, of a buzzer is very prominent when about to hatch and moves constantly. He imitated this with a separate 'bow tie' of white nylon wool tied on to the end of the leader with a slip knot. The buzzer body hung free on the leader and was prevented from being pulled off the end of the leader by the bow tie. To create the necessary translucent, almost luminous sheen of the body of a buzzer, it was made with an underbody of gold-coloured wire covered with a strip of silver foil. The wire also gave the fly enough weight to make it sink and then hang in the water but not continue sinking. The ends of four fibres from a browny-red cock pheasant tail feather formed a slipping shuck and the fibres themselves made the body. Sawyer fished the fly on a floating line with the leader well greased for half its length.

Conrad Voss Bark who was for many years the fishing correspondent for

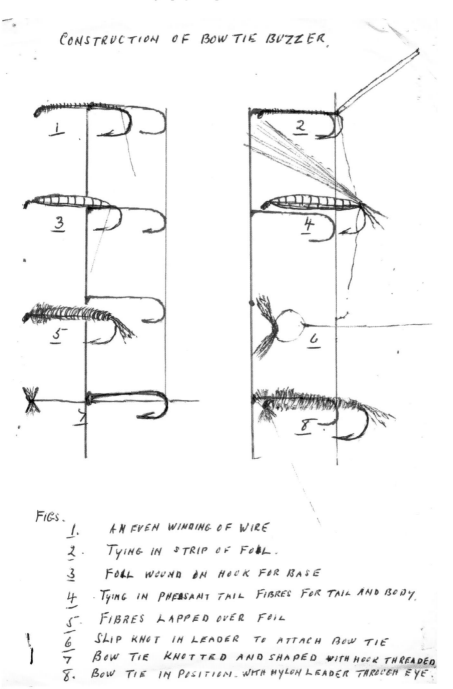

CONSTRUCTION OF BOW TIE BUZZER.

FIGS.
1. AN EVEN WINDING OF WIRE
2. TYING IN STRIP OF FOIL.
3 FOIL WOUND ON HOOK FOR BASE
4 TYING IN PHEASANT TAIL FIBRES FOR TAIL AND BODY.
5. FIBRES LAPPED OVER FOIL
6 SLIP KNOT IN LEADER TO ATTACH BOW TIE
7 BOW TIE KNOTTED AND SHAPED WITH HOOK THREADED
8. BOW TIE IN POSITION. WITH NYLON LEADER THROUGH EYE.

Frank Sawyer's drawing showing the construction of his innovative Bow Tie Buzzer

The Times enjoyed his still water fishing whether on Blagdon or at Two Lakes and elsewhere. His maternal grandfather was Willie Cox who fished at Blagdon from its opening until the middle 1920s. Willie Cox was an 'old time' fisherman who fished the lake when salmon and sea trout flies were used regularly and then during the transition to more imitative nymph fishing. Unlike his grandfather who would fish any method that would catch fish, Voss Bark was dedicated to the nymph: 'Nymph fishing for lake trout is . . . a delicate and difficult form of fishing which demands enormous concentration but which is exceptionally rewarding in terms of excitement and intellectual stimulation.' For him nymph fishing was true fly fishing and not to be confused with wet fly or lure fishing.

In his interesting and enjoyable book *Fishing For Lake Trout*, he stressed the vital importance of good presentation and the need for extreme concentration at all times. He was also one of the few writers to mention the importance of developing water-craft, an aspect of fly fishing that is as important on still waters as on running water. On presentation he wrote: 'Presentation is of such enormous importance that I must be forgiven if I emphasise again that no matter how perfect your pattern if you present it badly it will not be taken.' Concentration is required at all times one's fly is being fished because takes to a nymph are indicated by only the slightest movement of the line or leader.' As a last resort he did fish a large, heavy nymph on a long leader (but not as long as was to be advocated by other writers following in his path) for deep-lying fish but he felt that in so doing he was gradually losing the delicate quality of sub-surface and shallow water fishing

Three years after Conrad Voss Bark's book, Brian Clarke's important work *The Pursuit of Stillwater Trout* was published in 1975, coincidental with the boom in still water and lake fishing in England. In this book Clarke wrote about the 'three overriding factors on which practical nymph fishing on lakes is based'. Nymph fishing on still waters and lakes requires many of the skills required to fish nymphs successfully on rivers and additional skills as well. The first factor – as with nymph fishing in running water – is that the angler is endeavouring to imitate both the appearance and movement of the natural nymphs that are eaten by lake trout, at the same time as making sure that the fish can see their artificial nymphs. To be able to fish nymphs with any degree of success requires that the angler have at least a rudimentary knowledge of the behaviour of nymphs. The second factor is that as there is, in general, no or very little movement of water in a lake, the angler has to create movement to mimic the movement of the natural nymphs, by using different ways and speed of retrieve. Because most natural nymphs can only swim very slowly, retrieves must be correspondingly slow. His third factor was much more complex and less obvious. It is all to do with the way that a nymphing fish reacts to and takes an artificial nymph. As there are, but rarely, currents bringing food to the fish, trout have to hunt for their food and this movement uses energy. A fish will usually move only just fast enough to catch up with a food item before consuming it. This means that there will be only the most gentle impact on the artificial nymph and the line to which it is attached. In turn, it is often very difficult for the angler to register and respond to a take before the fish has ejected the nymph from its mouth. Everything possible needed to be done to make subtle takes as *visible* as possible, particularly when fishing the water. Such gentle takes require great concentration from the angler who must concentrate hard on the tip of his line and where the leader cuts through the water and respond immediately to the slightest of movements of line or leader. As Brian Clarke wrote: 'the primary rules of nymph fishing are that the angler's eyes should never leave his leader end and that, while the fly is in the water, he should tighten at anything that looks foreign to the normal state of the line, the leader, or the water around them.'

The best way to make takes visible is to fish with a floating line (there are times when a sinking or sink-tip line will have to be used, for example, to counter the effects of a strong wind). To the end of the line must be attached, for Brian Clarke, the most important part of the set-up: a very long leader. A sinking leader on the end of a floating fly line will sink in a curve and so, to reach bottom the leader must be considerably longer than the depth of water being fished. Clarke recommended a leader of twenty feet (6m) when fishing in water from ten to twelve feet (3m to 3.65m) and for water fifteen feet deep (4.5m) a leader will need to be up to twice as long – thirty feet (9+m). He maintained that this was about the maximum depth of water in which it is practical to fish a nymph.

In a similar way to Skues, who was very aware of and wrote about the significance of the different rise forms on rivers, so Brian Clarke wrote at length on the importance of the various rise forms to be seen on still waters. It is, after all, the rise of a trout to a fly that signals its position to the angler. And the still water nymph fisherman needs to know if the fish are feeding on nymphs. The water moves in response to movements of a fish's body and the observant angler who has a little knowledge of rise forms can learn much from studying them. Rise forms will vary depending on the state of the water, whether it is flat calm, there is some ripple or, on big waters, a good 'sea' running and will 'vary from the very obvious to the extremely subtle'. The 'classic' rise to a nymph in or just under the surface is the boil or whorl and is caused by a trout turning quickly, as it takes a nymph, and makes the water well up. Although Brian Clarke admitted that it is not an exact science, he maintained that the nature of the boil, or whorl, can give an indication of the depth of the fish. His 'rule-of-thumb' is that 'the more humped and silent the boil, the deeper the feeding fish; the broader and more shallow the whorl, the higher in the water and the more horizontally the fish has turned.' Knowledge of rise forms will help the angler to reduce some of the element of chance when casting to rising fish.

Another fisherman to have an enormous impact on still water fly fishing in the UK was Arthur Cove. He wrote *My Way with Trout* in which he shared his experiences of forty years of fishing small and large still waters. This book was published eleven years after Brian Clarke's book. Arthur Cove had started fishing reservoirs in 1952 and he gained invaluable knowledge by examining the contents of the stomachs of the fish that he caught. He started to tie his own flies because he could not find suitable patterns in tackle shops in the 1950s. Initially he tried to match exactly the shape and colour of natural nymphs. Comparing his tyings, when wet, with the natural showed him quickly that he was not getting the right colour combinations as his artificials were usually much too dark when wet. He was a great advocate of seal's fur for fly bodies as it is very versatile and he maintained that it looked even better when wet.

Although his early flies were passable imitations, he found out that it was the wrong technique and incorrect retrieves that stopped him catching fish. He then spent a lot of time watching how nymphs moved and he started to try different retrieves until he found the way to get the right movement, or *lack* of movement. This was to prove to be possibly more important than size, shape, profile or colour of fly fished. Flies that were 'rough impressions of the natural' when fished correctly proved the most successful at putting fish on the bank, particularly when fished at the most productive times. Cove also fished with very long leaders – average length was eighteen feet (6m) and often thirty feet (9+m) – and only used a tapered leader when fishing a single nymph. He preferred to fish with a team of three flies on a long, level leader. With the weight of the three flies distributed correctly – the heaviest fly on the point and the lightest on the top dropper – these long leaders were well balanced and would cast and turnover properly. For him it was the weight of the leader that mattered.

Arthur Cove soon became aware of how gentle a take could be, so light that the angler cannot afford to relax for a minute when his fly is in the water and fishing. Like Brian Clarke and everyone before him, he knew that the only indication of a take might be a very short dip of the end of the line when the hook must be set immediately.

In the USA in the 1950s Ted Trueblood preferred to fish imitative wet flies or nymphs but knew that they must be fished in a way that would produce the movement – or often lack of – that the trout would expect. For example, dragon fly nymphs can be moved in a series of very short jerks, with pauses in between, to imitate a natural taking in water and then squirting it out and moving forward, before pausing and going through the whole process again.

Knowing how nymphs move helped him to catch trout in difficult times when nothing else seemed to work, for example when trying to imitate a bottom crawler nymph. He fished with a sinking line and would cast well in front of a fish that he had seen, to give the fly and line enough time to reach bottom, before starting a very slow retrieve. If he could not see a fish, he would make a similar long cast, wait and then start retrieving. Waiting had two purposes, firstly it allowed the fly to sink fully, and secondly, it gave time for any disturbance from casting to disappear so fish would be less likely to be frightened by the splash of the line and the ripples on the surface.

Charles Brooks dealt with nymph fishing in pools, ponds and lakes in a chapter called 'The Leftovers'. In it he quoted the story of a doctor from Los Angeles who spent every June, July and August between 1946 and 1970 fishing Henry's Lake and claimed to catch an average of over one hundred fish a summer weighing more than five pounds (2.26kg). And what is more, he used but three patterns of fly: Ted Trueblood's Otter Shrimp, a Green Damsel nymph and a Woolly Worm with a green body. The method of fishing the Lake was to locate, from a boat, a channel of weeds, cast a long line down it, let the nymphs sink well and then retrieve them very slowly with a hand-twist retrieve. As he wrote, a simple method, and successful, but there could be many days when however well anyone fished, no or few fish would be caught. Brooks preferred to locate fish and then try for them as this was the key to catching fish. Once a fish had been found, observation of its position in the water and actions would dictate how to fish for it. If he could not locate a fish he would use a fast sinking or Hi-D line, a long leader and one of his weighted nymphs. He would then cast out as far as possible, let the line sink to the bottom before starting to retrieve, using a fast hand-twist retrieve with a short twitch every now and then. He would fish an area thoroughly and retrieve each cast until the leader was at the tip of his rod. He would know when he had found fish because the takes when using this method were always strong. He wanted to have only a small selection of flies, namely dragonfly nymphs in brown, tan and grey in sizes 4, 6 and 8, 2X long hooks, and damsels in green, tan and olive and hook sizes 6, 8 and 10, 2X long again. These flies were enough to fish any lake, based on the fact that if there were other flies available to fish, both dragon flies and damsels would be present as well.

In Australia in the 1970s John Sautelle recommended fishing still waters with a range of generic nymphs, tied with seal's fur, in black, brown and green. He also advocated fishing deep when the water is warm in summer and he allowed his fly to sink well before retrieving it *very* slowly. Twenty years earlier Ted Trueblood had discovered how effective it could be to fish deep and close to the bottom, in fifteen (5m) to twenty feet (6m) of water when nothing was happening near the surface. But he preferred to fish a sinking line as he felt that with a floater and even a long leader, his fly or flies would start moving towards the surface rather than staying near the bottom. He used the count-down method to time how long his flies were allowed to sink so that he could continue to fish at approximately the same depth – once he had found the correct depth at which to fish. He did not like his flies to be too heavy as they would not move as well as lighter ones. He also knew the importance of the retrieve, from as slow as possible up to very fast. He fished only a few sugges-tive nymph patterns and thought that the way a fly was fished was more important than the actual pattern. Most of his good nymphs were 'drab, dull, ragged-looking things in various shades of gray and brown'. A favourite fly was the Fledermaus nymph which he thought imitated the dragonfly nymph and was most successful on still waters and slow-flowing rivers where dragon flies were abundant but it accounted for fish nearly everywhere.

Note

1 David Burnett, who wrote the very interesting and informative introduction to the Fly Fisher's Classic Library version of Dr Mottram's book *Fly Fishing, Some New Arts and Mysteries*, told me an interesting story about Mottram fishing at Blagdon. The story was that he was nymph fishing from a boat and that he had spotted a large cruising rainbow trout. He watched the fish complete two circuits, each of which took forty-eight minutes, and then on the third circuit he cast his fly after forty-seven minutes. The result? A six pound (2.7kg) rainbow for a very patient fisherman as he had observed the fish for well over two hours.

9 Flies and fly tying

'These wire-bodied nymphs, an original and imaginative construction evolved by Sawyer, are the very foundation of modern nymph-fishing.'
Oliver Kite, *Nymph Fishing in Practice*, 1963

In 1953 Eric Taverner stated that an artificial nymph was, essentially, a wet fly but designed 'with more regard to the natural shape and to the translucence of the insect at that stage'. As we know, it was many years before trout fishermen realised and understood that upwinged flies do not arrive on the surface of a river from the air but hatch underwater. So it was that it took these same fisherman a long time to appreciate that the different nymphs move in different ways and at different speeds. Sir Joseph Ball, who opened the assault on Skues at The Debate on the ethics of nymph fishing on chalk streams, was still ignorant of the life and movements of nymphs as recently as 1938, as was Martin Mosely whose opinions tended to go unquestioned, except by Skues. Skues was able to refute some of them based on his own observations, for example, in a letter written to his friend C. A. N. Wauton on 30 August 1938, at the end of his last season on his beloved Itchen, about a large trout caught in McCaskie's Corner from which he extracted a living nymph. He put the nymph in a cup of water and proceeded to watch it. He saw it give 'short convulsive wriggles propelling him not so much as half an inch and then resting inert for several seconds. Mosely won't have it that this is a fair illustration of the nymph's behaviour, assuming that it must have been damaged in the trout's inside.' This was to be the only living nymph that Skues found inside a trout. How a nymph moves, or does not, in the water is of interest and concern to the nymph fisherman, unlike the dry fly man who, with the exception of fishing a dragging sedge, is unconcerned with the movement of the floating upwinged fly which, apart from the aforementioned sedge, does not move and simply floats along with the current.

Over the course of the development of nymph fishing the style, designs and range of materials used to tie nymphs have all changed and developed far beyond what Skues, in particular, and Mottram could ever have imagined. But while it is debatable if they are, strictly speaking, true nymphal patterns, there has been through all these many years one constant and that is the North

Country spider pattern, or soft hackle fly. Skues, as we know, wrote that 'The hackled North-Country pattern does not necessarily represent a submerged (or drowned) fly, but one in the process of hatching' or even 'wrecked in the moment of hatching' and that the early wet flies, used before dry fly fishing was developed, 'bore some resemblance to a nymph, a much closer resemblance than one finds in the North Country spiders'. And 'At the time I published *The Way of a Trout with a Fly* I thought it was advantageous to simulate nymphs with a good deal of precision, indicating wing cases and legs in due relative position and proportions. Subsequent experience has led me to realise that in practice such a precise simulation is not necessary, especially in water running with any speed.' We know that Skues, who started tying or dressing flies in 1887, did not like Mottram's flies which he thought were too rigid, dense and dull in colour and that because they had no hackles, they would land too heavily and he, Skues, thought that a pattern with a short, soft hackle would help break the fall of the hook on the water. Once again Mottram was ahead of his time as his flies looked forward to the patterns of Sawyer and Kite, with no hackles or legs (except in the case of his Resting nymph pattern), their quick entry and no encumbrance to sinking quickly. A pattern that lands with a plop or splash can often attract the attention of a fish and Brian Clarke and John Goddard promoted this as a 'minor tactic' for use under certain conditions. Again Mottram had got there first: he wrote in 1935 that leaded nymphs will fall with a plop and that if you could drop your leaded nymph at a trout's shoulder, it was then quite likely to turn sharply and take the nymph when all previous presentations had failed. One area where Skues and Mottram did agree was the desirability of having to hand examples of the natural to be imitated when tying. As referred to earlier, Venables commented on the importance of wetting tying materials when choosing the best colour to match the natural insect. Again, Mottram's dressings refer very specifically to the colour of materials 'when wet'.

In an article on tying flies, called 'Simple Flies', Mottram stressed the importance of making nicely shaped bodies that tapered towards the bend of the hook, with a well-formed thorax. Leaded nymphs could be made by adding lead foil and such nymphs could be used to imitate a real nymph rising from the river bed.

Skues maintained that his nymphs were very simple and could be tied quickly. He urged the fly tier to have a natural to hand and to ensure that the artificial nymph was a match in length, colour and proportions. 'If care be taken not to overdress the nymph and to secure the right taper of the body and the correct bulk of the pad of dubbing which is to suggest the wing cases, it is wonderful what a lifelike representation of the nymph may be secured.'

Eric Taverner described how 'Nymphs flash in the water in a most remarkable way as they attempt to avoid capture. This flash is caused by the strong contrast between the pale underside of the abdomen and the dark-olive or yellow of the upper parts. Thus, it will be seen that nymphs obey the law of the water that the parts of the body shaded from the light shall be pale and the exposed area of the body shall be dark.' He then went on to suggest that nymphs might be better ribbed with very narrow, flat gold tinsel, rather than gold wire. How impressed he would have been by woven-body Polish nymphs with their dark backs and light undersides. Skues was a great advocate of using dubbed seal's fur for the bodies of his nymphs 'as many of the nymphs are full of lights and glistenings'. Partly to enhance the 'lights and glistenings', and also for greater strength and durability, he also used fine gold or silver wire ribs. An interesting material that he used was blue Persian cat fur either natural or dyed in picric acid. William H. Lawrie was another fly tyer who also used blue cat fur.

Oliver Kite was to write: 'Pattern is of much less significance than size and careful construction to imitate the general appearance of natural nymphs in the water. The artificial nymph is dressed to sink quickly' and 'These wire-bodied nymphs, an original and imaginative construction evolved by Sawyer, are the very foundation of modern nymph-fishing.' Both Sawyer and Kite would have agreed that the thorax of a nymph should be represented

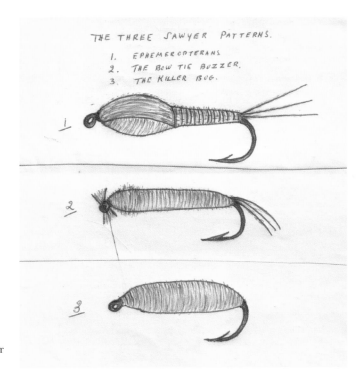

Drawings of Frank Sawyer's nymphs: ephemeropterans, the Bow Tie Buzzer and the Killer Bug

161

A selection of 'Polly' Rosborough's nymphs
Top left: Yellow Drake *Top right:* Big Yellow May
Bottom left: Near Enough *Bottom right:* Isonychia Velma

prominently and Kite dressed his Bare Hook nymph with nothing more than a thorax of copper wire.

It can be difficult to establish the definitive dressings of important nymphal patterns. Polly Rosborough admitted that he continued to develop his patterns as new materials became available. Skues also modified and developed many of his nymphal patterns over the decades. Moving right up to date, John Goddard is another fly tier and designer and developer of fly patterns whose published dressings are not always consistent. But he did admit to modifying and developing various patterns in his writings. Like Sawyer and his use of Chadwick's 477 wool, Goddard discovered for himself the effectiveness of some pink – about ten per cent – in his mixes of seal's fur for the bodies of his nymphs. But both of them were preceded in this knowledge by old Skues who had discovered the value of a touch of pink in a fly's dressing when he fished a fly invented by R. S. Austin, which Skues, christened Tup's Indispensable in 1900. This fly had a body of creamy pink dubbing and when fished wet, it was so effective for Skues that it became the foundation of his range of nymphs, although as a nymph he preferred it with a little less red seal's fur.

Sawyer in many cases stuck to his original dressings, once a pattern was established. His early version the Killer Bug, his grayling lure, was not tied with copper wire but with silver-coloured fuse wire for weight; he was still using fuse wire in 1960. He tied it for grayling in sizes 12 and 13. He used enough wire to produce a pronounced hump effect and wrapped the fuse wire underbody with darning wool, starting at the eye and finishing near the bend where he tied-off the wool with the fuse wire. Sawyer wrote in *Keeper of The Stream* that the colour of the wool was critical. While there was no mention of Chadwick's 477, the wool he chose was fawn with 'a definite pink tinge'. When wet, the wool turned a colour very like that of a shrimp. This was the significance of Chadwick's 477 darning wool. Sawyer admitted that it took him a very long time to get the dressing of the Killer Bug just right. There was no problem with the shape or weight but getting the colour right proved to be a time-consuming challenge until he found the Chadwick's wool. It is no longer available although cards of it do come on to the market every now and then and have been known to reach very high prices. This wool was also used to tie an imitation of a pale watery nymph which was one of Sawyer's early patterns that did not stand the test of time.

In an article on nymph fishing that Frank Sawyer wrote for Farlow's trout catalogue[1] of 1965, he wrote that he 'was never very successful [in constructing artificial nymphs] until discovering the use of fine copper wire as an aid in the dressing, when one could have the desired weight for sinking without in any way interfering with the neatness of the dressing'. It is interesting that Sawyer's

As well as his world-famous Pheasant Tail nymph, Frank Sawyer developed a number of other patterns, some of which failed the test of time. A well-chewed Pheasant Tail Red Spinner was the inspiration for the Pheasant Tail nymph
Top row: Pheasant Tail nymph, Grey Goose nymph
Middle row: SS nymph, Killer Bug, Bow Tie Buzzer
Bottom row: Spurwing and Procloeon Rufulum nymph, Pale Watery nymph

Oliver Kite's Bare Hook nymph, Reindeer and Red and New Forest Stream nymph

discovery and adoption of copper wire, and the world-wide success of his Pheasant Tail nymph in particular, does not seem to have been used by any fly designers or creators since. (In France in the early 1970s Jean Lysik created a nymph, the Nymphe Jeannot, that had an abdomen and thorax made from medium copper wire enamelled purple. Black tying thread was used. The abdomen was covered with peacock or heron herl and a wing case made from pheasant or heron fibres. The copper wire was bare on the underside of the thorax. This pattern was said to sink better so it could be fished deeper than Sawyer's Pheasant Tail or Grey Goose nymphs.) The designs of most of Sawyer's nymphs, with the exception of the Bow Tie Buzzer and SS nymph, were established by the late 1950s, although he did modify the tying of the Pheasant Tail nymph when he started tying them commercially. His flies were tied by his wife and two daughters Pat and Judy, his son Tim on occasions, and himself. The original Pheasant Tail nymph was finished off behind the eye of the hook but the commercial version was modified slightly so that the forward and backward lapping of the pheasant tail fibres that formed the wing case was finished behind the thorax. The fibres were secured with half a dozen turns of wire and then cut off. The wire was returned to the eye and finished off with a slip knot. It proved so successful that it was never altered. Any flies purported to have been tied by the Sawyers that have the fibres cut-off immediately behind the eye are not genuine Sawyer tyings.

Although Sawyer's nymphs were tied with copper wire, which added weight, and were tied very slim so that they would penetrate the surface film easily and sink quickly, the addition of lead under-bodies was not to be adopted generally by anglers and fly tiers until much later. Dr Barton had used copper wire to 'load' nymphs in the late 1920s but stopped using it as it was too springy. He was fishing when it was still thought to be essential to 'suppress the false cast' before presenting the nymph to a fish as false casting would dry the fly which would then fail to sink. He had fished with 'loaded nymphs' for some years and although the addition of lead wire 'may make the nymph a thought full-bellied' this was more than overcome by the fact that a loaded nymph sank instantly. Like Skues, Barton was also somewhat concerned about the splash made by a weighted nymph, but with careful casting and placing the nymph accurately, the problems of splash could be overcome.

164

Mottram used lead foil to load, or weight, his nymphs. Sawyer also experimented early on with using lead[2] to weight his flies but trial and error lead him to using copper wire which produced the right speed and depth of sink. His nymph fishing technique and his artificials were based on fishing after midsummer – which time he considered to be the most sporting for nymph fishing – and the nymphs that he would expect to find then. For some years he used three basic patterns, the Pheasant Tail nymph, a Pale Watery nymph and his third pattern, one which represented the spurwings and a Very Pale Watery nymph. He felt that these three patterns would be all that he needed and if he could not interest a trout in one of them, then there was no point in trying to attract the fish with any other patterns. Over time he was to revise his three basic patterns to the Pheasant Tail nymph, to represent dark naturals, the Grey Goose which represented lighter naturals, and the Killer Bug for both grayling and still waters. He even tied the Killer Bug as big as a size 8 for salmon. It has since proved a successful still water fly, as have the Grey Goose and Pheasant Tail nymphs. The Grey Goose nymph can be tied with died swan feathers if genuine grey farmyard goose feathers are not available.

Although many of the best and most effective nymph patterns are very simple, they must still be tied with due consideration to correct proportions and the right amount of material so that slender patterns are just that and do not end up as fat, bloated creations. Oliver Kite tied his nymphs with a small head, humped thorax, tapering abdomen and tails, to match these characteristics of the natural nymph. He made his bodies using herls, primarily from the long centre tail feather of an old cock pheasant but also used blue herls from a heron primary feather[3] or the grey herls from a goose feather. The fibres of the pheasant herl stand out suggesting the tracheal gills in a very realistic way. To begin with Kite had his flies tied for him by Mrs Bourton of Bulford, who also tied Sawyer's dry patterns, until 1958 when Sawyer taught him how to tie his own flies.

The American fly tier and designer André Puyans, who perfected his A. P. series of nymph in 1963, stated that size, shape and colour are the most important characteristics of an artificial nymph. The basic shape of a mayfly nymph is produced by making the tails about the length of the gape of the hook, or a little longer, the abdomen should be about fifty per cent of the overall length of the nymph, the thorax forty per cent and the head the remaining ten per cent. Because the heads of nymphs are usually a similar colour to their bodies, he dubbed the heads of his nymphs as he did not like heads resulting from varnished or lacquered tying thread. Skues was also against nymphs with a lot of exposed tying thread at the head as he felt that it gave them 'an unfinished effect' and he wound the hackle as near to the eye as possible.

John Goddard developed his PVC nymph in the mid-1960s from his experiences of fishing with Sawyer's Pheasant Tail nymph. He wanted a pattern with a lighter, translucent olive colour. The key to tying this pattern correctly lies in the choice of the PVC strip used to wrap the body. Goddard recommended using strips from an old olive or light green shower curtain as this material had the right combination of stretch and colour. Oliver Kite, who was a friend and fishing companion, helped him to perfect the pattern. Two other patterns that Goddard developed were the Gerroff nymph, in about 1976, and the Shrymph in 1993. The Gerroff was designed to sink very slowly and is tied on a biggish but unweighted hook and with a body tied on less than half the length of the hook shank, resulting in a fly with a very small silhouette. The Shrymph was developed for catching deep-lying grayling, although it also takes large trout lying in deep holes, and was a cross between a nymph and a shrimp. He wanted a pattern that could carry more weight, without looking ugly and unbalanced, than he felt he could produce when tying Killer Bugs.

Another significant and important development was the use of initially gold and then copper and other colours of metallic beads, for what were to become known as gold head or bead head nymphs. When and where bead heads were first used is unclear. Mackintosh's pike fly, as described in his book *The Driffield Angler*, had two small black beads for eyes. The Austrian fly fisherman Roman Moser has written that the use of gold or pearl beads may have originated in northern Italy around the turn of the nineteenth century. They were used on lures which were fished in teams using a very specific local but deadly technique. Roman Moser first saw some of these flies, with pearl bead heads, in 1978 and he was told that they were very successful when fished in murky, silty rivers. Because they were too light to be of much use in powerful rivers when used for fly fishing, Moser tied some nymphs with two layers of fine lead wire as an under-body and gold plastic beads. When he first fished them on Austria's river Traun, they were an instant success. The next development was to use small brass beads and a new fly was born which he called the gold head. He publicised these flies and the best way to fish them in the German magazine *Fliegenfischer* in 1985. Another promoter and populariser of gold heads was the Dutchman Theo Bakelaar. He confirms that beads have been around for many years, at least eighty or ninety, in areas of central Europe and were originally glass or metal. He first promoted goldheads at the Dutch Fly Fair of 1990 when he appeared with his head and face sprayed with gold paint. He had been tying flies with glass beads for some years before he saw his first fly with a gold bead on it. As Bakelaar says, although no fish has ever confirmed it for him, he believes that the gold bead is so effective because it works in four ways, providing weight, looking like an air bubble, fishes like a 'jig system' and the colour. The use of a bead provides good weight and a heavy bead will make the nymph hit the water with a distinct plop that will often attract the

The grayling is the preferred catch for most European and Scandinavian anglers. Its status in England is now very much improved and it is no longer considered to be vermin

attention of a nearby fish. This plop can be very effective on still waters. If a goldhead nymph is cast close to a rise the fish may be swimming away from where the nymph hits the water but the plop may make it turn round and investigate what attracted its attention. As regards the 'jig system' what this means is that when left alone to sink by itself, a goldhead nymph will sink head first. When the angler tightens the line and starts to retrieve line, the nymph will change attitude and start swimming head up. This up and down attitude can be devastatingly effective. Although Theo is confident that the gold colour attracts fish – sometimes from considerable distances – on a bright sunny day, there are times when the flash of a goldhead can frighten fish away.

Polly Rosborough always kept developing and trying to improve his fuzzy nymph flies, even after he had 'fixed' the design and dressing, and was always ready to try new materials as they came onto the market. He was one of the very few anglers not to use weighted flies although he did suggest tying flies on heavy-wire hooks for fishing in deep or fast water, with the exception of a pattern such as the light caddis emerger which should not be tied on heavy hooks as it was designed to be fished in the top foot (30cm) of water. All his nymphs were designed to be fished shallow as imitations of the naturals starting to emerge below the surface. He also tied his patterns with wing cases darker than the body as this is an important characteristic of a pre-emergent nymph.

Along with Ted Trueblood, he decided that shrimp patterns were best tied on straight hooks, rather than curved. Very much in contrast to current practice – particularly Czech shrimp patterns which are all tied on curved hooks. According to Polly Rosborough one of the last articles that Ted Trueblood wrote was on his research into the comparative effectiveness of shrimps and scuds tied on curved hooks and straight hooks. He caught some shrimps in a local lake and put them into an aquarium. Once in the water they straightened out and swam in a straight line like a minnow. That was the end of the experiment and Ted bought no more curved hooks.

A traditional material that was used for dry flies only for many years has made quite an impression when used for tying nymphs. That material is CDC or cul de canard, the fine feathers that are found surrounding the preen glands of ducks and other water birds. The use of CDC for dry flies in Europe has been traced back as far as the 1920s: Charles Bickel, of Vallorbe, tied flies with CDC feathers then, as did other tiers in the Swiss Jura mountain area. The French professional fly tier Henri Bresson is credited with coining the term cul de canard. Moving forward to 1986, the Frenchman Marc Petitjean, who lives in Switzerland, first introduced nymphs tied with CDC feathers. The idea of using a feather whose most important characteristics is its ability to float without any additional floatant, may seem contrary. After all a nymph is designed to sink. But the benefit of using CDC feathers for nymphs is that they are very mobile in the water and so when used as dubbing or for legs of nymphs – particularly transitional and floating nymphs – and emergers, they retain their mobility when this mobility is deemed to be a beneficial characteristic of an artificial nymph. CDC feathers can also be used to provide floatation for the thorax-end of a transitional nymph with the bulk of the body and tail submerged.

And in spite of all the new synthetic and natural materials available to the fly tier, the loss of many old, traditional materials that came from now-endangered species although there are many suitable substitutes, hare's ear or mask fur and the fibres or herls from a cock pheasant tail feather continue to be virtually unbeatable.

In the next chapter I have endeavoured to give – wherever possible – the original dressings of flies, or if not the original as near to that as possible. Too often one reads articles on particular flies or an individual and his flies where the author has not been able to resist adding his own variation to a pattern. Sometimes these additions may be an improvement but they do detract from the integrity of the original.

Notes

1 This catalogue listed a 'Sawyer Still Water Rod Power without effort on any open water. 9ft. 6in., 2-piece, 1 top, 6 1/2ozs #6 £18 18 0'. The rod was a Ritz parabolic made in France.

2 When writing about 'Sunk Nymphs' in his chapter on unorthodox trout flies in his book *Fly-Tying: Principles and Practice* which was published in 1940, Major-General Gerald Burrard referred his readers who 'wish[ed] to go in for more elaborate nymphs' than the basic sunk pattern that he described how to tie, to Mottram's *Fly Fishing, Some New Arts and Mysteries* as well as Skues' *The Way of a Trout With a Fly* and *Nymph Fishing For Chalk Stream Trout*.

3 Suitable feathers can often be found on the ground near a heronry or where herons are seen on or near rivers. I understand that in the USA it is illegal to even possess heron feathers.

10 Fly Dressings

G. S. Marryatt

Mayfly nymph

Hook: 12 or 14
Thread: Buff
Tail: Three short strands from a cock pheasant tail feather
Body and thorax: Buff wool ribbed with gold wire
Wing cases: Fibres from the dark part of a hen pheasant tail feather
Legs: Dark speckled grouse breast

G. E. M. Skues

The categories and dressings are those published in *Nymph Fishing for Chalk Stream Trout*

Large Dark Olive of Spring

April and early May

Hook: Down eye sneck bend, 12 or 14
Thread: Full yellow silk, waxed with brown harness-maker's wax
Hackle: Dark blue dun, hen or cockerel with woolly centre, long enough to suggest wing cases
Whisks/tails: Two strands of dark unspeckled guinea fowl neck feathers, dyed dark greenish
Rib: Fine gold wire
Body: Darkest green olive seal's fur, tapered from tail to shoulder and there definitely thickened

Medium Olive Dun

Early in season

HOOK: Down eye neck bend, 14

THREAD: Primrose silk, waxed with clear colourless wax

HACKLE: Short woolly blue feather from breast of bantam cock or hen, two, or at most, three turns

WHISKS/TAILS: Two strands of brownish blue unspeckled guinea fowl neck feathers, tied short

RIB: Optional, yellow silk, gold wire or none

BODY: Hare's ear fur or for lighter version hare's poll

Medium Olive Dun – 2

Early May

HOOK: Down eye sneck bend, 14

THREAD: Grey-brown, waxed with colourless wax

HACKLE: Light medium honey dun hen, short in the fibre. Two turns only

WHISKS/TAIL: Two strands pale-brownish blue cock guinea-fowl's neck, tied short

RIB: Optional, fine silver wire or none

BODY: Pale brown peacock quill, stripped

THORAX: Hare's poll

Medium Olive Dun – 3

June

HOOK: Down eye sneck bend, 15

THREAD: Primrose silk, waxed with brown harness-maker's wax

HACKLE: Dark blue cock, or hen

WHISKS/TAILS: Two strands of unspeckled pale-blue cock guinea-fowl's neck, tied short

RIB: Fine gold wire

BODY: Raw lamb's wool mixed with just enough brown olive seal's fur to shade it

THORAX: English squirrel's blue fur

Medium Olive Dun – 4

May, June and July

HOOK: Down eye sneck bend, 15 or 16

THREAD: Purple or grey brown silk, waxed with dark wax

HACKLE: Dark blue dun cock, or hen, to extend slightly beyond the dubbing of the thorax

WHISKS/TAILS: Two strands of dark unspeckled neck feathers from cock guinea fowl, tied very short

RIB: Optional, fine silver wire

BODY: Strand of brown quill from the stalk of the eye feather of a peacock stripped

THORAX: Small wad of dark hare's ear, close up to hackle

Medium Olive Dun – 5

June and July

HOOK: Down eye sneck bend, 15 or 16

THREAD: Pale orange silk, waxed with clear wax

HACKLE: Very short darkish blue cock hackle, one turn or, at the most, two

WHISKS/TAILS: Two strands of darkish unfreckled cock guinea-fowl's neck, tied short

BODY: Three or four strands of pale heron covert feathers dyed in picric acid, wound from tail to shoulder

THORAX: Small wad of English squirrel's blue fur, or dark hare's ear

Medium Olive Dun – 6

May and throughout season when small darkish watery dun is on

HOOK: Down-eye sneck bend, 16

THREAD: Bright yellow, waxed with colourless wax

HACKLE: Dark blue hen, short and no more than two turns

WHISKS: Two strands darkish blue unspeckled feather from neck of cock guinea-fowl, short

BODY: Thinly dubbed mole's fur mixed with yellow seal's fur

Medium Olive Dun – 7
July and August
HOOK: Down-eye sneck bend, 16
THREAD: Pale carrot, waxed with colourless wax, at shoulder only
HACKLE: Brownish with paler points, tied short
WHISKS: Two strands pale-brownish blue unfreckled cock guinea-fowl's neck feather, tied short
BODY: Pale-pinkish artificial silk tied in at shoulder and wound over its waste end and the whisk fibres and bare shank to near bend and then once under the whisks and back in successive turns to shoulder
THORAX: Hare's poll

July Dun
July and August
HOOK: Down eye sneck bend, 18
THREAD: Pale orange, waxed with clear wax
HACKLE: Rusty dun cock, very short in fibre, one turn
WHISKS/TAIL: Two strands cock guinea-fowl's neck feather dyed in picric acid, tied short
RIB: Fine gold wire
BODY: Medium blue fox fur, brightly dyed in picric acid
THORAX: Dark-brownish olive seal's fur or some darkish dun fur as a variation

Iron-blue Dun
HOOK: Down eye sneck bend, 18
THREAD: Crimson, waxed with clear wax
HACKLE: Shortest hackle from throat of a cock jackdaw, one turn or, at most, two
WHISKS/TAIL: Three strands of soft, white hen hackle, quite short
BODY: Mole's fur spun thinly on the tying silk, exposing two turns at the tail, tapering to thickest at shoulder

Pale Watery nymph
April and May, and again in July and August
Hook: Down eye sneck bend, 17
Thread: Primrose silk, waxed with colourless wax
Hackle: One turn of small very short darkish blue cockerel
Whisks/tail: Two strands pale unfreckled neck feather of cock guinea-fowl, tied short
Rib: Yellow silk, five turns.
Body: English squirrel's blue fur laid on thinly at tail and tapered to thickest at shoulder

Pale Watery nymph – 2
As above but with fine silver wire rib instead of yellow silk

Pale Watery nymph – 3
Hook: Down eye sneck bend, 16 or 18
Thread: White silk, waxed with colourless wax
Hackle: Very short honey dun cock, one turn only
Whisks/tails: Two strands pale unfreckled neck feather of cock guinea-fowl, tied short
Body: Cream-coloured fur from belly of baby seal
Thorax: Blue squirrel or hare's fur

Pale Watery nymph – 4
Hook: Down eye sneck bend, 16 or 18
Thread: Yellow, at shoulder only
Hackle: Pale honey dun cock, very short, one turn only
Whisks/tails: Pale-brownish blue neck feather of cock guinea-fowl tied in at shoulder so as to be short beyond body when body material wound on
Body: One strand from three-ply corded yellow silk, going greenish olive when wet, tied in at the shoulder with the waste end towards the tail, wound over the bare hook and whisks to tail, then once under whisks and back in taper to shoulder
Thorax: Hare's poll or, for variation, squirrel's blue fur

May to August
Hook: Down eye sneck bend, 16
Thread: Crimson or hot orange silk for head and thorax; white for rest of body. Both waxed with clear wax
Hackle: Pale-reddish centre with white points, tied quite short
Whisks/tail: Two strands palest (but not white) neck feather of cock guinea-fowl, tied short
Rib: Fine silver wire
Body: Cream colour baby seal's fur
Thorax: Rabbit's poll dyed in Red Ant dye

May to August – 2
Hook: Down eye sneck bend, 16
Thread: Cream, waxed with clear wax
Hackle: Medium dun hen with pale points, one turn
Whisks/tail: Two strands creamy neck feather of cock guinea-fowl
Rib: Fine silver wire
Body: Whitey grey fur from hare's shoulder
Thorax: Darker fur – in a variety of shades – from blue English squirrel or hare's fur

May to August – 3
Hook: Down eye sneck bend, 16
Thread: Cream, waxed with clear wax
Hackle: Palest ginger hen tied short, one turn
Whisks/tail: Two strands of palest creamy neck feather of cock guinea-fowl, tied short
Rib: Fine silver wire
Body: Pale rabbit's poll
Thorax: Hare's poll, or, for a variation, English squirrel's blue fur

Blue-winged Olive
Hook: Down eye round bend, 12 or 14
Thread: Hot orange
Hackle: Dark but definitely blue hen – as woolly in the fibre as can be had – two turns
Whisk: Three strands of dark hen hackle, tied short
Body: Cow-hair the colour of dried blood, dressed fat

Blue-winged Olive – 2
HOOK: Down eye round bend, 14
THREAD: Ordinary orange
HACKLE: Dark blue
WHISK: Three strands of close-freckled partridge hackle
BODY: Fur of blue Persian cat strongly dyed in picric acid, becoming a rich green

Blue-winged Olive – 3
HOOK: Down eye round bend, 14
THREAD: Orange
HACKLE: Greenish olive cock
WING CASES: Brownish-blue starling wing feather
WHISKS: Three strands of partridge closely freckled brown hackle
RIB: Fine gold wire
BODY: Mixture of a variety of seal's fur, olive and green and yellow with a hint of orange and red, all mixed with hare's poll and the green dyed fur (from variation 2) to make it spin easily

J. C. Mottram
Resting nymph
HOOK: Not specified. Wet fly, sizes 12, 14 or 16
THREAD: Same colour as thorax
TAIL: Three guinea fowl barbs
BODY: Peacock herl, to cover half hook shank
THORAX: Floss silk (Pearsalls' filoselle is recommended) of the correct shade when wet
LEGS: Four barbs from a hen pheasant primary wing feather

Swimming nymph
HOOK: Not specified. Wet fly, sizes 12, 14 or16
THREAD: Same colour as thorax
TAIL: Three guinea fowl barbs
BODY AND THORAX: Floss silk of the correct shade when wet, enough turns to make a fat body and thorax
WING CASES: The tips of two dark grey cock hackles tied on the top of the thorax

Caddis nymph

Hook: Not specified. Wet fly, sizes 14 or 16
Thread: Same colour as thorax
Body: Light brown floss silk
Thorax: Dark brown floss silk
Throat hackle: A few guinea fowl hackle barbs
Long antennae: Two long, thin fibres from the sword feather of a peacock

Diptera pupa or larva

Hook: Very lightweight
Thread: Brown or apple green
Tails / celia: Two or three barbs from an emu feather
Body / head of larva: Small wedge-shaped piece of cork, coloured black

William Lunn

Blue-Winged Olive nymph

Hook: Snecky Limerick, 15
Thread: Orange, shade 6
Tail: Fibre of Buff Orpington hackle cut short
Back: Strip a piece from coot wing feather, tie on at hook end of shank
Body: Two fibres from swan wing feather, dyed greeny-yellow, ribbed with gold twist
Hackle: Buff Orpington cock hackle. Bring coot feather over back, tie-in behind eye, cut ends off, give a few more turns and fasten off.

Watery Dun nymph

Hook: Snecky Limerick, 16 or 17
Thread: Orange, shade 6
Tail: Very light buff hackle, cut short
Back: Bleached starling wing, tie on at hook end of shank
Body: Two fibres from swan feather, dyed yellow
Hackle: Very pale buff, finish off as BWO Nymph

Pink nymph

Hook: Snecky Limerick, 14 or 15
Thread: Orange, shade 6
Tail: Fibres from Buff Orpington cock hackle, cut short
Back: Partridge hackle feather, fairly dark, tie on at hook end of shank
Body: Pink Sylvan artificial silk, shade 248, ribbed with gold twist
Hackle: Partridge hackle, cut short

Greenwell nymph
HOOK: Snecky Limerick, 14 or 15
THREAD: Orange, shade 6
TAIL: Fibres from Buff Orpington cock hackle, cut short
BACK: Strip from hen blackbird wing feather, tied as BWO Nymph
BODY: Yellow Sylvan artificial silk, shade 55, ribbed with gold twist
HACKLE: Coch-Y-Bonddu

Frank Sawyer
Pheasant Tail nymph
HOOK: Down eye Limerick, 16, 18 or20
WEIGHT/TYING THREAD: Fine red-colour copper wire
TAILS: Tips of four centre fibres from a browny-red cock pheasant tail feather
BODY: As tails
THORAX: As tails

Pale Watery nymph
HOOK: Down eye Limerick, 15 only
WEIGHT/TYING THREAD: Fine red-colour copper wire
TAILS: Four or five ginger cock hackle fibres
BODY: Fawny-pink darning wool, one third of a strand
WING CASE: Section from the dark edge of a woodpigeon primary feather

Spurwing and Very Pale Watery nymph
HOOK: Down eye Limerick, 14 or 16
WEIGHT/TYING THREAD: Fine, red-colour copper wire
BODY: Three browny-yellow fibres from condor wing feather
TAILS: Tips of condor fibres
THORAX: Gold wire
HEAD: A dozen turns of gold wire, as used for thorax

Grey Goose
HOOK: Down eye Limerick, 16, 18 or 20
WEIGHT/TYING THREAD: Fine, gold wire
TAILS: Herls from the primary wing feather of a farmyard grey goose
BODY: As tails
THORAX: As tails

SS nymph
Hook: Down-eye Limerick, 10 or 12
Weight/tying thread: Fine, dark red-colour copper wire
Tails: Grey goose herls from secondary wing feather of a farmyard grey goose
Body: As tails
Thorax: As tails

Killer Bug
Hook: Down-eye Limerick, 12, 14 or 16
Weight/tying thread: Medium copper wire (originally silver fuse wire)
Body: Chadwicks' 477 wool or beige wool with a pink or red thread in it

Bow Tie Buzzer
Hook: Down-eye Limerick, 12
Weight/tying thread: Gold wire
Underbody: Silver tinsel
Body/thorax: As tails
Tails: Four or five fibres from red cock pheasant tail feather
Celia: White nylon wool, tied to end of tippet

Oliver Kite
Bare Hook nymph
Hook: Down-eye Limerick, 14 or 16
Body: Fine copper wire to shape tapered abdomen and build-up thorax, or, just a thorax of copper wire

New Forest Stream nymph
Hook: Down-eye Limerick, 14 or 16
Weight: Copper wire on hook
Body: Black ostrich herl
Thorax: Pinch of reindeer hair as thorax tuft

Reindeer and Red
Hook: Size 14, 16 or 18
Thread: Fine copper wire
Body: Red wool from the pompom on traditional Lappish headgear
Thorax: Reindeer hair for thorax tuft

John Goddard

PVC nymph
HOOK: Partridge arrow point 12, 14, 16 or 18
THREAD: Brown
TAILS: Tips of three golden pheasant tippets
UNDERBODY AND THORAX: Copper wire
OVERBODY AND THORAX: One strand of olive coloured polypropylene yarn
BODY COVERING: ⅛" wide strip of clear PVC, dyed olive, wound and over-lapped up to the thorax
WING PADS: Three strands of dark pheasant tail herl, or black cock, doubled over

Mating shrimp
HOOK: Wide gape 8 to 12
THREAD: Brown
WEIGHT: Narrow strip of lead foil
BACK: Strip of olive-dyed PVC
RIB: Oval tinsel
BODY: Seal's fur, mixed, 50 per cent olive, 40 per cent mid-brown, 10 per cent fluorescent pink

The Gerroff
HOOK: wide gape 10 to 14
THREAD: Brown
BODY: Seal's fur or substitute, 50 per cent olive, 40 per cent mid-brown and 10 per cent fluorescent pink, blended well
WING CASE: Strip of olive PVC or latex

The Shrymph
HOOK: Wide gape, 8 to 12
THREAD: Brown
UNDERBODY: Lead wire wound on front half of hook shank to form a pronounced thorax
BODY AND THORAX: Seal's fur, or substitute, 50 per cent green, 40 per cent brown, 10 per fluorescent pink
RIB: Thick silver wire
WING CASE: Flue from a black crow feather doubled and re-doubled over the thorax

Suspender nymph
HOOK: Down eye, 14 or16
THREAD: Brown
TAILS: Three olive dyed golden pheasant tippets
RIB: Silver wire
BODY: Olive seal's fur or Sealex
HACKLE: Grizzle
WING PAD: Ethafoam ball, enclosed in nylon mesh, and coloured dark brown, Pantone shade 499M

Mayfly suspender nymph
HOOK: Long shank, 12
THREAD: Brown
TAILS: Three tips of cream ostrich herl
RIB: Brown monocord or silk
BODY: Seal's fur, mixed, ½ white, ¼ tan and ¼ yellow
WING CASES: Ethafoam ball, enclosed in nylon mesh, and coloured dark brown
THORAX: As body

Suspender hatching midge pupa
HOOK: Limerick bend or Drennan sedge, 12 or 14 (still waters), 18 (rivers)
THREAD: To match body colour, black, brown, green, red or orange; brown or green for rivers
FLOATATION BALL: White ethafoam ball, wrapped in white stocking material
TAG: White nylon filaments
RIB: Oval silver tinsel
BODY: Polypropylene yarn
THORAX: Peacock herl or brown dyed turkey herl
HACKLE: Natural red or grizzly tied parachute style

11 Bibliography

The publication date given is that of the edition used for research and reference and will not always that of the first edition.

Aston, Sir George, *Letters To Young Fly-Fishers*, Philip Allan & Co Ltd, 1926

Atherton, John, *The Fly and The Fish*, The Macmillan Company, New York, 1951

Babb, James R., *Crosscurrents, A Fly Fisher's Progress*, The Lyons Press, Connecticut, 1999

Baird, R. D., *A Trout Rose, Being a picture of the upper waters of the Itchen and something about fishing in those streams*, c1946

Barton, E. A., *Chalk Streams & Water-Meadows*, John Murray, 1932

Bergman, Ray, *Trout, The Trout Fisherman's Bible*, The Derrydale Press, Maryland, 2000

——*Just Fishing*, Hutchinson & Co (Publishing) Ltd, 1933

Borlase, G. W., *By Twinkling Streams*, Bennett Brothers, 1950

Bragg, Robert, *Introduction to Fishing in the British Isles and Overseas, 1915 – 1939*, Robert Bragg, Christchurch, New Zealand, 10 October 1989

Braithwaite, Andrew, The Wigram Legacy, Volume 9, 2004, *The Flyfisher*, Australian Fishing Network, Victoria

Bridgett, R. C., *Loch Fishing in Theory and Practice*, Herbert Jenkins Limited, 1924

——*Tight Lines*, Herbert Jenkins Limited, 1926

Brooks, Charles E., *Nymph Fishing For Larger Trout*, Lyons & Burford, New York, 1976

Bucknall, Geoffrey, *Modern Techniques of Still Water Fly-Fishing*, Frederick Muller Limited, 1980

——*The Bright Stream of Memory*, The Golden Years of *The Fishing Gazette*, Swan Hill Press, 1997

Burrard, Major General Gerald, *Fly-Tying: Principles and Practice*, Herbert Jenkins Limited, 1940

Carey, Brigadier General H. E., *One River*, The Falcon Press Limited, 1952

Chance, Jack and Paget, Julian, (eds) *The Flyfishers', An Anthology to Mark The Centenary of The Flyfishers' Club 1884 – 1984*, The Flyfishers' Club, 1984

Church, Bob, *This Fishing Life*, The Crowood Press Ltd, 2003

Clarke, Brian, *The Pursuit of Stillwater Trout*, Adam & Charles Black, 1975

Clarke, Brian and Goddard, John, *The Trout and the Fly, A New Approach*, Ernest Benn Limited, 1980

Clarkson, Joan, *Back Casts and Back Chat*, Game & Gun Ltd, 1936

Cove, Arthur, *My Way With Trout*, The Crowood Press Ltd, 1992

Cutcliffe, H. C., *Trout Fishing in Rapid Streams*, Porcupines, 1970

Dean, Roy, *Memories of the Shannon Rise 1936 – 1964*, Stevens Publishing Pty. Ltd, Tasmania, 1998

Dewar, G. A. B., *The Book of the Dry Fly*, Lawrence and Bullen, Ltd, 1897

Dick, Lenox, *The Art and Science of Fly Fishing*, D. Van Nostrand Company, Inc, New Jersey, 1966

Draper, Keith, *Trout Flies in New Zealand*, A. H. & A. W. Reed, Wellington, New Zealand, 1971

Dunne, J. W., *Sunshine And The Dry Fly*, A. & C. Black, Ltd 1924

Durnford, The Rev. Richard, *The Fishing Diary, 1809 – 1819*, Warren & Son, Ltd, 1911

Edmonds, Harfield H., and Lee, Norman N., *Brook and River Trouting*, published by the authors, 1916

Engle, Ed, Freestyle Nymphing, *Fly Fishing & Tying*, Winter 2003

Färnström, Nils *Fritidsfiskarnas 'Special'* 7, Fiske Med Nymf, Stockholm, nd c1975

——*Streamer mot Strömmen*, Almqvist & Wiksell/Gebers Förlag AB, Stockholm, 1965

Gierach, John, *Good Flies, Favorite Trout Patterns and How They Got That Way*, The Lyons Press, New York, 2000

Goddard, John, *Reflections Of A Game Fisher*, Robert Hale, 2002

——*John Goddard's Trout-Fishing Techniques*, A. & C. Black, 1996

——An eye on the fly down-under, *Salmon, Trout & Sea-Trout*, August, 1988

Grey, Viscount, *Fly Fishing*, J. M. Dent & Sons Ltd, 1931

Griffith, Mike, Sawyer Nymphing, So simple yet so effective, *Fly Fisherman*, September 1993

Halford, F. M., *An Angler's Autobiography*, Vinton & Co, Limited, 1903

——*Dry-Fly Fishing in Theory and Practice*, Barry Shurlock, 1973

——*The Dry-Fly Man's Handbook*, George Routledge & Sons, Limited, 1913

——*Floating Flies and How to Dress Them*, Barry Shurlock, 1974

Hammond, Bryn, *The New Zealand Encyclopaedia of Fly Fishing*, The Halcyon Press, Auckland, New Zealand, 1988

Hanna, T. J., *Angling, A Quarterly for Every Angler*, Country Life Limited, 1941

Harding, Colonel E. W., *The Fly Fisher and The Trout's Point of View*, Seeley Service & Co, 1931

Hartman, Robert, *About Fishing*, Arthur Barker, Ltd, 1935

Hayter, Tony, *F. M. Halford and the Dry-Fly Revolution*, Robert Hale, 2002

Herd, Andrew, *The Fly*, The Medlar Press, 2003

Hewitt, Edward Ringwood, *Telling On The Trout*, Charles Scribner's Sons, New York 1926

——*A Trout and Salmon Fisherman For Seventy-Five Years*, Charles Scribner's Sons, New York, 1948

——*Hewitt's Nymph Fly Fishing*, The Marchbanks Press, New York, 1934

Hickson, David, Indicator Nymphing, *Fly Fisherman*, March 1991

Hills, J. W., *River Keeper, The Life of William James Lunn*, Geoffrey Bles, 1934

——*My Sporting Life*, Philip Allan & Co, Ltd, 1936

——*A History of Fly Fishing For Trout*, Barry Shurlock, 1973

——*A Summer on The Test*, Andre Deutsch, 1989

Holbrook, Don, and Koch, Ed, *Midge Magic*, Stackpole Books, 2001

Hughes, Dave, *Nymph Fishing*, Frank Amato Publications, Inc, Oregon, 1995

Hunter, W. A., editor, *Fisherman's Pie, An Angling Symposium*, A. & C. Black, 1926

Jacobsen, Preben Torp,'The Sedge With The 'Built-In' Bubble', *Trout & Salmon*, December 1974

Jacques, David, *The Development of Modern Stillwater Fishing*, A. & C. Black, 1974

Journal of The Flyfishers Club, various issues including
   Volume 24, No. 94, Summer 1935
   Volume 26, No. 102, Summer 1937
   Volume 26, No. 103, Autumn 1937
   Volume 26, No. 104, Winter 1937/38
   Volume 27, No. 105, Spring 1938
   Volume 54, No. 212, Spring 1965

Kite, Major Oliver, *Nymph Fishing in Practice*, Herbert Jenkins, 1963

——*Nymph Fishing in Practice, With a new introduction and notes by Robert Spaight*, Swan Hill Press, 2000

——*A Fisherman's Diary*, Andre Deutsch, 1969

——*Elements of Nymph Fishing, Theory and Practice*, Herbert Jenkins Limited, 1966

——'Use a nymph for November grayling', *Trout & Salmon*, November 1960

——'October grayling day', *Trout & Salmon*, October 1965

——'November grayling pattern', *Trout & Salmon*, November 1965

——'When grayling reach their peak', *Trout & Salmon*, November 1966

Knight, J. A., *The Modern Angler*, Charles Scribner's Sons, New York, 1936

Krivanec, Karel, History of the Czech Nymph, http://shop.siman.cz/cl1801735975.htm

La Branche, George M. L., *The Dry Fly and Fast Water*, Van Cortland Press, New York, 1972

LaFontaine, Garry, *Caddisflies*, Winchester Press Nick Lyons Books, New York, 1981

Lawrie, William H., *Rough Stream Nymph*, Oliver and Boyd, 1947

Leisenring, James, *Art of Tying The Wet Fly*, Crown Publishers, Inc, New York, 1973

Links, Leon, *Tying Flies with CDC, The Fisherman's Miracle Feather*, Merlin Unwin Books, 2002

Lunn, Mick, with Clive Graham-Ranger, *A Particular Lunn*, Unwin Hyman Ltd, 1990

Mackie, Gordon, *Fly Leaves and Waterside Sketches*, Robert Hale, 1998

Mackintosh, Alexander, *The Driffield Angler*, published by the author, nd c1806

McCaskie, H.B., *The Guileless Trout*, The Cresset Press, 1950

McCaskie, Norman, *Fishing, My Life's Hobby*, Falcon Press Ltd, 1950

McClane, A. J., *The Practical Fly Fisherman*, Prentice-Hall, Inc, New York, 1953

——*The Complete McClean*, Truman Talley Books/E. P. Dutton, New York, 1988

McDonald, John, editor, *The Complete Fly Fisherman, The Notes and Letters of Theodore Gordon*, Jonathan Cape, 1949

Migel, J. Michael, and Wright Jr., Leonard M., editors, *The Masters On The Nymph*, Robert Hale, 1994

Mosely, Martin E., *The Dry-Fly Fisherman's Entomology*, George Routledge and Sons, Limited, nd c1932

Moser, Roman, Gold Head Nymphs, www.globalflyfisher.com , c2000

Mottram, Dr J. C., *Fly Fishing, Some New Arts and Mysteries*, The Flyfisher's Classic Library, 1994

——*Thoughts on Angling*, Herbert Jenkins Limited, nd c1945

Neale, Ian, 'Droppers without knots', *Trout & Salmon*

Ogden, James, *Ogden on Fly Tying*, John T. Norman, Cheltenham, 1879

Orman, Tony, *Trout on a Nymph*, The Halcyon Press, Auckland, 1991

Overfield, T. Donald, *Fifty Favourite Nymphs*, Ernest Benn Limited, 1978

——*GEM Skues, The Way of a Man with a Trout*, Ernest Benn Limited, 1977

——'Famous Fly-Dressers, Marryat', *Trout & Salmon*, May, 1971

——'The art of spinning dubbed bodies', *Trout & Salmon*, April 1972

Ovington, R., *How To Take Trout on Wet Flies and Nymphs*, Little, Brown and Company, Boston, 1954

Pain, C. Ernest, *Fifty Years on The Test*, Philip Allan, 1934

Parsons, John, *Four Seasons of Trout, A Fly-fisher's Year*, HarperCollins Publishers (New Zealand) Limited, New Zealand, 1994

Parsons, John and Hammond, Bryn, *One Hundred Years of Trout Fishing in New Zealand*, The Halcyon Press, Auckland, New Zealand, 1999

Penn, Richard, *Maxims and Hints on Angling, Chess, Shooting and Other Matters*, John Marway, 1855

Pequegnot, Dr Jean-Paul, *French Fishing Flies*, Nick Lyons Books, New York, 1987

Pope, Steve, Looking Back as Blagdon Celebrates 100 years, *The Buzzer* 2003

Pritt, T. E., *North-Country Flies*, Smith Settle, 1995

Plunket-Greene, H., *Where The Bright Waters Meet*, André Deutsch Limited, 1983

Puyans, André, Tying The A. P. Nymph Series, http://andrepuyans.com/APNymph.htm

Radcliffe, William, *Fishing From The Earliest Times*, John Murray, 1921

Reid, John, *Clyde-Style Flies and their dressings*, David & Charles, 1971

Ritz, Charles, *A Fly Fisher's Life*, Max Reinhardt, 1959

Roberts, John, *The World's Best Trout Flies*, Tiger Books International, 1995

——*Flyfishing for GRAYLING*, Excellent Press, 1999

Robson, Kenneth, editor, *The Essential GEM Skues*, A. & C. Black, 1998

Ronalds, Alfred, *The Fly-Fisher's Entomology*, Herbert Jenkins Limited, 1921

Rosborough, E. H. 'Polly', *Tying and Fishing the Fuzzy Nymphs*, Stackpole Books, Harrisburg, P. A., 1988

Rose, R. N., *The Field, 1853 – 1953*, Michael Joseph, 1953

Salmon and Trout Magazine, various issues including:
    July, 1913
    April, 1914
    September, 1929
    September, 1933
    May, 1945
    September, 1949

Sautelle, John, *Fishing for the Educated Trout*, Murray Book Distributors Pty, Limited, Ultimo, Australia, 1978

Saville, Tom, *Reservoir Trout Fishing with Tom Saville*, H. F. & G. Witherby Ltd, 1991

Sawyer, Frank, *Nymphs and The Trout, New applications of a technique for fly fishermen*, Stanley Paul, 1958

——*Keeper of the Stream, The life of a river and its trout fishery*, George Allen & Unwin, 1985

——'A new idea for the Buzzer', *Trout & Salmon*

    July on the chalk streams, *Trout & Salmon*, July 1956

September trout flies, *Trout & Salmon*, September 1956

When I go fishing, *Trout & Salmon*, April 1957

April on the river, *Trout & Salmon*, April 1957

October on the river, *Trout & Salmon*, October 1957

Nymph fishing in North Sweden, *Trout & Salmon*, December 1959 and January 1960

A study in contrasts, *Trout & Salmon*, May 1960

With the nymph in Bavaria, *Trout & Salmon*, March, April and May 1963

Nymph Fishing, *Farlow's Trout Catalogue 1965*, C. Farlow & Co. Ltd.

Sawyer, Frank, and Vines, Sidney, *Frank Sawyer, Man of the Riverside*, George Allen & Unwin, 1984

Schwiebert, Ernest, *Nymphs*, Winchester Press, New York, 1973

Shepherd, Alan, The Pot Scrubber Nymph (Dick Wigram), www.flyanglersonline.com/features/oldflies.part24l.html

Sikora, Adam, Fishing Czech Nymph *1*, http://shop.siman.cz/cl1801735976.htm

Skues, G. E. M., *Minor Tactics Of The Chalk Stream*, A. and C. Black, 1930

——*Silk, Fur and Feather: The Trout-Fly Dresser's Year*, The Flyfisher's Classic Library 1993

——*The Way of a Trout with a Fly*, A. & C. Black, 1949

——*Itchen Memories*, Robert Hale, 1999

——*Nymph Fishing for Chalk Stream Trout*, A. & C. Black, 1960

——*The Chalk-Stream Angler, Sidelines, Sidelights and Reflections* , Barry Shurlock, 1976

Sturgis, W. B., and Taverner, E., *New Lines for Fly-fishers*, Seeley, Service & Co, Limited, 1946

Swisher, Doug, and Richards, Carl, *Selective Trout, A Dramatically New and Scientific Approach to Trout Fishing on Eastern and Western Rivers*, Crown Publishers Inc, New York, 1971

Taverner, Eric, *Trout Fishing From All Angles*, Seeley, Service & Co, Ltd, 1929

——*An Introduction To Angling*, Beaufort Library, 1953

——*Fly Tying for Trout*, Seeley Service & Co. Ltd, 1957

Taverner, John, *Certaine Experiments Concerning Fish and Fruite*, Salmon and Trout Magazine, No. 50 January, 1928 and No. 51 April, 1928

Taylor, J. Paul, *Fishing and Fishers*, Ward, Lock and Co Limited, undated c1898

Taylor, Steve, *Amber Nymph at Blagdon*, notes dated 1941 for an unpublished article, *The Buzzer* 2003

The Field, 12 December, 1857

——3 and 10 October, 1891

——January, 1898

——30 December, 1899

——21 April, 1906

——17 July and 18 September, 1909

——1 April, 1911

——5 and 19 October, 1912

——27 October, 1913

——14 February, 1914

——12 November, 1959

Trench, Charles Chenevix, *A History of Angling*, Hart-Davis, MacGibbon, 1974

Trueblood, Ted, Wet Fly Tackle and tactics, *Field & Stream*, April 1956, Boise State University Library, Ted Trueblood collection

——Wet Fly Tactics, *Field & Stream*, June 1945, Boise State University Library, Ted Trueblood collection

——Deep Stuff, *Field & Stream*, May 1954, Boise State University Library, Ted Trueblood collection

——Letter to Leon L. Martuch, Mss 89, Box 18, Folder 13, Boise State University Library, Ted Trueblood collection

——Ted Trueblood extols the virtues of the wet fly for trout and explains the technique of fishing it, *Field & Stream*, February 1956, Boise State University Library, Ted Trueblood collection

——Taking The Mystique Out Of Fly Fishing, Box 14, Folder 35, 1973 draft of article, Boise State University Library, Ted Trueblood collection

——Wet Flies and Nymphs, *Ted Trueblood's Fishing Handbook*, Boise State University Library, Ted Trueblood collection

Turing, H. D., *Trout Problems*, A. & C. Black, 1948

——*Fly Fishing*, Country Books, Nicholson and Watson, 1951

Turner, Eric Horsfall, *Angler's Cavalcade*, A. & C. Black, 1966

Venables, Colonel Robert, *The Experienced Angler: or Angling Improved*, Antrobus Press, 1969

Veniard, John, *Fly Dresser's Guide*, Adam & Charles Black, 1968

Voss Bark, Conrad, *The Encyclopaedia of Fly Fishing*, B. T. Batsford Ltd, 1968

——*Fishing for Lake Trout with Fly and Nymph*, H. F. & G. Witherby Ltd, 1972

Walker, C. F., editor, *The Complete Fly-Fisher*, Herbert Jenkins, 1963

——*The Angling Letters of GEM Skues*, A. & C. Black, 1975

Walton, Izaak, and Cotton, Charles, *Walton and Cotton's Complete Angler*, edited by Ephemera, George Routledge and Sons, 1881

Webster, D., *The Angler and The Loop Rod*, William Blackwood and Sons, 1885

West, Leonard, *The Natural Trout Fly and its Imitation*, William Potter, 1921

Welsh, Stephen, Will the real brown nymph please stand up?, wwww.flyflickers.com/ff/flybox/replete_mangler/nymphs/brownnymphs.htm

Whitlock, Dave, *A Guide To Aquatic Trout Food*, Swan Hill Press, 1994

Wigram, R. H., *Trout and Fly in Tasmania*, Angus & Robertson Limited, Sydney, 1938

——*The Uncertain Trout*, Georgian House Pty. Ltd, Australia, 1951

——*Nymph Fishing in the Southern Hemisphere*, Angling And Gun Sport, Sydney, Australia, 1992

——*The Fly*, Stevens Publishing Pty. Ltd, Tasmania, 2002

Wulff, Lee, *Trout on a Fly*, Nick Lyons Books, New York, 1986

Younger, John, *River Angling for Salmon and Trout*, The Flyfisher's Classic Library, 1995

Index